SO-AZO-262

APPLIED

AND

DECORATIVE ARTS

APPLIED
AND
DECORATIVE ARTS

A Bibliographic Guide to Basic Reference Works, Histories, and Handbooks

Donald L. Ehresmann

1977

Libraries Unlimited, Inc.
Littleton, Colo.

Copyright © 1977 Donald L. Ehresmann
All Rights Reserved
Printed in the United States of America

LIBRARIES UNLIMITED, INC.
P.O. Box 263
Littleton, Colorado 80160

Library of Congress Cataloging in Publication Data

Ehresmann, Donald L   1937-
  Applied and decorative arts.

  Includes indexes.
  1. Art industries and trade—Bibliography.
I. Title.
Z5956.A68E47   [NK1110]   016.745   76-55416
ISBN 0-87287-136-3

To the Germanisches Nationalmuseum

on its

One Hundred and Twenty-fifth Anniversary

TABLE OF CONTENTS

PREFACE 14

CHAPTER ONE–APPLIED AND DECORATIVE ARTS–GENERAL 17
   Dictionaries and Encyclopedias 17
   General Histories and Handbooks 19
   Modern Applied and Decorative Arts (19th and 20th Centuries) 20
   American Applied and Decorative Arts (U.S. and Canada) 21
   European Applied and Decorative Arts 22
      General Histories and Handbooks 22
      National Histories and Handbooks 23
         Denmark 23
         France 23
         Germany 24
         Great Britain 25
         Italy 25
         Norway 26
         Poland 26
         Scotland 26
         Spain 26
         Sweden 27
         Switzerland 27
   Oriental Applied and Decorative Arts 27
   African Applied and Decorative Arts 29

CHAPTER TWO–ORNAMENT 30

CHAPTER THREE–FOLK ART 33
   Bibliographies 33
   General Histories and Handbooks 33
   American Folk Art 33
   European Folk Art 34
      General Histories and Handbooks 34
      National Histories and Handbooks 34
         Austria 34
         Bulgaria 35
         Czechoslovakia 35
         Denmark 35
         France 35
         Germany 36

CHAPTER THREE–FOLK ART (cont'd)

Great Britain 36
Hungary 37
Italy 37
Norway 37
Poland 37
Rumania 38
Russia 38
Spain 38
Switzerland 38
Oriental Folk Art 39

CHAPTER FOUR–ARMS AND ARMOR 40
Dictionaries and Encyclopedias 40
General Histories and Handbooks 41
Ancient Arms and Armor 41
Western Arms and Armor 42
Oriental Arms and Armor 45
Edged Weapons 46
Firearms 46

CHAPTER FIVE–CERAMICS 49
Bibliographies 49
Dictionaries and Encyclopedias 49
General 49
Dictionaries of Marks and Signatures 51
General Histories and Handbooks 52
Pre-Columbian Ceramics 53
Ancient and Medieval Ceramics 54
American Ceramics (U.S., Canada and Latin America) 56
European Ceramics 57
General Works 57
France 58
Germany, Austria and Switzerland 59
Great Britain 60
Scandinavia 62
Spain and Portugal 63
Eastern European Countries 63
Oriental Ceramics 64
Islamic Ceramics 64
Far Eastern Ceramics 64
General Works 64
China 65
Japan and Korea 66

CHAPTER FIVE–CERAMICS (cont'd)

Porcelain 67
  General Histories and Handbooks 67
  American Porcelain (U.S. and Canada) 68
  European Porcelain 68
    General Works 68
    France 69
    Germany, Austria and Switzerland 70
    Great Britain 71
    Italy 71
    Netherlands 72
    Eastern European Countries 72
  Oriental Porcelain 73
Pottery, Faience, Majolica, Stoneware 74
  General Histories and Handbooks 74
  American Pottery, etc. (U.S. and Canada) 74
  European Pottery, etc. 75
    General Works 75
    France 75
    Germany, Austria and Switzerland 76
    Great Britain 77
    Italy 77
    Netherlands 78
    Portugal 79
    Scandinavia 79
  Australian Pottery, etc. 79

CHAPTER SIX–CLOCKS, WATCHES AND AUTOMATA 80
Bibliographies 80
Dictionaries and Encyclopedias 80
  General 80
  National Dictionaries of Clock and Watchmakers 81
    France 81
    Italy 81
    Netherlands 81
    Russia 81
    Spain 82
    Sweden 82
General Histories and Handbooks 82
National Histories 84
  France 84
  Great Britain 84
  Italy 85
  Netherlands 85
  Switzerland 85
  United States 86
Automata 86

CHAPTER SEVEN—COSTUME 88
   Bibliographies 88
   Dictionaries and Encyclopedias 89
   General Histories and Handbooks 90
   Ancient and Medieval Costume 94
   Modern Costume (19th and 20th Centuries) 95
   American Costume (U.S. and Canada) 96
   European Costume 96
      France 96
      Great Britain 96
   Oriental Costume 98
   African and Australian Costume 99

CHAPTER EIGHT—ENAMELS 101
   Bibliographies, Dictionaries and Encyclopedias 101
   General Histories and Handbooks 101
   Western Enamels 101
   Oriental Enamels 103

CHAPTER NINE—FURNITURE 104
   Dictionaries and Encyclopedias 104
   General Histories and Handbooks 104
   Ancient Furniture 107
   American Furniture (U.S., Canada and Latin America) 107
   European Furniture 110
      General Works 110
      France 111
      Germany, Austria and Switzerland 115
      Great Britain 116
      Italy 121
      Low Countries 122
      Scandinavia 123
      Spain and Portugal 124
   Oriental Furniture 125

CHAPTER TEN—GLASS 126
   Bibliographies 126
   Dictionaries and Encyclopedias 126
   General Histories and Handbooks 126
   Ancient and Byzantine Glass 128
   Modern Glass (19th and 20th Centuries) 128
   American Glass (U.S. and Canada) 130

CHAPTER TEN–GLASS (cont'd)
European Glass 131
   General Works 131
   France and Belgium 132
   Germany, Austria and Switzerland, with Czechoslovakia 133
   Great Britain 133
   Italy 135
   Scandinavia 135
   Spain 136
Oriental Glass 136

CHAPTER ELEVEN–IVORY 137
General Histories and Handbooks 137
Western Ivory 137
Oriental Ivory (including Netsuke) 140

CHAPTER TWELVE–JEWELRY 141
General Histories and Handbooks 141
Ancient Jewelry 142
Western Jewelry 143
   General Histories and Handbooks 143
   National Histories and Handbooks 144
     France 144
     Great Britain 144
     Italy 144
     Netherlands 145
     Spain 145
Oriental Jewelry 145
Cameos and Intaglios 145

CHAPTER THIRTEEN–LACQUER 147

CHAPTER FOURTEEN–LEATHER AND BOOKBINDING 149

CHAPTER FIFTEEN–MEDALS AND SEALS 154

CHAPTER SIXTEEN–METALWORK 157
General Histories and Handbooks 157
Brass and Copper 158
Gold and Silver 159
   Dictionaries of Marks 159
   General Histories and Handbooks 160
   Ancient and Medieval Gold and Silver 162
   Modern Gold and Silver (19th and 20th Centuries) 163
   American Gold and Silver (U.S., Canada and Latin America) ... 163
     United States 163
     Canada 165
     Latin America 166

CHAPTER SIXTEEN—METALWORK (cont'd)

European Gold and Silver 166
    France 166
    Germany, Austria and Switzerland 168
    Great Britain 170
    Italy 173
    Netherlands 174
    Scandinavia 175
    Spain and Portugal 176
Oriental Gold and Silver 176
Iron 176
Pewter 178
    General Histories and Handbooks 178
    American Pewter (U.S. and Canada) 179
    European Pewter 180
    General Histories and Handbooks 180
    National Histories and Handbooks 181
        Czechoslovakia, 181
        France, 181
        Germany, 182
        Great Britain, 182
        Netherlands, 183
        Russia, 183
        Scandinavia, 183
        Scotland, 183
        Switzerland, 184

CHAPTER SEVENTEEN—MUSICAL INSTRUMENTS 185

CHAPTER EIGHTEEN—TEXTILES 187
Bibliographies 187
Dictionaries and Encyclopedias 187
General Histories and Handbooks 188
Pre-Columbian Textiles 189
American Textiles (U.S.) 190
European Textiles 190
Oriental Textiles 193
African Textiles 194
Carpets and Rugs 195
    General Histories and Handbooks 195
    European Carpets and Rugs 196
    Oriental Carpets and Rugs 196
    General Histories and Handbooks 196
    Caucasian and Central Asian Carpets and Rugs 200
    Chinese Carpets and Rugs 201

CHAPTER EIGHTEEN—TEXTILES (cont'd)

Embroidery 201
    Dictionaries and Encyclopedias 201
    General Histories and Handbooks 201
    National Histories and Handbooks 203
        Germany 203
        Great Britain 203
        Italy 203
        United States 204
Lace 204
    Dictionaries and Encyclopedias 204
    General Histories and Handbooks 204
    National Histories and Handbooks 207
        Belgium 207
        Italy 207
        Spain 207
        United States 207
Tapestry 208
    Bibliographies 208
    General Histories and Handbooks 208
    National Histories and Handbooks 211
        France 211
        Germany 211
        Low Countries 212

CHAPTER NINETEEN—TOYS AND DOLLS 213

AUTHOR INDEX 217

SUBJECT INDEX 227

PREFACE

This volume is the first classified and annotated bibliography of books on the history of the applied and decorative arts. Bibliographic access to the large and complex literature on the subject until now has been restricted to the limited and out-of-date sections in the general fine arts bibliographies of Chamberlin and Lucas and to the uneven coverage of the material, chiefly periodical literature, in such annual bibliographies as the *Répertoire d'art et d'archéologie* . . . and the *Art Index*.[1] As a critical and descriptive guide to the basic reference works, histories, and handbooks, this bibliography is directed to scholars, librarians, and collectors. It has been designed as a pendant to my *Fine Arts: A Bibliographic Guide to Basic Reference Works, Histories, and Handbooks* (Littleton, Colo., Libraries Unlimited, 1975) and as the second in a series of critical bibliographies devoted to books on the history of art.

DEFINITION OF THE APPLIED AND DECORATIVE ARTS

Because of their position between art and technology and between the fine arts and craft, there is no clear and universally accepted definition of what constitutes the applied and decorative arts. Although the designations "applied" and "decorative" arts are in some sense exclusive, they tend to be used interchangeably. They are understood differently in Britain and the United States, and the Continental designations *Kunstgewerbe* and *l'art décoratif* connote still different groupings of media.[2] For the purposes of this bibliography I have combined two definitions: the narrow definition that concentrates on the so-called minor arts of ceramics, enamels, furniture, glass, ivory, leather, metalwork and textiles, as well as the broader definition that takes in the more applied mixed media of arms and armor, clocks and watches, costume, jewelry, lacquer, medals and seals, musical instruments, and toys. The unifying quality in each of these various art forms is that all possess a significant artistic history, significant both in quality of artistic expression and persistence in the history of the world's art.

Objects or media of pure technology or craft are excluded. So are those media that are essentially adjuncts of the major arts, such as drawing, the graphic arts, mosaic, ancient vase painting, medieval manuscript illumination and stained glass, bronze sculpture and landscape architecture. These important art forms will be covered in projected bibliographies devoted to painting, sculpture and architecture.

BIBLIOGRAPHIC SCOPE

Included in the bibliography are books written in Western European languages, published between 1875 and 1975. Of works published before 1900 only classic or pioneering works have been selected. Pamphlets, periodical articles, museum and exhibition catalogs are not included. Within these parameters every effort has been made to include books representative of the broad spectrum of literature on the applied and decorative arts. Books for the general reader and beginning collector are included, together with exhaustive reference works and scholarly histories and handbooks. Although the vast majority of books contained in this bibliography are of interest to the collector, books devoted exclusively to the collecting, investing, restoring, or preserving of the applied and decorative arts have not been included.

CLASSIFICATION SYSTEM AND ANNOTATIONS

The various media and mixed media are arranged alphabetically. However, certain major media—namely, ceramics, metalwork and textiles—are subdivided into submedia. Thus porcelain and various forms of pottery are classified under ceramics; gold and silver, pewter, iron and brass are found under metalwork; and carpets, embroidery, lace and tapestry come under textiles. Within the media classifications the literature is classified along principles used in my bibliography on the fine arts. Bibliographies, dictionaries and other reference works are grouped at the beginning, followed by histories and handbooks classified according to periods and countries. In the few cases where reference works are listed under national headings, notes have been provided to guide the user. The classification stops at national histories; excluded are histories and handbooks restricted to regions, cities or the work of individual artists. The latter will be incorporated in the forthcoming bibliography of artists' monographs. The annotations, using a uniform, stylized approach, are designed to provide as much information as possible in few words.

SECTIONS ON ORNAMENT AND FOLK ART

Because of their intimate association with applied and decorative arts, the histories of ornament and folk art are included.

INDEXES

The chief purpose of the subject index is to complement the table of contents, which is the book's primary subject access tool. The non-specialist should be the primary benefactor of the subject index, because it expands the vocabulary of the applied and decorative arts by supplying synonyms to terms used in the table of contents and by indexing under variant terminologies the individual arts treated within the broad classification system. As examples, "decoration" and "designs" refer to Chapter Two, Ornament, and "wrought iron" refers to books found in the Metalwork section under iron. Thus, the subject index functions as a cross-reference tool and, indirectly, as a lexicon. It should be understood, however, that the subject index is not necessarily an index to the contents of the books.

The author index is to all authors and to titles that are main entries.

ACKNOWLEDGMENTS

As in the preparation of the first volume the author is grateful to numerous colleagues in the academic and museum worlds for their expert advice. I would especially like to acknowledge the assistance of my wife, Julia M. Ehresmann, for her constant advice and editing and for preparing the section on bookbinding, and to my research assistant Debra Mancoff for her help in the annotation of the sections on costume and musical instruments. And again I owe special gratitude to the staff of the Ryerson Library of the Art Institute of Chicago, without whose cooperation and support it would have been impossible to compile this bibliography.

NOTES

[1] For a full citation and evaluation of these basic bibliographic tools, see entries 2, 7, 22, and 155 in Donald L. Ehresmann, *Fine Arts: A Bibliographic Guide to Basic Reference Works, Histories, and Handbooks.* (Littleton, Colo., Libraries Unlimited, 1975).

[2] For an excellent discussion of the definition of applied and decorative arts, see the preface in Harold Osborne, *The Oxford Companion to the Decorative Arts* cited here as entry 12.

CHAPTER ONE

APPLIED AND DECORATIVE ARTS—GENERAL

DICTIONARIES AND ENCYCLOPEDIAS

1   Boger, Louise A., and Batterson H. Boger. **The Dictionary of Antiques and the Decorative Arts; a Book of Reference for Glass, Furniture, Ceramics, Silver, Periods, Styles, Technical Terms, Etc.** New York, Scribner's, 1967. 662p. illus. LC 67-18131.

A good, serious dictionary well illustrated with line drawings and plates of museum pieces and items accessible to the collector. First published in 1957; this edition provides a supplement, pp. 569-662. Bibliography, pp. 559-66, is a good classified list of books, mostly in English, with supplement of more recent literature, pp. 661-62.

2   Bosc, Ernest. **Dictionnaire de l'art, de la curiosité et du bibelot.** Paris, Firmin-Didot, 1883. 695p. illus.

Older, serious dictionary of the applied arts covering arms and armor, ceramics, glass, gold and silver, jewelry, metalwork and musical instruments. Perhaps its most useful feature, for the specialist, is the list of nineteenth century collectors, pp. 671-90.

3   Bradford, Ernle. **Dictionary of Antiques.** London, English Universities Press, 1963. 151p. illus.

Popular, pocket-sized dictionary covering terms relating to ornament, technique, material, styles and objects of the decorative and applied arts. Appendices give lists of major designers, craftsmen and artists.

4   Cameron, Ian, and Elizabeth Kingsley-Rowe, eds. **Collins Encyclopedia of Antiques.** London, Collins, 1973. 400p. illus.

Popular encyclopedia covering the various objects and media of the decorative and applied arts as they interest the collector. Illustrated with major museum pieces and pieces accessible to collectors. Bibliography of basic books of reference, pp. 391-98.

5   **The Complete Encyclopedia of Antiques.** New York, Connoisseur, 1962. 1472p. illus. index. Reprint: New York, Hawthorn, 1967. LC 62-9526.

Good, serious encyclopedia of American and European, especially English, applied arts directed to the beginning and experienced collector. Each chapter is devoted

to a particular medium or class of antique object. Each consists of a brief introductory survey followed by a glossary and collection of plates. Good, classified
bibliography, pp. 1410-22, of books in all languages. List of principal museums
and galleries in America and Europe.

6   **The Connoisseur's Complete Period Guides to Houses, Decoration,
      Furnishing and Chattels of the Classic Periods.** Edited by Ralph Edwards
      and L. G. G. Ramsey. London, The Connoisseur, 1968. 1536p. illus.
      index.

Originally published in six volumes. Good, serious encyclopedia of Western applied
arts and interior decoration from 1500 to 1860. Emphasis is on English and American
work. Arrangement is by periods, with essays on the various media by experts in the
field of antique collecting. Well illustrated with line drawings and plates. Some of
the chapters have bibliographical footnotes and short bibliographies at their end.
An alphabetical list of contemporary sources mentioned in the text is given,
pp. 1503-05.

7   Coysh, A. W. **The Antique Buyer's Dictionary of Names.** New York,
      Praeger, 1970. 278p. LC 70-125355.

Useful bibliographical dictionary of the applied arts arranged by media and then
alphabetically by the name of the artist or artisan. Entries give basic biographical
data and brief comment on the artistic activity of the person. No bibliography.

8   Doane, Ethel M. **Antiques Dictionary.** Brockton, Mass., 1949. 290p. illus.

Popular dictionary of short definitions. Not illustrated. Bibliography, pp. 283-90,
lists basic books in English.

9   Havard, Henry. **Dictionnaire de l'ameublement.** Paris, Librairies-Imprimeries
      Réunies, 1887-90. 4v. illus.

Comprehensive dictionary of furniture and related decorative and applied arts
(ceramics, silver, etc.). An older work illustrated with cuts and line drawings, still
useful because of its large scope. Bibliographical references are included in some
of the major entries.

10   Hughes, Therle. **Antiques, an Illustrated A to Z.** New York, World, 1972.
      175p. illus. LC 70-183094.

Popular dictionary covering styles, media, objects, techniques and ornament relating
to antiques. Illustrated with line drawings. No bibliography.

11   Macdonald-Taylor, Margaret S. **A Dictionary of Marks: Metalwork,
      Furniture, Ceramics; the Identification Handbook for Antique Collectors.**
      New York, Hawthorn, 1962. 318p. illus. index. LC 62-17114.

Popular, pocket-sized handbook of major marks found on American and British
metalwork, English and French furniture, English, European and Oriental ceramics.
Bibliography, pp. 309-10, lists books in English.

12 Osborne, Harold, ed. **The Oxford Companion to the Decorative Arts.**
   Oxford, Clarendon, 1975. 865p. illus.
Excellent dictionary covering all aspects of the decorative and applied arts. Longer
entries cover the major media, periods, and nations and cultures. Shorter entries
treat the biographies of major artists and craftsmen, techniques, materials, objects,
decoration and styles. Entries have bibliographical references to list of basic books.

13 Phillips, Phoebe, ed. **The Collectors' Encyclopedia of Antiques.** New York,
   Crown, 1973. 704p. illus. index. LC 73-76934.
Good, well-illustrated popular encyclopedia covering arms and armor, ceramics,
clocks and watches, furniture, glass, jewelry, metalwork, musical instruments,
scientific instruments and toys. Each section has an introductory historical essay
followed by collection of plates with good descriptive captions, glossary of terms,
advice on collecting and restoration, and bibliography of basic books.

14 Savage, George. **Dictionary of Antiques.** New York, Praeger, 1970. 534p.
   illus. LC 75-107216.
Good, serious dictionary of objects, techniques, materials, media, ornament, styles,
and artists and craftsmen relating to antiques. Well illustrated. Bibliography, pp.
504-34, is a good classified list of books and catalogs in all languages.

15 Seling, Annemarie, ed. **Keysers Antiquitätenlexikon.** 3rd ed. Munich,
   Keyser, 1969. 328p. illus.
Good, comprehensive dictionary of the applied arts directed to the needs of
collectors. More than two thousand entries cover styles, techniques, materials,
objects and major artists. Well illustrated. Appendix with outline history of
style in applied arts as an aid to identification.

16 Seling, Helmut, ed. **Keysers Kunst- und Antiquitätenbuch.** Heidelberg and
   Munich, Keyser, 1967-70. 3v. illus.
Excellent, comprehensive handbook of the applied arts directed to the needs of
collectors. Volume one covers books, paintings and frames, boxes and miniatures,
prints, faience, glass, tapestries, furniture, Oriental carpets, Far Eastern decorative
arts, sculpture, porcelain, silver and pewter. Volume two: coins, medals, arms and
armor, drawings, jewelry, clocks and watches, scientific instruments, and modern
art. Volume three: folk furniture, folk painting, folk prints, autographs, old maps,
bookbindings, bronzes, copper and brass, old toys, and ancient, pre-Columbian,
African and Oceanic applied arts. Well illustrated. Chapters written by various
German specialists.

GENERAL HISTORIES AND HANDBOOKS

17 Bossert, Helmuth T. **Geschichte des Kunstgewerbes aller Zeiten und**
   Völker . . . Berlin, Wasmuth, 1928-35. 6v. illus. index.
Excellent, scholarly history of the applied arts covering all civilizations and periods
from prehistoric times through the nineteenth century. Authoritative text by various

renowned experts. Well illustrated with museum pieces. Each chapter concludes with an excellent bibliography of books and periodical articles in all languages. A standard work.

18   Bucher, Bruno. **Geschichte der technischen Künsten.** Stuttgart, Spemann, 1875-93. 3v. illus. index.
Good, older, scholarly history of Western applied arts from antiquity through the nineteenth century. Arranged by media with separate bibliographies at the end of each chapter.

19   Drepperd, Carl W. **First Reader for Antique Collectors.** Garden City, N.Y., Doubleday, 1946. 274p. illus. index.
Popular handbook covering ceramics, furniture, glass, metalwork, etc. Good selection of illustrations. Short bibliographies of basic books given at the end of each chapter. Glossary of terms.

20   Harper, George W., ed. **Antique Collectors Guide and Reference Handbook** . . . New York, Harper, 1939. 87p. illus.
Useful handbook containing, among other essays of dated value, "A Bibliography for Antiques," by Alice Winchester (annotated list of some 150 basic books); "Collecting Societies"; "Why and How to Collect Antiques," by Thomas Ormsbee; and "Antique Names and Terms," by G. W. Harper (a glossary of terms).

21   Lehnert, Gustav, *et al.*, eds. **Illustrierte Geschichte des Kunstgewerbes.** Berlin, Oldenbourg, n.d. 2v. illus. index.
Excellent, scholarly history of the applied arts. Volume one covers Western ceramics, bronze, gold and silver, terra cotta, engraved gems, glass, wood, mosaic, and stained glass from ancient times through the Renaissance. Volume two covers the same arts to the early twentieth century and the minor arts of Islam and the Far East. Thoroughly illustrated with museum pieces. Authoritative text by renowned experts. Excellent bibliography, Vol. 2, pp. 795-817, arranged by chapters and covering books and periodical articles in all languages.

22   Marangoni, Guido. **Storia dell'arredamento.** Milan, Società Editrice Libraria, 1952. 3v. illus.
Serious history of minor and applied arts from prehistory to about 1950. Arranged by media and techniques within a chronological framework. Treats ornament, furniture, fabric, needlework, lace, costume, jewelry, accessories, ceramics, bookbindings, and others.

MODERN APPLIED AND DECORATIVE ARTS
(19th and 20th Centuries)

23   Bourgeois, Emile. **Le style empire, ses origines et ses caractères.** Paris, Laurens, 1930. 131p. illus. index.
Good, serious history of neo-classical decorative art from its origins in Tuscan art of the eighteenth century through the second decade of the nineteenth century. Emphasis is on French interior decoration and furniture. Bibliographical footnotes.

24   Lichten, Frances. **Decorative Art of Victoria's Era**. New York, Scribner's, 1950. 274p. illus. index.
Popular, illustrated history of English and American Victorian decorative arts. Arranged by broad cultural classes (e.g., "World of Industry") and illustrated chiefly with engravings from contemporary books and pamphlets. Bibliography, pp. 265-70, is primarily a list of Victorian illustrated books on the decorative arts.

25   McClinton, Katharine M. **Art Deco: A Guide for Collectors**. New York, Potter, 1972. 288p. illus. index.
Popular handbook of art deco furniture, silver, ceramics, glass, textiles, metalwork, jewelry and graphics. Illustrated with collectibles, it gives suggestions on where and how to buy. Bibliography of basic books and periodical articles.

26   Norbury, John. **The World of Victoriana: Illustrating the Progress of Furniture and Decorative Arts in Britain and America, 1837-1901**. London, Hamlyn, 1972. 128p. illus. index.
Popular pictorial survey of American and British decorative arts of the Victorian period. Covers furniture, interior decoration, glass, ceramics and textiles. Brief bibliography of basic books.

27   **The Random House Collector's Encyclopedia: Victoriana to Art Deco**. New York, Random House, 1974. 302p. illus. LC 74-5380.
Good, popular dictionary of Western applied arts covering persons, styles, materials, techniques, objects, major works and movements. Illustrated with collectibles. Bibliography, pp. 297-302, is arranged according to the entries and lists chiefly books in English.

28   Wood, Violet. **Victoriana; a Collector's Guide**. London, Bell, 1960. 175p. illus. index.
Popular handbook with chapters on ceramics, furniture, glass, jewelry, textiles and metalwork. One-page bibliography of basic books. Emphasis is on English Victoriana.

29   Woodhouse, Charles P. **The Victoriana Collector's Handbook**. New York, St. Martin's, 1970. 237p. illus. index. LC 70-156345.
Popular handbook covering ceramics, furniture, glass, jewelry and metalwork with chapters on collecting and Victorian artists and craftsmen. Appendix with major assay marks.

AMERICAN APPLIED AND DECORATIVE ARTS
(U.S. and Canada)

30   Comstock, Helen, ed. **The Concise Encyclopedia of American Antiques**. New York, Hawthorn Books, n.d. 2v. illus. index. LC 58-5628.
Good, popular encyclopedia consisting of essays on the various media and styles by experts in the antique collecting field. Good selection of plates. Each chapter concludes with a bibliography of basic books.

31   Hornung, Clarence P. **Treasury of American Design**. New York, Abrams, n.d. 2v. illus. index. LC 76-142742.
Popular, pictorial survey of American "articles of daily use" from Colonial times to the end of the nineteenth century. Grouped in broad classes—for example, objects associated with the sea, tavern, etc.—but also has chapters on specific classes like cigar store Indians. No bibliography.

32   Lessard, Michel, and Huguette Marquis. **Encyclopédie des antiquités du Québec**. Montreal, Les Éditions de l'Homme, 1971. 526p. illus. LC C71-4511.
Good popular encyclopedia covering all aspects of the applied and deocrative arts of French Canada including furniture, ceramics, metalwork, textiles. General bibliography of reference books, pp. 511-18.

33   Stillinger, Elizabeth. **The Antiques Guide to Decorative Arts in America, 1600—1875**. New York, Dutton, 1972. 463p. illus. LC 77-158605.
Popular history/handbook covering furniture, ceramics, glass, metalwork and silver. Illustrated with pieces accessible to the collector. Bibliography, pp. 459-63, is a classified list of basic books.

34   Webster, Donald B., ed. **The Book of Canadian Antiques**. New York and Toronto, McGraw-Hill, 1974. 352p. illus. index. LC 74-10381.
Excellent collection of essays by various experts on the major Canadian applied and decorative arts including chapters on dating and identification, restoration and care, fakes and investment. List of museum and collections and good, classified bibliography of books and catalogs, pp. 343-46.

EUROPEAN APPLIED AND DECORATIVE ARTS

General Histories and Handbooks

35   Alexandre, Arsène . . . **Histoire de l'art décoratif du XVIe siècle à nos jours**. Preface by Roger Marx. Paris, Laurens, 1892. 336p. illus.
Older history of Western applied arts from the sixteenth century through the nineteenth century. Covers wood, metal, ceramics, glass and textiles. Most noted for the chromolithographs by Lemercier.

36   Kohlhaussen, Heinrich. **Europäisches Kunsthandwerk**. Frankfurt am Main, Umschau, 1969-72. 3v. illus.
Excellent, illustrated survey of Western European applied arts from the early Middle Ages to the end of the baroque. Volume one covers the Romanesque; Volume two, the Gothic; and Volume three, the Renaissance and baroque periods. Each volume provides a good introductory essay followed by excellent plates with thorough descriptive notes which have bibliographies. General classified bibliographies at the end of each volume.

37   Labarte, Jules. **Histoire des arts industriels au moyen âge et à l'époque de la renaissance.** Paris, Morel, 1864-66. 4v. (text) 2v. (illus.).
Older, serious history of Western applied arts from the early Middle Ages through the Renaissance. Bibliographical footnotes.

38   Molinier, Émile. **Histoire générale des arts appliqués à l'industrie du Ve à la fin du XVIIIe siécle.** Paris, Lévy, 1896-1919. 6v. illus.
Volume five never published. Good, comprehensive history of Western applied arts through the eighteenth century. Volume one treats ivories; Volume two, furniture of the Middle Ages and Renaissance; Volume three, furniture of the seventeenth and eighteenth centuries; Volume four, gold and silver from the fifth through the fifteenth century; and Volume six, tapestries. Bibliographical footnotes. An old standard work.

National Histories and Handbooks

Denmark

39   Gelfer-Jørgensen, Miriam. **Dansk Kunsthandvaerk, 1730-1850: Rokoko, Klassicisme.** Copenhagen, Gyldendal, 1973. 23p. illus. LC 74-304735.
Illustrated survey of Danish silver, ceramics, furniture and textiles of the period 1730 to 1850. Bibliographical references.

40   Nielsen, Kay R. **Danske antikviteter.** Copenhagen, Reitzel, 1963. 2v. illus. index. LC 65-30994.
Popular history/handbook of Danish applied arts to the mid-nineteenth century. Volume one covers furniture; Volume two, clocks, ceramics, glass, silver and pewter. A brief bibliography of basic books in Danish is given on p. 70 in Volume two. A useful pocket handbook for the collector.

France

41   Eriksen, Svend. **Early Neo-Classicism in France: The Creation of the Louis XVI Style in Architecture, Decoration, Furniture, Ormolu, Gold and Silver, and Sèvres Porcelain in the Mid-18th Century.** London, Faber, 1973. 432p. illus. index.
Good, serious history of French interior decoration and applied arts from 1740 to 1770. Well illustrated with major interiors and museum objects. Bibliographical footnotes.

42   Gonzalez-Palacios, Alvar. **The French Empire Style.** London, Hamlyn, 1966. 157p. illus.
Popular history covering architecture, sculpture, painting, furniture, metalwork, porcelain and textiles. Good color plates. No bibliography.

43   Oglesby, Catherine. **French Provincial Decorative Art**. New York, Scribner's, 1951. 214p. illus. index.
Popular history/handbook of French provincial furniture, ceramics, metalwork and textiles. Bibliography of basic books in all languages, pp. 212-14.

44   Savage, George. **French Decorative Art, 1638-1793**. New York, Praeger, 1969. 189p. illus. index. LC 79-81560.
Good, serious history covering furniture, ceramics, metalwork and tapestry with chapters on Versailles and the French court style, development of French decorative art, style and interior decoration. Appendices offer useful lists and inventories from contemporary documents. Bibliography, pp. 179-80, lists basic books and catalogs in all languages.

45   Strange, Thomas A. **An Historial Guide to French Interiors . . . During the Last Half of the Seventeenth Century, the Whole of the Eighteenth Century and the Earlier Part of the Nineteenth**. London, Methuen, 1950. 370p. illus.
Popular illustrated survey concentrating on restored interiors featuring furniture, wall decorations and objets d'art. No bibliography.

46   Viollet-le-Duc, Eugène E. **Dictionnaire raisonné du mobilier français de l'époque carlovingienne à la renaissance**. Paris, Morel, 1868-75. 6v. illus. index.
Old comprehensive encyclopedia of French applied arts of the Middle Ages and Renaissance. Contents: t. 1, p. 1, Meubles; t. 2, pt. 2, Ustensiles; pt. 3, Orfèvrerie; pt. 4, Instruments de musique; pt. 5, Jeux, passe-temps; pt. 6, Outils, outillages; t. 3-4, pt. 7, Vêtements, bijoux de corps, objets de toilette; t. 5-6, pt. 8, Armes de guerre offensives et défensives.

Arranged in dictionary form within the volumes. A scholarly source much out of date but still valuable as a pioneering, classic work affording insight into the neo-Gothic taste of the influential author.

Germany

47   Klingenburg, Karl-Heinz. **Vom Steinbell bis zum Schönen Brunnen. Angewandte Kunst in Deutschland bis zur Mittelalter**. Berlin, Zentralinstitut für Formgesaltung, 1964. 462p. illus. (Abriss der Angewandten Kunst, 1)
Good illustrated survey of German applied arts from the early Middle Ages to the present. Arranged by function, it features pieces from East German museums.

48   Kohlhaussen, Heinrich. **Geschichte des deutschen Kunsthandwerks**. Munich, Bruckmann, 1955. 591p. illus. index. (Deutsche Kunstgeschichte, Band V)
Excellent, scholarly history of German applied and decorative arts from the sixth century to circa 1952. Illustrated with museum pieces. Good classified bibliography of books and periodical articles in German, pp. 577-590. A standard history.

49   Passarge, Walter. **Deutsche Werkkunst der Gegenwart**. Berlin, Rembrandt, n.d. 154p. illus.

Popular survey of German applied arts of the late nineteenth and early twentieth century covering enamels, gold and silver, metalwork, textiles, leather, glass and ceramics. No bibliography.

Great Britain

(for Scotland, see no. 61)

50   Beard, Geoffrey W. **Georgian Craftsmen and Their Work**. South Brunswick, N.J., A. S. Barnes, 1967. 206p. illus. index. LC 67-20199.

Good, serious history of interior decoration in England from 1700 to 1800. Emphasis is on technical and financial aspects of major projects. Appendix with list of major craftsmen and specimen costs. Good, classified bibliography, pp. 190-98, that includes manuscript and archival sources.

51   Gloag, John. **Victorian Comfort: A Social History of Design from 1830-1900**. Newton Abbot, David & Charles, 1973. 252p. illus. index. First published in 1961 (London, A. & C. Black).

Popular illustrated survey of British Victorian applied and decorative arts with emphasis on the social context. No bibliography.

52   Lavine, Sigmund A. **Handmade in England. The Tradition of British Craftsmen**. New York, Dodd Mead, 1968. 148p. illus. index. LC 68-16179.

Popular history of English furniture, glass, pottery, porcelain and silver from the Middle Ages through the eighteenth century. Good classified bibliography of basic books and catalogs, pp. 135-137.

53   Strange, Thomas A. **English Furniture, Decoration, Woodwork and Allied Arts During the Last Half of the Seventeenth Century, the Whole of the Eighteenth Century, and the Earlier Part of the Nineteenth**. New York, Scribner's, 1950. 368p. illus.

Popular illustrated survey of English furniture and interior decoration. Illustrations feature restored interiors and major pieces of furniture and wall decoration. No bibliography.

Italy

54   Chiesa, G. **Il Cinquecento: Mobili, arti decorative, costume**. Milan, Görlich, 1972. 96p. illus.

Popular illustrated survey of Italian applied and decorative arts of the sixteenth century.

55   Chiesa, G. **Il Quattrocento: Mobili, arti decorative, costume**. Milan, Görlich, 1972. 96p. illus.

Popular illustrated survey of Italian applied and decorative arts of the fifteenth century.

56   Chiesa, G. **Il Seicento: Mobili, arti decorative, costume.** Milan, Görlich, 1973. 111p. illus.
Popular illustrated survey of Italian applied and decorative arts of the seventeenth century. Illustrated with museum pieces and historic interiors.

57   Cito Filomarino, Anna M. **L'arredamento in Italia ieri e oggi.** Milan, Görlich, 1972. 2v. illus. LC 73-33343.
Well-illustrated, comprehensive history of Italian applied and decorative arts from the Middle Ages to the present with emphasis on interior decoration.

58   Rosa, Gilda. **La decorazione dell'età barocca.** Milan, Fabbri, 1967. 156p. illus. LC 68-100576.
Popular illustrated survey of European decorative arts of the baroque with emphasis on Italian examples. Bibliography of basic books and catalogs, pp. 152-53.

Norway

59   Hopstock, Carsten. **Norwegian Design, from Viking Age to Industrial Revolution.** Oslo, Dreyer, n.d. 212p. illus. LC 59-20547.
Popular illustrated survey of Norwegian applied and decorative arts. No bibliography.

Poland

60   Bochnak, Adam. **Decorative Arts in Poland.** Warsaw, Arkady, 1972. 331p. illus. index. LC 72-171720.
Popular illustrated history covering folk art as well as the major applied and decorative arts. Illustrated with museum pieces. Brief bibliography of basic books in Polish and Western European languages.

Scotland

61   Finlay, Ian. **Scottish Crafts.** London, Harrap; New York, Chanticleer, 1948. 128p. illus. index.
Good, serious history covering architecture and sculpture as well as the applied arts of metalwork, textiles, ceramics, glass and the art of the book from the Middle Ages to the present. No bibliography.

Spain

62   Sanchez-Mesa, Martin D. **L'arredamento spagnolo.** Milan, Fabbri, 1967. 158p. illus. LC 68-111877.
Popular illustrated survey of Spanish applied and decorative arts from the Middle Ages through the nineteenth century. Brief bibliography of basic books in all languages.

Sweden

63 Plath, Iona. **The Decorative Arts of Sweden.** New York, Dover, 1966.
     218p. illus. index. LC 65-20487.
First published in 1948. Good, popular history of Swedish textiles, ceramics, metalwork, glass, wood sculpture and wall painting from the Middle Ages to the present.
Emphasis is on folk art with a few select examples of modern applied arts. No
bibliography.

Switzerland

64 Lüthi, Max. **Bürgerliche Innendekoration des Spätbarock und Rokoko in
     der deutschen Schweiz.** Zurich, O. Füssli, 1927. 92p. illus.
Good, popular illustrated survey of German Swiss interiors with major works of
furniture and objets d'art of the eighteenth century. Good bibliography of basic
books and some periodical articles, pp. 80-89.

ORIENTAL APPLIED AND DECORATIVE ARTS

65 Bowes, James Lord. **Japanese Marks and Seals** . . . London, Sotheran, 1882.
     379p. illus. index.
Useful index of marks and seals found on Japanese pottery, illuminated manuscripts,
printed books, lacquer, enamel, metal, wood, ivory, etc. "The zodiacal cycle and
year periods," pp. 342-53.

66 Cohn-Wiener, Ernst. **Das Kunstgewerbe des Ostens.** Berlin, Verlag für
     Kunstwissenschaft, n.d. 256p. illus. index.
Good, serious history of Oriental minor arts covering Near, Middle and Far East
from ancient Egypt through the nineteenth century. Bibliography, pp. 255-56,
is a classified list of basic books chiefly in German.

67 Dupont, Maurice. **Décoration hindoue** . . . Paris, A. Calavas, 1924. 6p.
     text, 48 plates.
Illustrated survey of Indian applied and decorative arts. No bibliography.

68 Feddersen, Martin. **Chinese Decorative Arts; a Handbook for Collectors
     and Connoisseurs.** New York, T. Yoseloff, 1961. 286p. illus. index.
     LC 61-9623.
Good, serious handbook/history of Chinese ceramics, furniture, lacquer, ivory,
metalwork and textiles from earliest dynastic times until the end of the nineteenth
century. Brief bibliography of basic books in all languages.

69   Feddersen, Martin. **Japanisches Kunstgewerbes: Ein Handbuch für Sammler
      und Liebhaber.** Braunschweig, Klinkhardt & Biermann, 1960. 320p. illus.
      index. LC A61-874. (Bibliothek für Kunst- und Antiquitätenfreunde, Band 2)
Good, serious history/handbook of Japanese applied and decorative arts covering
furniture, ceramics, metalwork, lacquer, ivory and textiles. Chapter on collecting
and good classified bibliography of basic books in all languages, pp. 288-305.

70   Kühnel, Ernst. **The Minor Arts of Islam.** Ithaca, N.Y., Cornell University
      Press, 1971. 255p. illus. index. LC 75-110331.
Excellent, serious handbook covering furniture, manuscript illumination, book
binding, pottery, glass, metalwork, ivory, wood and stone carving. Well-selected
illustrations of museum pieces. List of public collections and good, classified and
annotated bibliography of basic books in all languages, pp. 247-50.

71   Kümmel, Otto. **Ostasiatisches Gerät.** Berlin, Cassirer, 1925. 62p. (text)
      140 plates.
Good, illustrated survey of Far Eastern lacquer, bronze, and ceramics. Introductory
essay with descriptive notes to the plates which illustrate museum pieces. No
bibliography.

72   Lee, Sherman E. **Japanese Decorative Style.** New York, Abrams, 1961.
      161p. illus. index. LC 61-9910.
Excellent, scholarly history of Japanese decorative arts. Chapter one gives an analysis
of the nature of Japanese decorative style; subsequent chapters treat the development by periods. Good selection of illustrations with descriptive notes. Bibliography,
pp. 155-58, lists books and periodicals articles in Japanese and Western languages.

73   Migeon, Gaston. **Les arts plastiques et industriels.** Paris, A. Picard, 1907.
      476p. illus. index. (Manuel d'art musulman, tome II)
Good but older comprehensive history of Islamic sculpture and applied arts
including furniture, ceramics, glass, metalwork and textiles. Bibliographies at the
end of the chapters. A pioneering work; still indispensable.

74   Turk, Frank. **Japanese Objets d'Art.** New York, Sterling, 1963. 156p. illus.
      index. LC 63-11584.
Popular handbook on Japanese decorative arts with chapters on the historical background, periods and styles and subject matter. Glossary and brief bibliography of
general works. Illustrated with pieces accessible to the average collector.

75   Yamada, Chisaburoh F., ed. **Decorative Arts of Japan.** Tokyo, Kodansha
      International, 1964. 262p. illus. LC 63-22011.
Good, serious survey history consisting of chapters on ceramics, metalwork, lacquer
and textiles by various Japanese specialists. Well illustrated with color plates of
major museum pieces with descriptive captions. Chronological table but no
bibliography.

AFRICAN APPLIED AND DECORATIVE ARTS

76   Trowell, Kathleen M. **African Design**. New York, Praeger, 1960. 78p. illus. LC 60-71832.

Good, serious handbook of the applied arts of the major sub-Saharan peoples of Africa. Covers wall decoration, mats and screens, textiles, basketry, leather, cicatrization and body painting, calabash decoration, wood and ivory carving, metalwork and pottery. Good chapter on motifs in African design. Good plates with descriptive captions. Bibliographical footnotes.

CHAPTER TWO

ORNAMENT

77   Berliner, Rudolf. **Ornamentale Vorlageblätter des 15. bis 18. Jahrhunderts.** Leipzig, Klinkhardt & Biermann, 1926. 182p. (text), 450 plates. index.
Excellent, scholarly collection of decorative engravings from the fifteenth through the eighteenth century. Thoroughly indexed by artist, publishers, and collections from which the illustrations were taken.

78   Bossert, Helmuth T. **An Encyclopedia of Colour Decoration from the Earliest Times to the Middle of the XIXth Century . . .** New York, Weyhe, 1928. 34p. (text), 120 plates.
Illustrated survey of colored decoration, mostly wall painting, from antiquity to the middle of the nineteenth century. Plates with descriptive notes.

79   Bossert, Helmuth T., ed. **Ornament in Applied Art** . . . New York, Weyhe, 1924. 35p. (text), 122 plates. index.
Good, illustrated survey of world ornament with introductory essay and descriptive notes to the plates. No bibliography. A new German edition was published in 1956.

80   Brønsted, Johannes. **Early English Ornament; the Sources, Development and Relationship to Foreign Styles of Pre-Norman Ornamental Art in England** . . . London, Hachette; Copenhagen, Levin & Munksgaard, 1924. 352p. illus. index.
Good, scholarly history of English ornament from the introduction of Christianity to the Norman Conquest, with a chapter on "Southern Europe: Oriental Animal Ornament in the Pre-Norman Period." Bibliographical footnotes.

81   Christensen, Erwin O. **The Index of American Design.** New York, Macmillan, 1950. 229p. illus. index.
Pictorial survey of American applied, popular and folk arts consisting of some four hundred illustrations recorded in the *Index of American Design* at the National Gallery of Art. Subject list, pp. 209-17, covers the entire collection, not solely those watercolors reproduced. Bibliography, pp. 219-21, lists basic books. This work has been reprinted in Clarence Hornung's *Treasury of American Design* (31).

82   Debes, Dietmar. **Das Ornament, Wesen und Geschichte: Ein Schriftenverzeichnis.** Leipzig, Seemann, 1956. 101p.
Excellent, classified bibliography of some 2,026 books and periodical articles on all aspects of the history and nature of ornament. Thoroughly indexed. A basic reference tool.

83   Evans, Joan. **Pattern: A Study of Ornament in Western Europe from 1180 to 1900**. Oxford, Clarendon Press, 1931. 2v. illus. index.
Good, scholarly history of ornament. Well illustrated. Bibliographical footnotes.

84   Fořtova-Sámalová, Pavla. **Egyptian Ornament**. London, A. Wingate, 1963. 162p. illus. LC 64-2811.
Popular handbook of ancient Egyptian ornament with plates and line drawings taken from architecture, applied and decorative arts.

85   Glazier, Richard. **A Manual of Historic Ornament** . . . 6th ed. rev. and enl. London and New York, Batsford, 1948. 184p. illus.
Good, popular history/handbook illustrated with line drawings and plates. Bibliography, pp. 177-81, lists basic books to the time of publication.

86   Guilmard, Désiré. **Les maîtres ornemanistes, dessinateurs, peintres, architectes, sculpteurs et graveurs; écoles française, -italienne, -allemande, et des Pays-Bas** . . . Paris, Plon, 1880-81. 560p. illus. index.
Pictorial handbook of decorative designs arranged according to schools and subdivided by masters, listed chronologically. Bibliography of works consulted in the Bibliothèque de Paris, pp. 523-27. Indexes by motif and artist follow each school. General index of authors at end. Old but still useful for reference to specific artists.

87   Hamlin, Alfred D. F. **A History of Ornament**. New York, Century, 1916-23. 2v. illus. index. Reprint: New York, Cooper Square, 1973.
Good, comprehensive history of Western ornament illustrated with line drawings and plates. Volume one covers ancient and medieval ornament; Volume two, Renaissance and modern. Bibliographies at the end of each section. Index in each volume. A standard history of ornament.

88   Jones, Owen. **The Grammar of Ornament** . . . London, Quaritch, 1910. 157p. illus.
Older but good general handbook of world ornament. Consists of essays by various scholars with coverage of Oriental and primitive ornament as well as the main periods of Western ornament. Short bibliographies of basic books at the end of each chapter.

89   Leeds, E. T. **Celtic Ornament in the British Isles down to A.D. 700**. Oxford, Clarendon, 1933. 170p. illus. index.
Good, scholarly history with emphasis on metalwork. Bibliographical footnotes.

90   Meyer, Franz S. **A Handbook of Ornament** . . . Chicago, Wilcox & Follett, 1945. 548p. illus. index. Reprint: New York, Dover, 1975.
First published in 1888. Old, comprehensive handbook of ornament. Part one treats the elements of ornament; Part two, applied ornament; Part three, ornament on decorative objects. Within the parts the brief text and numerous illustrations are arranged by formal qualities.

91   Petrie, Flinders. **Decorative Patterns of the Ancient World.** London, Quaritch, 1930. 88 plates.

Illustrated survey of ancient ornament from ancient Egypt through La Tène Celtic. Consists of plates of line drawing details with brief notes.

92   Racinet, Albert C. A., ed. **L'ornement polychrome; deux cents vingt planches en couleur** . . . Paris, Firmin Didot, 1888. 2v. illus. index.

Illustrated handbook of colored ornament from antiquity through the eighteenth century. General introduction and notes to the plates. An old standard work.

93   Rettelsbusch, Ernst. **Stilhandbuch: Ornamentik, Möbel, Innenausbau von den ältesten Zeiten bis zum Biedermeier.** 3rd ed. Stuttgart, Hoffmann, 1937. unpaged.

Illustrated survey of Western ornament from ancient Egypt to the middle of the nineteenth century consisting of line drawings of ornamental details on furniture and interior decoration with descriptive notes. No bibliography.

94   Speltz, Alexander. **Styles of Ornament, Exhibited in Designs, and Arranged in Historical Order** . . . New York, Grosset and Dunlap, 1935. 647p. illus. index. Reprint: New York, Dover, 1959.

Good, comprehensive pictorial history of ornament from ancient Egypt through Neoclassicism. Brief text introduces each period followed by corpus of line drawings of ornament with captions indicating source. Alphabetical list of reference books, pp. 627-29.

95   Stafford, Maureen, and Dora Ware. **An Illustrated Dictionary of Ornament.** New York, St. Martin's, 1974. 246p. illus. index. LC 74-21095.

Good, popular dictionary of world ornament covering types, motifs, styles, periods, and illustrated with line drawings. Bibliography, pp. 243-44, lists basic books in English.

CHAPTER THREE

FOLK ART

BIBLIOGRAPHIES

96   **Internationale Volkskundliche Bibliographie. International Folklore Bibliography. Bibliographie internationale des arts et traditions populaires.** V. 1– . Basel, Société Suisse des Traditions Populaires, 1942– . Edited by Robert Wildhaber. Succeeds: *Volkskundliche Bibliographie* (Strasbourg and Berlin, 1917-41).
Comprehensive annual bibliography covering all aspects of folk and popular culture including folk art. Lists books, catalogs and periodical articles in all languages. A standard reference tool for serious study of folk art.

GENERAL HISTORIES AND HANDBOOKS

97   **Art populaire; travaux artistiques et scientifiques du Ier congrès international des arts populaires.** Paris, Éditions Duchartre, 1932. 2v. illus.
Excellent collection of essays covering all aspects of world folk art written by renowned experts. Part one deals with basic questions of origins and definition; Part two provides an excellent series of essays on major regional classes of folk art; and Part three deals with matters of technique. Includes dance and music. No bibliography.

AMERICAN FOLK ART

98   Christensen, Erwin O. **American Crafts and Folk Arts.** Washington, R. B. Luce, 1964. 90p. illus.
Good, popular history from Colonial times to the present with a chapter on American Indian crafts. Good list of basic books, catalogs and bulletins, pp. 88-90.

99   Lipman, Jean, and Eve Meulendyke. **American Folk Decoration.** New York, Oxford University Press, 1951. 163p. illus. index. Reprint: New York, Dover, 1972.
Good, popular history/handbook covering furniture, tinware, textiles, architectural decoration, coach and sign painting, and fractur designs. Appendix with selected list of public collections. Good, classified bibliography of books and periodical articles, pp. 157-59.

100   Lipman, Jean, and Alice Winchester. **The Flowering of American Folk Art, 1776-1876.** New York, Viking, 1974. 288p. illus. LC 73-6081.
Good, serious, illustrated survey based on an exhibition organized by the Whitney Museum of American Art. Covers folk painting and sculpture in addition to the usual decorative and applied arts. Well illustrated. Appendix with biographical index to artists. Bibliography, pp. 284-87, provides a good classified list of basic books, catalogs, and periodical articles.

101   Polley, Robert L., ed. **America's Folk Art.** New York, Putnam, 1968. 192p. illus. LC 68-31615.
Popular illustrated survey of American folk arts and crafts of the eighteenth and nineteenth century. Chapters treat media (i.e., glass, ceramics, metalwork, painting) and classes of objects (i.e., lighting devices, weathervanes, toys, and guns). Appendix with list of major museums and collections. No bibliography.

EUROPEAN FOLK ART

General Histories and Handbooks

102   Bossert, Helmuth T. **Peasant Art in Europe** . . . London, Benn, 1927. 44p. (text), 132 plates. index.
Good, pictorial survey arranged by country. List of dated examples. Bibliography, pp. 40-43, lists basic books in all languages. Slightly expanded German edition was published in 1941.

103   Hansen, H. J., ed. **European Folk Art in Europe and the Americas.** New York and Toronto, McGraw-Hill, 1967. 281p. illus. index. LC 68-16683.
Good, serious handbook consisting of short essays on various regions by experts covering Western and Eastern Europe and America. Excellent illustrations. Bibliography, pp. 261-64, lists basic books.

National Histories and Handbooks

Austria

104   Haberlandt, Michael. **Werke der Volkskunst mit besonderer Berücksichtung Österreichs.** Vienna, J. Löwy, 1914. 2v. illus. index.
Good, serious history/handbook of Austrian folk art covering painting, furniture, ceramics, textiles and costume. Bibliographical footnotes.

105   Holme, Charles, ed. **Peasant Art in Austria and Hungary.** London, Paris, New York, The Studio, 1911. 54p. (text), 816 plates.
Good, illustrated survey covering Austrian, Hungarian, Rumanian, Croatian, and Slavonian folk art. Essays on the major regions by experts accompanied by good collections of illustrations of peasant houses and examples of various crafts, including folk costume. No bibliography.

106   Schmidt, Leopold. **Volkskunst in Österreich**. Vienna and Hanover, Forum
        Verlag, 1966. 200p. illus. index. LC 67-76390.
Good, serious history/handbook of Austrian folk art covering all major media
including architecture painting and sculpture. Good bibliography of books and
periodical articles, pp. 189-196.

Bulgaria

107   Boschkov, A. **Die bulgarische Volkskunst**. Recklinghausen, Bongers, 1972.
        384p. illus. index.
Good, serious history/handbook of Bulgarian folk arts covering costume, furniture,
ceramics and metalwork. Well illustrated, including maps. Brief bibliography of
basic books.

Czechoslovakia

108   Mrlian, Rudolf, ed. **Slovak Folk Art**. Prague, Artia, 1953-54. 2v. illus.
Good pictorial survey with English introduction but captions and notes in Czech.
No bibliography.

109   Sourek, Karel. **Folk Art in Pictures**. London, Spring, n.d. 45p. (text),
        271 illus.
Popular pictorial survey covering all classes of folk art in Czechoslovakia with
examples dating from the seventeenth century through the twentieth century.
No bibliography.

Denmark

110   Uldall, Kai. **Dansk folkekunst**. Copenhagen, Thaning & Appel, 1963.
        298p. illus. index. LC 66-32747.
Good, serious history/handbook of Danish folk art covering furniture, ceramics,
metalwork, textiles and costume. Bibliography of basic books and catalogs,
pp. 297-98.

France

111   Ducharte, Pierre L., and René Saulnier. . . . **L'imagerie populaire; les
        images de toutes les provinces françaises du XVe siècle au second Empire**.
        Paris, Libraire de France, 1925. 447p. illus. index.
Excellent, scholarly dictionary of the subject matter found in French popular and
provincial art. Although based upon and illustrated by popular graphics, this work
is very useful for the study of French folk art motifs and subjects. Bibliography
of basic books and periodical articles, pp. 443-45.

Germany

112   Brückner, Wolfgang. **Deutschland, vom 15. bis zum 20. Jahrhundert.**
       Munich, Callwey, 1969. 248p. illus. index.
Good, popular survey of German folk art covering furniture, costume, textiles,
metalwork and ceramics. Bibliography, pp. 236-45, is a good list of basic books,
catalogs and periodical articles.

113   Karlinger, Hans. **Deutsche Volkskunst.** Berlin, Propyläen, 1938. 505p.
       illus. index.
Excellent scholarly handbook of German folk art covering all types, including
popular sculpture and architecture. Introductory text followed by good corpus
of illustrations with descriptive notes. No bibliography. A standard work on
German folk art.

114   Lehmann, Otto. **Deutsches Volkstum in Volkskunst und Volkstracht.**
       Berlin, W. de Gruyter, 1938. 125p. illus. index.
Good, serious history/handbook of German folk art with emphasis on the general
cultural context. Reflects the National-Socialist point of view that was current at
the time of publication.

115   Meyer-Heisig, Erich. **Deutsche Volkskunst.** Munich, Prestel, 1954. 17p.
       (text) 102 plates.
Good, serious introduction to German folk art, with excellent plates of works in
the Germanisches Nationalmuseum in Nuremberg. Chapters treat folk art in its
functional context—i.e., interior decoration, religious work, utilitarian objects,
etc. No bibliography.

116   Spiess, Kurt von. **Bauernkunst, ihre Art und Sinn.** 2nd ed. Berlin,
       Stubenrauch, 1943. 338p. illus. index.
Good, scholarly study of world folk art with emphasis on Central Europe. Chapters
treat materials and techniques, content and style. Poor quality illustrations. Good
classified bibliography, pp. 324-30, lists books and periodical articles in all languages.

Great Britain

117   Lambert, Margard, and Enid Marx. **English Popular Art.** London and New
       York, Batsford, 1951. 120p. illus. index.
Good, popular survey of both folk and popular art in England from the Middle
Ages to the present. Chapters on carvings, metal signs and ornaments, painting,
textiles, pottery, glass and printing. No bibliography.

Hungary

118   Gink, Károly, and Ivor S. Kiss. **Folk Art and Folk Artists in Hungary**. Budapest, Corvina, 1968. 112p. illus. LC 72-5032.
Popular illustrated survey covering costume, ceramics, furniture, metalwork and textiles. No bibliography.

119   **Hungarian Decorative Folk Art**. 2nd ed. Budapest, Corvina, 1955. 36p. (text) 208 plates.
Pictorial survey with brief introduction followed by plates with descriptive captions. No bibliography.

Italy

120   Holme, Charles, ed. **Peasant Art in Italy**. London, Paris, New York, The Studio, 1913. 39p. (text), 449 plates.
Good, illustrated survey with an introduction and chapters on folk art in the Abruzzi, women's crafts, peasant jewelry, and the "Presepe." Good collection of plates. No bibliography.

121   Toschi, Paolo. **Arte popolare italiana**. Rome, Bestetti, 1960. 451p. illus.
Good, serious study of Italian folk and popular arts with important chapter on popular graphics. Well illustrated and with good bibliography, pp. 439-48, of books and periodical articles.

Norway

122   Hauglid, Roar, *et al*. **Native Art of Norway**. New York and Washington, D.C., Praeger, 1967. 176p. illus. index.
Good, popular history/handbook with essays written by Norwegian specialists on the various media. Concentrates on wood carving, rose painting, art weaving and folk costumes. Well illustrated. No bibliography.

123   Stewart, Janice S. **The Folk Arts of Norway**. Madison, Wisc., University of Wisconsin Press, 1953. 246p. illus. index.
Good, serious history/handbook with a chapter on the sources of Norwegian folk art. Good bibliography, pp. 231-35, lists books and periodical articles in all languages.

Poland

124   Czarnecka, Irena. **Folk Art in Poland**. Warsaw, Polonia, 1957. 9p. (text), 234 plates.
Pictorial survey. No bibliography.

125   Jackowski, Aleksander, and Jadwiga Jarnuszkiewicz. **Polnische Volkskunst.**
       Vienna and Munich, Schroll, 1968. 216p. illus. LC 70-363375.
Good, popular survey of Polish folk art, including furniture, metalwork, ceramics
and textiles. Well illustrated. Brief bibliography of basic books chiefly in Polish
and German.

Rumania

126   **Folk Art in Rumania.** Bucharest, Rumanian Institute for Cultural Relations
       with Foreign Countries, 1955. unpaged. illus.
Pictorial survey covering interior decoration (including churches), national costume
and folk jewelry, textiles and pottery. No bibliography.

Russia

127   Holme, Charles, ed. **Peasant Art in Russia.** London, Paris, New York, The
       Studio, 1912. 52p. (text), 550 plates.
Good, popular, illustrated survey covering Great and Little Russia, Russian Poland
and Lithuania. Essays on various crafts including folk costume. No bibliography.

128   Pronin, Alexander, and Barbara Pronin. **Russian Folk Arts.** South Brunswick,
       N.J., A. S. Barnes, 1975. 192p. illus. index.
Popular history covering icons, lubki, lacquer ware, wood and bone carving, ceramics,
metalwork and textiles from the ninth through the nineteenth century. Glossary of
Russian terms. Bibliography, p. 184, lists basic books in English and Russian.

Spain

129   Galter, Juan S. **El arte popular en España.** Barcelona, Barral, 1948. 623p.
       illus.
Good, serious handbook of Spanish folk and popular art including folk sculpture
and architecture. Well-selected plates with good notes. No bibliography.

Switzerland

130   Baud-Bovy, Daniel. **Peasant Art in Switzerland.** London, The Studio, 1924.
       72p. (text), 431 plates.
Good, illustrated survey with plates of individual pieces, entire interiors and works
of eighteenth and nineteenth century art depicting folk art and architecture.
Bibliography, pp. xvii-xix, lists basic books in all languages.

131   Creux, René. **Volkskunst in der Schweiz.** n.p., Éditions de Fontainemore, 1970. 328p. illus. LC 72-558264.

Good, serious illustrated survey of Swiss folk art covering all major media. Good introductory essay followed by excellent selection of plates. Brief bibliography of basic books.

ORIENTAL FOLK ART

132   Munsterberg, Hugo. **The Folk Arts of Japan.** Rutland, Vt., Tuttle, 1958. 168p. illus. index. LC 58-7496.

Popular survey of Japanese folk pottery, baskets, lacquer, metalwork, textiles as well as sculpture, painting, and architecture. No bibliography.

133   Muraoka, Kageo, and Kichiemon Okamura. **Folk Arts and Crafts of Japan.** New York and Tokyo, Weatherhill/Heibonsha, 1973. 164p. illus. (Heibonsha Survey of Japanese Art, Nr. 26)

Good, popular survey mostly of seventeenth, eighteenth and nineteenth century examples, with emphasis on general appreciation of folk art. Well illustrated. No bibliography.

CHAPTER FOUR

ARMS AND ARMOR

DICTIONARIES AND ENCYCLOPEDIAS

134   Gardner, Robert E. **Small Arms Makers: A Directory of Fabricators of Firearms, Edged Weapons, Crossbows and Polearms.** New York, Crown, 1963. 378p. illus. index. LC 62-20058.
Good, comprehensive dictionary providing basic biographical data, reference to major works and bibliographical references. General bibliography, pp. 375-78.

135   Gelli, Jacopo. **Guida del raccoglitore e dell'amatore di armi antiche.** Milan, Hoepli, 1968. 434p. illus. LC 77-407935.
Good, well-illustrated dictionary of antique arms and armor. Bibliography of basic books in all languages, pp. 429-34.

136   Gyngell, Dudley S. H. **Armourers' Marks: Being a Compilation of the Known Marks of Armourers, Swordsmiths and Gunsmiths.** London, Thorsons, 1959. 131p. illus. LC 59-41997.
Good dictionary of armorers' marks from the sixteenth through the eighteenth century, directed to the serious collector. Bibliography, p. 129-131, has separate list of important English sales catalogs.

137   Musciarelli, Letterio. **Dizionario delle armi.** Milan, Mondadori, 1971. 731p. illus.
Good, comprehensive dictionary of world arms and armor covering types, material, techniques, decoration and major makers. Well illustrated with museum pieces and works of art depicting arms and armor.

138   Peterson, Harold L., ed. **Encyclopedia of Firearms.** New York, Dutton, 1964, 367p. illus. index. LC 64-25937.
Good, comprehensive dictionary covering all aspects of the manufacture and use of firearms including types, mechanisms, materials and makers. Longer entries have good bibliographies. Illustrated with plates and line drawings.

139   Støckel, Johan F. **Haandskydevaabens Bedømmelse.** Copenhagen, Nordlundes bogtrykkeri, 1938-43. 2v. illus. index. LC 44-18923.
Excellent scholarly handbook of European armorers' marks and other control marks used on arms and armor. Danish text with summary translations in German. Useful English, French and German glossaries. A standard reference work in the field.

140   Stone, George C. **A Glossary of the Construction, Decoration, and Use of Arms and Armor in All Countries and in All Times.** Portland, Me., Southworth, 1934. 694p. illus.
Useful, popular dictionary illustrated with line drawings. Bibliography, 687-94, lists basic books chiefly in English.

GENERAL HISTORIES AND HANDBOOKS

141   Ashdown, Charles H. **Arms & Armour.** New York, Dodge, n.d. 384p. illus. index.
Older, popular history from prehistoric times through the sixteenth century. Illustrated with plates of museum pieces and works of art illustrating arms and armor. No bibliography.

142   Blackmore, Howard L. **Arms and Armour.** New York, Dutton, 1965. 160p. illus.
Popular illustrated history of world arms and armor.

143   Maindron, Maurice. **Les armes.** Paris, Picard & Kaan, 1890. 343p. illus.
Older, popular history from prehistoric times through the eighteenth century, with an epilogue on nineteenth century arms. Occasional bibliographical footnotes.

ANCIENT ARMS AND ARMOR

144   Bonnet, H. **Die Waffen der Völker des alten Orients.** Berlin, Leipzig, J. C. Hinrichs, 1926. 223p. illus. index.
Good, scholarly history of the arms and armor of ancient Egypt and Mesopotamia, illustrated with plates of museum pieces and line drawings. Bibliographical footnotes.

145   Couissin, Paul. **Les armes romaines; essai sur les origines et l'évolution des armes individuelles du légionnaire romain.** Paris, H. Champion, 1926. 569p. illus. index.
Good, scholarly history of ancient Roman arms and armor illustrated with line drawings. Thorough bibliographical footnotes refer to specialized literature.

146   Salonen, Erkki. **Die Waffen der alten Mesopotamier; eine lexikalische und kulturgeschichtliche Untersuchung.** Helsinki, Societas Orientalis Fennica, 1965. 215p. illus. (Studia Orientalis Edidit Societas Orientalis Fennica, 33) LC 67-9.
Scholarly history/handbook of the arms and armor of ancient Mesopotamia, illustrated with line drawings and plates of works of art depicting arms. Thorough bibliographical footnotes.

147   Snodgrass, Anthony M. **Arms and Armour of the Greeks**. Ithaca, Cornell
       University Press, 1967. 151p. illus. index. LC 67-20632.
Excellent, serious history of ancient Greek arms and armor from Mycenaean times
through the second century B.C. Thorough bibliographical footnotes and good,
general classified bibliography, pp. 131-132, listing major books in all languages.

148   Snodgrass, Anthony M. **Early Greek Armour and Weapons, from the End
       of the Bronze Age to 600 B.C.** Edinburgh, Edinburgh University Press,
       1964. 280p. illus. index.
Excellent, scholarly history arranged by types and well illustrated with actual pieces
and works of art depicting arms and armor. Extensive bibliographical footnotes and
excellent general bibliography of basic works, pp. 213-268.

149   Wolf, Walther. **Die Bewaffnung des altägyptischen Heeres**. Leipzig,
       J. C. Hinrichs, 1926. 108p. illus. index.
Scholarly study of ancient Egyptian arms and armor, illustrated with line drawings
and plates of works of art depicting arms. Bibliographical footnotes.

WESTERN ARMS AND ARMOR

150   Aroldi, Aldo M. **Armi e armatore italiane fino al XVIII sécolo**. Milan,
       Bramante, 1961. 543p. illus. index. LC 62-43141.
Good, serious history of Italian arms and armor from the early Middle Ages to the
end of the eighteenth century, illustrated with major museum pieces. Good bibliography of books and periodical articles in all languages, pp. 535-44.

151   Blair, Claude. **European and American Arms, c. 1100-1850**. New York,
       Crown, 1962. 134p. illus. index. LC 62-11803.
Good, popular history/handbook treating the development of forms and decoration.
Dictionary of marks. Bibliography of basic books in English, pp. 123-127.

152   Blair, Claude. **European Armour, c. 1066 to c. 1700**. New York, Macmillan,
       1959. 248p. illus. index. LC 59-24447.
Good, popular history with well-chosen illustrations of major museum pieces.
Bibliography, pp. 230-36, lists basic books and catalogs in all languages.

153   Boccia, Lionello G., and E. T. Coelho. **L'arte dell'armatura in Italia**. Milan,
       Bramante, 1967. 549p. illus. index. LC 68-119207.
Good, serious history of Italian arms and armor from the Middle Ages through the
eighteenth century. List of major armorers' marks. List of basic books, catalogs
and periodical articles, pp. 545-49. A well-illustrated history.

154   Boeheim, Wendelin. **Handbuch der Waffenkunde. Das Waffenwesen in seiner historischen Entwicklung vom Beginn des Mittelalters bis zum Ende des 18. Jahrhunderts.** Leipzig, Seemann, 1890. Reprint: Graz, Akademische Druck-und Verlagsanstalt, 1966. 694p. illus. index. LC 67-78549.
Good, older scholarly history of Western arms and armor from the early Middle Ages through the eighteenth century. Illustrated with line drawings and arranged by class with chapters on technique, collecting and excellent list of makers' marks by country and initials. A classic pioneering work.

155   Boeheim, Wendelin. **Meister der Waffenschmiedekunst vom XIV. bis ins XVIII. Jahrhundert; ein Beitrag zur Geschichte der Kunst und des Kunsthandwerks.** Berlin, W. Moeser, 1897. 246p. illus. index.
Older scholarly history of European armor from the fourteenth to the middle of the eighteenth century with emphasis on the major makers. A pioneering and classic work.

156   Bruhn de Hoffmeyer, Ada. **Arms and Armour in Spain. A Short Survey. Volume 1: The Bronze Age to the End of the High Middle Ages.** Madrid, Instituto de Estudios Sobre Armas Antiquas, 1972. 199p. illus. index.
Good, serious history of arms and armor in Spain from early Bronze Age to the end of the thirteenth century. Bibliographical footnotes.

157   Calvert, A. F. **Spanish Arms and Armour.** London, Lane, 1907. 142p. illus.
Older, popular history from the early Middle Ages through the sixteenth century. No bibliography.

158   Demmin, August. **Die Kriegswaffen in ihren geschichtlichen Entwicklungen von den ältesten Zeiten bis auf die Gegenwart.** 4th ed. Leipzig, Seemann, 1893. 2v. illus. index. Reprint: Hildesheim, Olms, 1964. LC 66-97580.
English translation of the first edition: *An Illustrated History of Arms and Armour from the Earliest Period to the Present Time.* (London, 1877).

Good, older history of arms and armor from pre-historic times to the mid-nineteenth century. Chapters treat the major periods and cultures and, in more detail, the development of specific types. Appendix with dictionary of major armorers and their marks. A classic pioneering work.

159   Ffoulkes, C. **The Armourer and His Craft from XIth to XVIth Century.** London, Methuen, 1912. 199p. illus. index. Reprints: New York, B. Blom, 1967. LC 67-13328; and New York, Ungar, 1967. LC 67-25838.
Older, popular history/handbook with chapters on manufacture and use, list of major armorers of Europe with short biographies and list of marks. Useful polyglot glossary of terms. Appendices with documents concerning armorers' guilds and ordinances. Bibliography, pp. xx-xxii, lists the basic books of the older literature.

160   Fryer, Douglas J. **Antique Weapons A–Z**. New York, T. Nelson, 1971.
       114p. illus. LC 70-160145.
Popular pictorial survey with emphasis on European and American weapons–i.e.,
both firearms and edged weapons of the eighteenth and nineteenth centuries.
Bibliography, pp. 113-14, lists basic books chiefly in English.

161   Gardner, J. Starkie. **Armour in England from the Earliest Times to the
       Reign of James the First**. London, Seeley, 1897. 98p. illus. index.
Older, popular history illustrated with major museum pieces. No bibliography.

162   Hewitt, J. **Ancient Armour and Weapons in Europe**. Oxford and London,
       Parker, 1855-60. 3v. illus. index. Reprint: Graz, Akademische Druck-und
       Verlagsanstalt, 1967. LC 67-105989.
Good, older, serious history of Western arms and armor from the beginning of the
Iron Age through the seventeenth century. Most illustrations are engravings from
dated tomb sculpture. Bibliographical footnotes. Invaluable as a corpus of dated
illustrations.

163   Laking, Guy F. **A Record of European Armour and Arms through Seven
       Centuries**. London, Bell, 1920-22. 5v. illus. index.
Good, serious and comprehensive history from the eleventh century through the
seventeenth century. Volume one provides a general history; subsequent volumes
treat the development of major types. Well illustrated with museum pieces and
works of art illustrating arms and armor. Appendices with notes on forgeries and
armor in English churches. Good bibliography, v. 5, pp. 275-304, lists books and
periodical articles in all languages. A standard work.

164   Martin, Paul. **Arms and Armour, from the 9th to the 17th Century**.
       Rutland, Vt., Tuttle, 1968. 298p. illus. index. LC 67-28906.
Good, popular survey of Western arms and armor from the time of Charlemagne to
Louis XIV with emphasis on material in French collections. Well illustrated. Bibliography, pp. 289-92, lists basic books, catalogs and some periodical articles in all
languages.

165   Nickel, Helmut. **Arms and Armour Through the Ages**. Rev. ed. London,
       Collins, 1971. 122p. illus. index.
Good, popular history from the ancient world to the end of the nineteenth century,
illustrated with good plates of objects in the collections of the Metropolitan Museum
of Art in New York. Brief one-page bibliography.

166   Nickel, Helmut. **Ullstein Waffenbuch. Eine kulturhistorische Waffenkunde
       mit Markenzeichen**. Frankfurt/Main and Berlin, Ullstein, 1974. 323p. illus.
       index.
Good, popular history of European arms and armor from the Middle Ages to the
nineteenth century. List of major marks. Brief bibliography of basic works chiefly
in German.

167   Norman, Vesey. **Arms and Armour**. London, Octopus, 1972. 96p. illus.
Good, but brief, popular history of Western arms and armor from the eleventh
through the fifteenth century. Well illustrated with museum pieces and works of
art depicting arms and armor. No bibliography.

168   Peterson, Harold L. **Arms and Armour in Colonial America, 1526-1783**.
       Harrisburg, Pa., Stackpole, 1956. 350p. illus. index.
Good, serious history arranged by periods and covering firearms, ammunition, and
edged weapons and armor. Illustrated with actual pieces and line drawings of their
mechanism. Extensive bibliographical footnotes. Bibliography of basic books,
pp. 337-45, is thorough but unclassified.

169   Reitzenstein, Alexander von. **Der Waffenschmied. Vom Handwerk der
       Schwertschmiede, Plattner und Büchsenmacher**. Munich, Prestel, 1964.
       96p. illus. (Bibliothek des Germanischen Nationalmuseums Nürnberg
       zur deutschen Kunst- und Kulturgeschichte, Band 23)
Excellent, serious illustrated history of Western arms and armor with emphasis on
the artistic, technical and use aspects. Excellent illustrations of major museum
pieces and works of art depicting the manufacture and use of arms and armor.
Good bibliography of basic books in all languages, p. 88.

170   Thomas, Bruno, Ortwin Gamber, and Hans Schedelmann. **Arms and
       Armour of the Western World**. New York, McGraw-Hill, 1964. 251p.
       illus. LC 64-22727.
Good, serious illustrated history from the thirteenth to the nineteenth century.
Brief introductory essay followed by excellent plates of museum pieces accompanied with good descriptive notes. Glossary of terms and additional notes on
major armorers with bibliographical references.

ORIENTAL ARMS AND ARMOR

171   Creswell, K. H. C. **A Bibliography of Islamic Arms and Armour**. London,
       Royal Asiatic Society, 1956. 79p.
Excellent, classified and in part annotated bibliography of some 497 books and
periodical articles on all aspects of Islamic arms and armor. This material has
been incorporated in the author's comprehensive bibliography: *A Bibliography
of the Architecture, Arts and Crafts of Islam to 1960* (New York, 1961); see
item 103 in Ehresmann, *Fine Arts*.

172   Egerton, Wilbraham E. **Indian and Oriental Armour**. Harrisburg, Pa.,
       Stackpole, 1968. 178p. illus. index. LC 68-16504.
Reprint of revised edition of book first published in 1880.

Older, popular history of East Indian arms and armor through the eighteenth
century. Brief bibliography of basic books, p. vi.

173   Holstein, Prosper P. H. **Contribution à l'étude des armes orientales**. Paris, Lévy, 1931. 2v. illus. index.
Scholarly study of Indian and Southeast Asian arms. Volume one gives the history; Volume two is a detailed catalog of the major illustrated pieces. General bibliography, tome 1, pp. ix-xxiii, and reference to more specialized literature in the catalog and footnotes.

174   Robinson, H. Russell. **Oriental Armour**. New York, Walker, 1967. 257p. illus. index. LC 67-13231.
Good, serious history covering the Islamic world, Central Asia, India, Southeast Asia, China, Korea and Japan. Glossary of terms. Bibliography, pp. 216-17, is an alphabetical list of books and articles chiefly in English.

175   Vianello, Gianni. **Armi in Oriente**. Milan, Fabbri, 1967. 158p. illus. LC 68-112093.
Popular illustrated survey of Oriental arms and armor featuring major museum pieces. Bibliography of basic books in all languages, pp. 154-55.

EDGED WEAPONS

176   Oakeshott, R. Ewart. **The Sword in the Age of Chivalry**. New York, Praeger, 1965. 152p. illus. index. LC 65-14185.
Good, popular history of edged weapons in the West arranged by types from the tenth through the sixteenth century. List of major blade marks. Bibliography, pp. 144-45, lists basic books chiefly in English.

177   Seitz, Heribert. **Blankwaffen**. Braunschweig, Klinkhardt & Biermann, 1965-68. 2v. illus. index. LC 67-35206. (Bibliothek für Kunst- und Antiquitätenfreunde, Band 4-4A)
Excellent, serious history/handbook of Western edged weapons from prehistoric times to the nineteenth century. Excellent bibliography of books and periodical articles in all languages, v. 1, pp. 415-26, and v. 2, pp. 395-410.

178   Wilkinson, Frederick J. **Edged Weapons**. Garden City, N.Y., Doubleday, 1970. 256p. illus. index. LC 72-113989.
Popular general history of world edged weapons from prehistoric times to the present. Brief bibliography of basic books.

FIREARMS

179   Blackmore, Howard L. **Firearms**. London, Dutton, 1964. 158p. illus. index.
Popular history from the late Middle Ages to the mid-nineteenth century, arranged by loading system.

180   Blackmore, Howard L. **Guns and Rifles of the World.** New York, Viking, 1965. 134p. illus. LC 65-17169.
Good, popular, illustrated history from the fifteenth through the nineteenth centuries arranged by loading system. Bibliography of basic books, pp. 125-26.

181   Ffoulkes, Charles J. **The Gun-Founders of England.** Cambridge, Cambridge University Press, 1937. 133p. illus. index.
Good, comprehensive list of English gunsmiths from the fourteenth through the nineteenth centuries providing basic biographical data and facsimiles of marks. General bibliography, pp. 126-28.

182   Hayward, John F. **The Art of the Gunmaker.** New York, St. Martin's 1962-64. 2v. illus. index. LC 62-5869 rev.
Excellent, serious history of European and American firearms. Volume one covers the development in Europe from 1500 to 1660; volume two treats the development in Europe and America from 1660 to 1830. Good treatment of artistic or ornamental aspects and thorough descriptions of mechanisms. Bibliographical footnotes.

183   Jackson, Herbert J., and Charles E. Whitelaw. **European Hand Firearms of the Sixteenth, Seventeenth and Eighteenth Centuries.** London, Holland Press; Chicago, Quadrangle, 1960. 108p. illus. index. LC 60-980.
Popular, illustrated survey.

184   Lindsay, Merrill. **One Hundred Great Guns: An Illustrated History of Firearms.** New York, Walker, 1967. 379p. illus. index. LC 67-23653.
Good, serious history of firearms from the invention of gunpowder to the mid-nineteenth century, with a chapter on decoration and a section devoted to control marks. Good bibliography of basic books, including older illustrated source books, pp. 310-65.

185   Pollard, Hugh B. C. **A History of Firearms.** London, G. Bles, 1926. 320p. illus. index.
Popular history of world firearms written from the standpoint of the general history of warfare.

186   Satterlee, Leroy D., and Arcadi Gluckman. **American Gun Makers.** Buffalo, N.Y., Ulbrich Co., 1940. 186p. illus.

_____. *Supplement to American Gun Makers.* Buffalo, N.Y., Ulbrich Co., 1949. 66p.
Popular but useful dictionary of American gun makers from early Colonial times to the twentieth century. General bibliography, pp. 185-86.

187   Schedelmann, Hans. **Die grossen Buchsenmacher: Leben, Werke, Marken.** Braunschweig, Klinkhardt & Biermann, 1972. 325p. illus. index. LC 73-304998.
Good, serious history/handbook of European firearms from the fifteenth through the nineteenth century, with emphasis on major makers. Illustrated with major

signed museum pieces and facsimiles of marks. Good general bibliography, pp. 322-25.

188   Wilkinson, Frederick J. **Antique Firearms**. Garden City, N.Y., Doubleday, 1969. 256p. illus. index.

Popular history of world firearms from the sixteenth century through the nineteenth century. Brief bibliography of basic books.

CHAPTER FIVE

CERAMICS

BIBLIOGRAPHIES

Note: For bibliographies of Swiss ceramics, see
         nos. 256 and 258.

189   Champfleury, Jules F. H. **Bibliographie céramique; nomenclature analytique
       de toutes les publications faites en Europe et en Orient sur les arts et
       l'industrie céramiques depuis le XVIe siècle jusqu'à nos jours.** Paris,
       Quantin, 1881. 352p.
Old but thorough classified bibliography of books and periodical articles on all
aspects of world ceramics, with the exception of ancient Greek, Roman and Gallo-
Roman. Part one covers general works and is arranged alphabetically; Part two treats
works on various countries and civilizations, arranged geographically. Entries in
Part two are annotated. A standard reference work for specialized research.

190   Solon, Louis M. E. **Ceramic Literature: An Analytical Index to the Works
       Published in All Languages on the History and the Technology of the
       Ceramic Art . . .** London, Griffin, 1910. 660p.
Good, annotated bibliography of books, periodicals and catalogs on all aspects of
ceramics. Main part, an annotated list by author, is followed by a classified list of
the same works. A supplement was published in the *Transactions of the Ceramic
Society* (Stoke-on-Kent, v. VI, 1911-12, pp. 65-104). A useful tool for gaining
access to older literature, particularly that on the history of ceramic technology.

DICTIONARIES AND ENCYCLOPEDIAS

General

191   Barber, Edwin A. **The Ceramic Collectors' Glossary.** New York, Walpole
       Society, 1914. 119p. illus. Reprint: New York, Da Capo, 1967. LC 67-
       27448.
General dictionary of ceramic terms covering techniques, materials, ornament,
types. Illustrated with line drawings. Old but still useful for basic and antiquated
terms.

192   Boger, Louise A. **The Dictionary of World Pottery and Porcelain.** New York, Scribner's, 1971. 533p. illus. LC 72-123829.
A good, popular dictionary of world ceramics covering potters, marks and signatures, types, techniques, places, countries, styles and periods. Short entries with informative notes and good illustrations. Bibliography, pp. 525-33, is a good list of basic books in all languages.

193   Cinotti, Mia. **Dizionario della ceràmica dalla preistoria all'Ottocento.** Milan, Ideal-Standard, 1967. 253p. illus. LC 76-372706.
Comprehensive dictionary covering all aspects of world ceramics including techniques and materials, styles and periods, countries and centers of manufacture and types. General bibliography, pp. 241-53, lists basic books in all languages.

194   Garnier, Édouard. **Dictionnaire de la céramique; faïences-grès-poteries . . .** Paris, Librairie de l'Art, 1893. 258p. illus.
Comprehensive dictionary of ceramics covering makers, places, types and terms, with an alphabetical list of marks and monograms. Appendix of figurative marks. Older, pioneering work of interest chiefly to the scholar and antiquarian-historian.

195   Haggar, Reginald G. **The Concise Encyclopedia of Continental Pottery and Porcelain.** New York, Praeger, 1968. 533p. illus. LC 68-28656.
Good, illustrated dictionary of Continental pottery and porcelain treating periods, countries, centers, artists, decorative motifs and techniques. Plates illustrate museum pieces. Entries on major manufacturers give facsimiles of marks and signatures. Major entries have own bibliographies. Good classified bibliography of general works in all languages, pp. 523-33.

196   Jervis, William P., comp. **The Encyclopedia of Ceramics . . .** New York, Canal Street, n.d. (c. 1902). 673p. illus. index.
Older, popular dictionary covering countries, style, materials, techniques, centers and objects. List of major American and European marks, pp. 657-73.

197   Minghetti, Aurelio. **Ceramisti.** Milan, Istituto Editoriale Italiano B.C. Tosi, 1939. 451p. illus. (Enciclopedia biografica e bibliografica "Italiana" serie XLI)
A good biographical dictionary of ceramic artists from the eleventh century to the early twentieth century. Bibliographical references given in most entries.

198   Savage, George, and Harold Newman. **An Illustrated Dictionary of Ceramics.** New York, Van Nostrand Reinhold, 1974. 320p. illus. LC 73-17999.
Comprehensive dictionary of ceramic terms covering technique, decoration, types, subjects, major styles and countries in short entries. Good illustrations. No bibliography.

Dictionaries of Marks and Signatures

Note: Only general dictionaries are included in this section.
For dictionaries of ceramic marks of specific countries,
see the national categories below.

199   Behse, Arthur. **Porzellanmarken-Brevier für Sammler und Kunsthändler.**
3rd ed. Braunschweig, Klinkhardt & Biermann, 1965. 50p. illus. LC 66-
74730.
Good, popular pocket-sized dictionary of European porcelain marks illustrated with
facsimiles. Bibliography, pp. 49-50, lists basic handbooks in German.

200   Burton, William, and Robert L. Hobson. **Handbook of Marks on Pottery
& Porcelain.** Rev. ed. London, Macmillan, 1928. 213p. illus. index.
General dictionary of ceramic marks covering Europe, the Orient and America.
Arranged geographically with brief introductions to each country followed by out-
line and facsimiles of major marks. An older pocket dictionary of marks.

201   Chaffers, William. **Collector's Hand-Book of Marks and Monograms on
Pottery & Porcelain of the Renaissance and Modern Periods . . . 4th ed.**
Revised by Frederick Litchfield. London, Reeves, 1968. 367p. illus.
LC 68-143078.
Good, comprehensive dictionary of world ceramic marks; a condensed version of
the author's larger work (202).

202   Chaffers, William. **Marks and Monograms on European and Oriental
Pottery and Porcelain . . . 15th rev. ed.** London, Reeves, 1965. 2v.
illus. index. LC 66-38182.
Comprehensive dictionary of ceramic marks arranged first by country then by place,
giving facsimiles of marks. Short histories and descriptions at the beginning of each
section. Volume 2 of this edition, treating British pottery and porcelain marks, has
been greatly expanded by G. A. Godden. In spite of inaccuracies, still the most used
dictionary of ceramic marks.

203   Cushion, John P., and William B. Honey. **Handbook of Pottery and
Porcelain Marks.** 3rd rev. ed. London, Faber and Faber, 1965. 477p.
illus. index. LC 66-1611.
Comprehensive dictionary of ceramic marks of Europe and the Orient, with
especially good coverage of British marks. Illustrated with facsimiles of marks
and signatures. Arranged by country with a brief introduction to each and a useful
general introduction on the historical use of ceramic marks. Appendices provide
dating letters for Wedgwood, Minton, and Staffordshire ceramics.

204   Thorn, C. Jordan. **Handbook of Old Pottery and Porcelain Marks.** New
York, Tudor, 1947. 176p. illus. index.
Popular dictionary of American, European and Oriental ceramic marks, arranged
geographically. Most useful for nineteenth century marks.

GENERAL HISTORIES AND HANDBOOKS

205   Berges, Ruth. **From Gold to Porcelain; the Art of Porcelain and Faience.**
New York, Yoseloff, 1964. 239p. illus. index. LC 63-18243.
Popular history of world ceramics, with emphasis on the beginnings and early
development of Western European porcelain and faience of the seventeenth and
eighteenth centuries. Illustrated with museum pieces. Section on music in porcelain.
Bibliography, pp. 226-27, is an unclassified list of basic books in all languages.

206   Chaffers, William. **The New Keramic Gallery.** . . . 3rd ed. London, Reeves
and Turner, 1926. 2v. illus.
Illustrated survey of world ceramics, intended as a supplement to the author's
Marks and Monograms (202).

207   Charleston, Robert J., ed. **World Ceramics: An Illustrated History.** New
York, McGraw-Hill, 1968. 352p. illus. index. LC 68-24604.
Well-illustrated, popular history of world ceramics from ancient times to the present.
Has brief section on African, Oceanian and pre-Columbian ceramics. No bibliography.

208   Cooper, Emmanuel. **A History of Pottery.** New York, St. Martin's, 1972.
276p. illus. index. LC 72-85262.
Good, popular history of world pottery from prehistoric times to the present.
Arrangement is chronological, with special chapters on British and American
pottery. Illustrated with museum pieces, excellent maps and chronological table.
Useful glossary of terms. Bibliography, pp. 265-70, is a good, classified list of
major books in English.

209   Cox, Warren E. **The Book of Pottery and Porcelain.** Rev. ed. New York,
Crown, 1970. 2v. illus. index. LC 75-127511.
Popular general history of world ceramics from prehistoric times to the present.
Emphasis is on the techniques of manufacture. Many but poor illustrations.
Section on marks. No bibliography.

210   Eberlein, Harold D., and Roger W. Ramsdell. **The Practical Book of
Chinaware.** Rev. ed. Philadelphia, Lippincott, 1948. 320p. illus. index.
Good, popular history of world china and porcelain, with emphasis on pieces
accessible to the average collector. Covers the period from ancient times to 1840.
Bibliography, pp. 307-10, is a good list of basic books chiefly in English.

211   Grässe, Johann G. T. **Führer für Sammler von Porzellan und Fayencen,
Steinzeug, Steingut** . . . 21st ed. Braunschweig, Klinkhardt & Biermann,
1967. 736p. illus. index. LC 68-140703.
An excellent, serious handbook of European and Oriental ceramics for the experienced collector. Arranged geographically, with facsimiles of marks and a most
comprehensive corpus of plates illustrating both museum quality objects and
pieces within the reach of the serious collector. Thoroughly indexed by initials,
places of manufacture, and makers' and designers' names. A standard collector's
handbook.

212   Hannover, Emil. **Pottery and Porcelain, a Handbook for Collectors** . . .
       London, Benn, 1925. 3v. illus. index.
Good, older handbook of world ceramics from ancient Egypt to the end of the
nineteenth century. Volume one covers earthenware and stoneware of Europe
and the Near East; Volume two, Far Eastern ceramics; Volume three, European
porcelain. Good bibliographies of the early literature at the end of each volume.
An older standard handbook.

213   Hughes, George B. **The Collector's Pocket Book of China**. New York,
       Hawthorn Books, 1967. 376p. illus. index. LC 66-20615.
Popular, pocket-sized handbook of world ceramics for the beginning collector.
Chapters on the history of china, terminology and techniques, ornament and a
dictionary of major potters and their marks.

214   Jacquemart, Albert. **History of Ceramic Art**. 2nd ed. London, S. Low,
       Marston, Low and Seale, 1877. 628p. illus. index.
General history of world ceramics from antiquity to the mid-nineteenth century.
A pioneering, classic work in the history of ceramics.

215   Marryat, Joseph. **History of Pottery and Porcelain**. 3rd ed. London,
       Murray, 1868. 549p. illus. index.
An early pioneering history of world ceramics.

216   Savage, George. **Ceramics for the Collector; an Introduction to Pottery
       & Porcelain**. London, Rockliff, and New York, Macmillan, 1954. 224p.
       illus. index.
Popular handbook for the beginning collector covering both Western and Oriental
ceramics. Provides a glossary of terms and bibliographies at the end of each chapter.

217   Savage, George. **Pottery Through the Ages**. Harmondsworth, Penguin,
       1959. 247p. illus. index.
Good, popular history of world pottery from prehistoric times through the nineteenth century illustrated with museum pieces. Arranged by countries with
bibliographies at the end of each chapter. Appendix lists marks on Wedgwood
ceramics.

PRE-COLUMBIAN CERAMICS

218   Bushnell, G. H. S., and Adrian Digby. **Ancient American Pottery**. London,
       Faber and Faber, 1955. 51p. (text) 80p. (illus.) index.
A good but brief serious history of pottery in South America, Central America and
the southwestern United States from the earliest times to the Spanish conquest.
Illustrated with museum pieces. Basic bibliography of books and periodical
articles, pp. 47-48.

219   Harcourt, Raoul d', and Marguerite d'Harcourt. **La céramique ancienne du Pérou**. Paris, Morancé, 1924. 45p. illus.
Good illustrated survey of pre-Columbian ceramics including figurines of Peru. Brief bibliography of basic books and periodical articles, p. 3.

220   Lehmann, Henri. **Pre-Columbian Ceramics**. New York, Viking, 1962. 127p. illus. index. LC 61-5481.
Good, popular survey with emphasis on figurative ceramics. Well-chosen illustrations.

221   Salazar Bondy, Sebastian. **La cerámica peruana prehispánica**. Mexico City, Universidad Nacional Autónoma de Mexico, 1964. 25p. (test), 40p. illus.
Illustrated survey of pre-Columbian Peruvian ceramics including terra cotta figurines. Bibliography of basic books in Spanish, p. 21.

222   Wuthenau, Alexander von. **The Art of Terra Cotta Pottery in Pre-Columbian Central and South America**. New York, Crown, 1967. 203p. illus. index. LC 75-103627.
Good serious history-study of terra cotta sculpture in pre-Columbian South and Central America. Treated by regions, with additional chapters on technique and symbolism. Bibliography, pp. 192-95, lists books and periodical articles in all languages.

ANCIENT AND MEDIEVAL CERAMICS

Note: Only general histories and handbooks are included here. For a serious study of the complex archaeological literature dealing with the ancient ceramics of specific sites, peoples and periods consult the bibliographies: *Archäologische Bibliographie* and *Fasti Archaeologici* (Ehresmann, *Fine Arts*, Nos. 34 and 36).

223   Ballardini, Gaetano. **L'eredità ceramistica dell'antico mondo romano** . . . Rome, Istituto Poligrafico dello Stato, 1964. 303p. illus. index. LC 68-141986.
Good, serious illustrated history of ancient Roman ceramics from early Republican times to the fifth century A.D. Well illustrated with museum pieces. Brief bibliography of basic works, chiefly in Italian.

224   Buschor, Ernst. **Griechische Vasen**. Munich, Piper, 1940. 213p. illus.
Good, serious history of ancient Greek vase painting from the Geometric period through the second century B.C. Illustrated with representative museum pieces. No bibliography. A classic, personal account by one of the greatest scholars of ancient art.

225   Charleston, Robert J. **Roman Pottery**. London, Faber & Faber, 1955. 48p.
        illus. index. LC 55-2952.
Good, serious handbook of ancient Roman pottery with brief but factual historical
introduction, good collection of plates and excellent, classified bibliography,
pp. 41-44, listing books and periodical articles in all languages.

226   Dugas, Charles. **La céramique des Cyclades**. Paris, E. de Boccard, 1925.
        292p. illus. index. (Bibliothèque des Écoles françaises d'Athènes et de
        Rome . . . fasc. 129)
Good, scholarly history/handbook of ancient pottery of the Cyclades. Thorough
bibliographical footnotes.

227   Folsom, Robert S. **Handbook of Greek Pottery; A Guide for Amateurs**.
        Greenwich, Conn., New York Graphic Society, 1967. 213p. illus. index.
        LC 68-25740.
Popular history of ancient Greek ceramics from 1050 to 145 B.C., written in outline form and directed to the beginning collector. Select bibliography of major
books in English; an appendix lists terminology of the major shapes of ancient
Greek pottery.

228   Furumark, Arne. **The Mycenaean Pottery: Analysis and Classification**.
        Stockholm, Kungl. Vitterhets Historie och Antikvitets Akademien, 1941.
        2v. illus.
Excellent scholarly handbook/history of ancient Mycenaean pottery. Volume one
provides a chronology of the development of Mycenaean pottery; Volume two is a
detailed system of classification of most known pieces according to form, color,
decoration, etc. Illustrated mainly with line drawings. Extensive bibliographical
references. A standard handbook.

229   Lacy, A. D. **Greek Pottery in the Bronze Age**. London, Methuen, 1967.
        303p. illus. index. LC 67-108472.
Good, serious history/handbook of ancient Greek pottery directed to the student
and archaeologist. Good classified and partly annotated bibliography of basic
books and periodical articles, pp. 288-90.

230   Lane, Arthur. **Greek Pottery**. 3rd ed. London, Faber, 1971. 64p. illus.
        LC 75-852836.
Good, brief outline history of ancient Greek pottery useful to the beginning
student and collector. Bibliography, pp. 59-61, is a good classified list of books
and periodical articles in all languages.

231   Mingazzini, Paolino. **Greek Pottery Painting**. London and New York,
        Hamlyn, 1969. 157p. illus.
Popular history of ancient Greek vase painting from late Mycenaean times through
the third century B.C. No bibliography.

232   Oswald, Felix. **Index to Potters' Stamps on Terra Sigillata "Samian Ware."**
       Liverpool, Author, 1931. Reprinted: Farnborough, Gregg Press, 1964. 428p.
The 1964 reprint includes addenda from the edition of 1936. Good, scholarly index
of potters' marks found on ancient Roman terra sigillata (incised ware), arranged by
name of the potter. Reference is given to dates and examples. A standard handbook
index to Roman pottery.

233   Stiles, Helen E. **Pottery of the Ancients.** New York, Dutton, 1938. 128p.
       illus. index.
Popular history of ancient Egyptian, Greek, Roman, Etruscan and Far Eastern
ceramics. Illustrated with museum pieces. No bibliography.

234   Villard, François. **Les vases grecs.** Paris, Presses Universitaires de France,
       1956. 109p. illus. LC A57-199.
Popular illustrated survey of ancient Greek vase painting from the Geometric
style through the Hellenistic period. Bibliography, pp. 103-105, lists basic books
in all languages.

235   Wallis, Henry. **Byzantine Ceramic Art.** London, Quaritch, 1907. 40p.
       (text), 41 plates.
Older, illustrated survey of Byzantine ceramics with concentration on middle and
late Byzantine ceramics.

AMERICAN CERAMICS
(U.S., Canada and Latin America)

       Note: see also nos. 266 and 270 listed under "European
                Ceramics."

236   Barber, Edwin A. **Marks of American Potters.** . . . Philadelphia, Patterson
       and White, 1904. 174p. illus. index. Reprint: Southhampton, N.Y.,
       Cracker Barrel Press, 1973. LC 70-21077.
Dictionary of marks on American pottery, arranged by regions: Pennsylvania, New
Jersey, New York, New England, Ohio, southern states and western states with
facsimiles of marks. Each region is introduced with a brief historical sketch. Short
commentaries on major factories. Old, but still a basic reference tool.

237   Barber, Edwin A. **The Pottery and Porcelain of the United States; an
       Historical Review of American Ceramic Art from the Earliest Times to
       the Present Day.** New York, Putnam, 1909. 621p. illus. index. Reprint:
       Watkins Glen, N.Y., Century House, 1971. LC 79-96939.
A once-standard, popular history of American ceramics. Still useful to the specialized
collector and student.

238   Collard, Elizabeth. **Nineteenth-Century Pottery and Porcelain in Canada**.
       Montreal, McGill University Press, 1967. 441p. illus. index. LC 67-30576.
Scholarly history of Canadian nineteenth century ceramics, including French-
Canadian. Provides an appendix of marks and a check list of Canadian nineteenth
century potters. Bibliography provided in the footnotes. Standard work on nineteenth century Canadian ceramics.

239   Ketchum, William. **The Pottery and Porcelain Collector's Handbook; a
       Guide to Early American Ceramics from Maine to California**. New York,
       Funk & Wagnalls, 1971. 204p. illus. index. LC 71-137487.
Handbook of American ceramics for the beginning collector arranged by type and
region. Appendix provides a list of early American potteries. Illustrates pieces within
reach of the average collector.

240   Pileggi, Aristides. **Cerâmica no Brasil e no mundo**. São Paulo, Martins,
       1958. 290p. illus. index. LC 61-30502.
Popular history of Brazilian pottery from Colonial times to the present. Bibliography of books and periodical articles, pp. 201-202.

241   Ramsay, John. **American Potters and Pottery**. New York, Tudor, 1947.
       309p. illus. index.
Popular history of pottery in the United States through the late nineteenth century.
Illustrations of pieces within reach of average collector. Check list of major American
potters.

242   Rivero, Manuel R. **Lozas y porcelanas en Venezuela**. Caracas, n.p. 1972.
       150p. illus. LC 72-225341.
Popular, illustrated survey of pottery and porcelain of Venezuela since the Conquest.
No bibliography.

243   Schwartz, Marvin. **Collector's Guide to Antique American Ceramics**. Garden
       City, N.Y., Doubleday, 1969. 134p. illus. index. LC 69-10989.
Popular history of ceramics in America from 1650 to 1910 directed to beginning
collectors. Arranged by types, with a short introductory history and a section of
advice to the collector. Illustrated with pieces in museums and historical sites.

EUROPEAN CERAMICS

General Works

244   Dexel, Walter. **Keramik. Stoff und Form**. Berlin and Braunschweig,
       Klinkhardt & Biermann, 1958. 141p. illus. index. LC A59-3167.
Good, serious history of Western ceramics from ancient times to the present with
emphasis on the interrelationship between form and technique.

245   Hillier, Bevis. **Pottery and Porcelain, 1700-1914: England, Europe and North America.** New York, Meredith, 1968. 386p. illus. index. LC 68-27001.
Good, popular history of Western ceramics since 1700, with emphasis on the cultural context of ceramic design. Excellent bibliography, pp. 361-68, and further bibliography in the footnotes. Good illustrations.

246   Honey, William B. **European Ceramic Art, From the End of the Middle Ages to about 1815.** 2nd ed. London, Faber and Faber, 1963. 2v. illus. LC 68-128038.
A good, serious survey history of European ceramics. Illustrated with museum pieces. Dictionary of factories and artists, index to marks and general bibliography, (v. 2, pp. 17-27).

247   Litchfield, Frederick. **Pottery and Porcelain; a Guide to Collectors.** 6th ed. London, Black, 1953. 356p. illus. index.
An older, popular history/handbook of Western ceramics from the Middle Ages to the end of the nineteenth century. Section on the major European factories gives some facsimiles of marks. Includes a glossary of terms and a bibliography, pp. 331-34, useful for the older literature.

248   Tardy (firm). **Les poteries, les faiences et les porcelaines européenes ...** Paris, Tardy, 1953-55. 2v. illus. index. LC 62-32073 rev.
General handbook/history arranged by countries giving historical survey and list of chief marks for each. Illustrated with both museum pieces and items accessible to the collector.

France

249   Cushion, John P. **Pocket Book of French & Italian Ceramic Marks.** London, Faber and Faber, 1965. 199p. illus. LC 66-36391.
Useful pocket-sized dictionary of major ceramic marks. Illustrated with facsimiles.

250   Ernould-Gandouet, Marielle. **La céramique en France au XIXe siècle ...** Paris, Gründ, 1969. 192p. illus. index. LC 76-415743.
Popular history of French nineteenth century ceramics with lists of marks. Illustrated with museum pieces. Bibliography, pp. 88-90, lists basic books and periodical articles in French.

251   Fontaine, Georges. **La céramique française.** Paris, Presses Universitaires de France, 1965. 186p. illus. index. LC 66-72503.
Good, popular history of French ceramics from Gallo-Roman times to the present, illustrated with museum pieces. No bibliography.

252   Frantz, Henri. **French Pottery and Porcelain**. London, Batsford; New York, Scribner's, 1913. 176p. illus. index.
Older, popular history from the Middle Ages through the nineteenth century. One-page bibliography of basic books.

253   Peyre, Roger R. **La céramique française: fayences, porcelaines, biscuits, grès, dates de la fondation des ateliers, caractéristiques, marques et monogrammes** . . . Paris, E. Flammarion, 1910. 310p. illus. index.
Good, older, serious history/handbook of French ceramics covering porcelain, faience, soft paste and stoneware. Provides lists of major marks and signatures and much useful factual information concerning the operation of various centers and workshops.

Germany, Austria and Switzerland

254   Cushion, J. P. **Pocket Book of German Ceramic Marks and Those of Other Central European Countries**. London, Faber and Faber, 1961. 184p. illus. index. LC 62-2187.
Popular, pocket-sized dictionary of German and Central European ceramic marks with facsimiles.

255   Ducret, Siegfried. **German Porcelain and Faience**. New York, Universe, 1962. 466p. illus. index. LC 62-13886.
A good, serious handbook/history of German porcelain and faience through the late nineteenth century. Arrangement is by place and factory. Concise text with excellent illustrated catalog of museum quality pieces accompanied by good descriptive notes. Short dictionary of marks and excellent but unclassified bibliography, pp. 452-56, listing books, catalogs, and periodical articles in all languages.

256   Früh, Margit. **Bibliographie der schweizerischen Keramik, 1947-1968**. n.p., Keramik-Freunde der Schweiz, 1960. 24p.
Classified bibliography of books and periodical articles in all languages and on all aspects of Swiss ceramics published between 1947 and 1968. Continues the bibliography of Swiss ceramics by W. A. Staehelin (258).

257   Pazaurek, Gustav E. **Deutsche Fayence- und Porzellan-Hausmaler**. 2nd ed. Stuttgart, Hiersemann, 1971. 2v. illus. index. LC 72-329340.
Reprint of 1925 edition. Excellent scholarly history/handbook of German painted porcelain and faience. Arranged by place, it emphasizes major porcelain and faience painters. Illustrated with pieces in museums and major private collections. Emphasis is on the seventeenth and eighteenth centuries, although porcelain painting since the Biedermeier period is given a chapter. Facsimiles of signatures and thorough bibliographical footnotes. A standard work on German ceramic painters.

258   Staehelin, Walter A. **Bibliographie der schweizerischen Keramik vom Mittelalter bis zur Neuzeit.** Basel, Hirzen-Verlag, 1947. 39p.
Excellent comprehensive bibliography of 350 books and periodical articles covering all aspects of Swiss ceramics. Covers publications through 1947. Continued in Früh (256).

Great Britain

259   Cushion, John P. **Pocket Book of English Ceramic Marks and Those of Wales, Scotland and Ireland.** 154p. illus. LC 59-3962.
Useful pocket-sized dictionary of major ceramic marks, illustrated with facsimiles.

260   Fisher, Stanley W. **British Pottery and Porcelain.** London, Arco, 1962. 162p. illus. index. LC 63-2362.
Popular history of British ceramics, with emphasis on the eighteenth and nineteenth centuries. Arranged by manufactory and types, with sections on identification and collecting. Bibliography, pp. 154-55, lists basic books in English.

261   Fisher, Stanley W. **English Ceramics: Earthenware, Delft, Stoneware, Creamware, Porcelain** . . . New York, Hawthorn, 1966. 256p. illus. index. LC 66-17842.
Popular handbook of British ceramics for the beginning collector. Part one has a brief history and advice to the collector; Part two contains chapters on major kinds of ceramics ware, with reference to the chief factories. Illustrated with pieces within reach of average collector.

262   Godden, Geoffrey A. **British Pottery and Porcelain: 1780-1850.** [South Brunswick, N.J.], A. S. Barnes, 1963. 144p. illus. index.
Good, serious history of English pottery and porcelain of the "classic" period, 1780 to 1850. A general historical survey of the period is followed by chapters on the major centers and manufactories, technique, fakes, marks, and dating and care of porcelain and pottery. Good, classified bibliography of books, pp. 138-40. Illustrated with pieces in museums and private collections.

263   Godden, Geoffrey A. **Encyclopedia of British Pottery and Porcelain Marks.** New York, Crown, 1964. 765p. illus. LC 64-22014.
A good, comprehensive dictionary of British ceramic marks. Alphabetical arrangement by name of maker, designer, factory or region with facsimiles of marks and occasional illustrations of pieces. Appendix of unidentified marks. Glossary of terms and bibliography, pp. 741-44, of books listed by date of publication.

264   Godden, Geoffrey A. **The Handbook of British Pottery and Porcelain Marks.** New York, Praeger, 1968. 197p. illus. index. LC 68-19134.
Good pocket-sized handbook of British ceramics marks. Arranged alphabetically by name of maker with index by initials. Special chronological list of Staffordshire potters since 1780.

265   Godden, Geoffrey A. **An Illustrated Encyclopedia of British Pottery and Porcelain.** New York, Crown, 1966. 390p. illus. index. LC 66-23065.
Excellent illustrated guide to British ceramics. Brief historical sketch and glossary of terms are followed by an excellent corpus of illustrations of both museum pieces and pieces accessible to the collector; arrangement is by maker, artist, and/or place of manufacture. Intended to be a companion to the author's *Encyclopedia of British Pottery and Porcelain Marks* (263).

266   Godden, Geoffrey A. **Victorian Porcelain.** New York, Universe, 1970. 22p. illus.
Good, popular illustrated history of British and American porcelain from circa 1840 to the beginning of art nouveau. Good selection of illustrations. Brief bibliography of basic works.

267   Honey, William B. **English Pottery and Porcelain.** 6th ed. rev. by R. J. Charleston. London, A. and C. Black, 1969. 287p. illus. index. LC 76-484125.
Good, popular history of English ceramics from the fourteenth through the nineteenth century. Illustrated with examples in British museums and major private collections. Bibliography, pp. 257-61.

268   Hughes, Bernard, and Therle Hughes. **English Porcelain and Bone China, 1743-1850.** New York, Praeger, 1968. 254p. illus. index. LC 68-21583.
Popular history of English ceramics, 1743 to 1850, arranged by centers and illustrated with examples within reach of the average collector. Provides short list of marks and good bibliography, pp. 244-48, of books and periodical articles, classified by centers.

269   Hughes, George B. **Victorian Pottery and Porcelain.** New York, Macmillan, 1960. 184p. illus. index. LC 60-930.
Popular history/handbook with emphasis on British examples. Chapter on collecting, brief bibliography of basic works.

270   Mankowitz, Wolf, and Reginald G. Haggar. **The Concise Encyclopedia of English Pottery and Porcelain.** 2nd ed. New York, Praeger, 1968. 312p. illus. LC 68-28655.
Good, comprehensive dictionary covering factories, places of manufacture, artists, techniques, materials, and ornament. Illustrated with museum pieces, pieces accessible to the collector and numerous facsimiles of marks and signatures. Appendixes with lists of: museums in Britain and America having good collections of English ceramics, engravers for pottery and porcelain, British potters on foreign soil. Good classified bibliography, pp. 300-11, lists basic books and periodical articles.

271   Ormsbee, Thomas H. **English China and Its Marks**. London, Allen, 1962.
       200p. illus. index. LC 63-5978.
Popular history/handbook of English pottery and porcelain from earliest times to
circa 1880. Introductory chapter treats the development to 1750; succeeding
chapters cover the work of major makers active between 1750 and 1880. Facsimiles
of major makers' marks. A good introduction for the beginning collector.

272   Rackham, Bernard, and Herbert Read. **English Pottery**. London, Benn,
       1924. 142p. illus. index. Reprint: Wakefield, E. P. Publishing, 1972.
An old but good, serious history of English pottery from earliest times to the end
of the eighteenth century. Illustrated with pieces in museums. A bibliography of
general works is given on p. xxiv and of specialized literature at the end of chapters.

273   Rackham, Bernard. **Medieval English Pottery**. 2nd ed. London, Faber and
       Faber, 1972. 39p. (text), 96p. (plates). index.
Brief but serious history of English medieval ceramics, illustrated with pieces in
British museums.

274   Sandon, Henry. **British Pottery and Porcelain**. New York, Arco, 1969.
       175p. illus. LC 72-108999.
Popular history from the Middle Ages to the late nineteenth century. Illustrated
with museum quality pieces. Appendices provide list of major collections, list of
marks, and very brief bibliography.

275   Savage, George. **English Pottery and Porcelain**. New York, Universe, 1961.
       431p. illus. LC 61-11039.
Popular, well-illustrated history of English ceramics arranged by centers and illustrated
with museum pieces. Descriptive notes to the plates, short list of marks and brief
bibliography of basic works, p. 428.

276   Wills, Geoffrey. **The Book of English China**. South Brunswick, N.J.,
       A. S. Barnes, 1966. 96p. illus. index. LC 65-24846.
Popular illustrated survey covering both porcelain and pottery.

Scandinavia

277   Hernmarck, Carl. **Fajans och poslin; svenska keramik före 1850**. Stockholm,
       Wahlström & Widstrand, 1959. 164p. illus. index. LC 62-67457.
Good, popular illustrated survey of Swedish ceramics dating before 1850. List of
major works and brief bibliography of basic reference works.

278   Mårtenson, Gunnar G. **Gammal finländsk keramik**. Helsinki, Söderström,
       1958. 146p. illus. index. LC A59-7458 rev.
Popular history/handbook of Finnish ceramics, with brief list of marks and bibliography of basic works.

Spain and Portugal

279   González Martí, Manuel. **Cerámica del Levante español, siglos medievales.** Barcelona, Labor, 1944-52. 3v. illus. index.
Excellent, scholarly history of Spanish medieval ceramics. Contents: t. 1: Loza; t. 2: Alicatados y azulejos; t. 3: Azulejos, "socarrats," y retablos. Good bibliographies at end of each section.

280   Llubiá Munné, Luis M. **Cerámica mediieval española.** Barcelona, Labor, 1967. 194p. illus. index. LC 73-270660.
Popular illustrated survey of Spanish medieval ceramics. Illustrated with museum pieces.

281   Valente, Vasco. **Cerâmica artística portuense dos séculos XVIII e XIX.** Porto, Machado, n.d. 244p. illus. index.
Serious history of Portuguese ceramics of the eighteenth and nineteenth centuries arranged by major centers and factories. Lists of marks; illustrated with museum pieces.

Eastern European Countries

282   Csányi, Karl. **Geschichte der ungarischen Keramik, des Porzellans und ihre Marken.** Budapest, Verlag des Fonds für bildende Künste, 1954. 160p. illus.
Good, serious history/handbook of Hungarian faience, stoneware and porcelain arranged by place. Good dictionary of marks. Bibliography, pp. 124-26, lists mostly Hungarian books.

283   Meyer, Hans. **Böhmisches Porzellan und Steingut.** Leipzig, Hiersemann, 1927. 332p. illus. index.
Good, scholarly history of porcelain and stoneware in Bohemia from the early eighteenth century to the mid-nineteenth century, arranged by centers. Thoroughly documented, illustrated with museum pieces and provided with tables of marks.

284   Strauss, Konrad P. **Die Geschichte der Töpferkunst vom Mittelalter bis zur Neuzeit und die Kunsttöpfereien in Alt-Livland (Estland und Lettland).** Basel, P. H. Heitz, 1969. 272p. illus. index. LC 79-519605.
Good, scholarly history of ceramics of Estonia, Latvia and Lithuania from the early Middle Ages to the present. Bibliographical footnotes.

ORIENTAL CERAMICS

Islamic Ceramics

285   Butler, Alfred J. **Islamic Pottery; a Study Mainly Historical**. London, Benn, 1926. 179p. illus. index.
A serious older history of Islamic pottery from its beginnings through the eighteenth century. Good plates of museum quality pieces and bibliography, pp. xxi-xxiv, of the basic older literature.

286   Lane, Arthur. **Early Islamic Pottery; Mesopotamia, Egypt and Persia**. London, Faber and Faber, 1947. 52p. (text), 100p. (illus.). index.
An excellent, brief but serious history of Islamic pottery to the end of the thirteenth century. There is a companion volume on later Islamic pottery by same author (287). Illustrated with museum pieces. Good basic bibliography, pp. 51-52.

287   Lane, Arthur. **Later Islamic Pottery**. 2nd ed. London, Faber and Faber, 1971. 133p. illus. index. LC B72-179330.
Good, brief but factual history of pottery in Persia, Syria, Egypt and Turkey from the fourteenth through the nineteenth century. Bibliography, pp. 124-27, is good in basic books and periodical articles.

288   Rivière, Henri. **La céramique dans l'art musulman**. Paris, E. Lévy, 1913. 2v. illus.
Good illustrated survey of Islamic ceramics featuring museum pieces. Brief bibliography in Volume one, pp. 19-20.

289   Yoshida, Mitsukuni. **In Search of Persian Pottery**. New York, Weatherhill, 1972. 161p. illus. LC 72-76402.
Popular general history of pottery in Iran from prehistoric times to the present. No bibliography.

Far Eastern Ceramics

General Works

290   Honey, William B. **The Ceramic Art of China, and Other Countries of the Far East**. London, Faber and Hyperion Press, 1945. 238p. illus. index.
Good, serious history of the ceramics of China, Korea, Japan and Indochina from prehistoric times to the end of the nineteenth century. Noteworthy collection of plates showing museum pieces. Appendices: lists of marks, glossary of Chinese ceramic terms, discussion of fakes and copies, and patterns and subjects in Far Eastern ceramic decoration. Good bibliography, pp. 218-26, lists books and periodical articles in Western and Oriental languages. Although it is dated in parts, it is still the best general history of Far Eastern ceramics.

291   Koyama, Fujio, and John Figgess. **Two Thousand Years of Oriental Ceramics**. New York, Abrams, 1961. 379p. illus. LC 60-10344.
A good, pictorial history of ceramics in China, Japan, Korea and Indochina from earliest times to the beginning of the twentieth century. Brief outline history introduces the excellent collection of plates with good descriptive captions. Pieces illustrated are in museums and major private collections. Brief bibliography, p. 379, lists basic books in all languages.

292   Penkala, Maria. **Far Eastern Ceramics; Marks and Decoration**. The Hague, Mouton, 1963. 263p. illus. index. LC 65-375.
Serious handbook/history of Far Eastern ceramics, arranged by countries and consisting of brief introductory histories followed by lists of marks. Provides glossaries of Chinese, Korean and Japanese terms and a good, comprehensive bibliography, pp. 235-41, of books and periodical articles.

China

293   Beurdeley, Michel, and Cécile Beurdeley. **A Connoisseur's Guide to Chinese Ceramics**. New York, Evanston, San Francisco and London, Harper & Row, 1974. 318p. illus. index. LC 74-1792.
Popular handbook/history covering all types of Chinese ceramics from prehistoric times to the late nineteenth century. Illustrated chiefly with pieces in private collections and the trade.

294   Du Boulay, Anthony. **Chinese Porcelain**. London, Octopus, 1973. 95p. illus.
Popular illustrated survey from earliest examples to about 1912. No bibliography.

295   Goidsenhoven, J. P. van. **La céramique chinoise: Commentaires sur son évolution**. Brussels, Connaissance, 1954. 213p. illus. index.
Popular history of Chinese ceramics, including figurines, from Neolithic times to 1912 with emphasis on the evolution of forms and decoration. Illustrated with museum pieces. Brief list of marks.

296   Gray, Basil. **Early Chinese Pottery and Porcelain**. London, Faber and Faber, 1953. 48p. (text), 75p. (plates). index. LC 53-27387.
Good, serious history from the Shang through the Yüan dynasty. Good collection of representative museum pieces. Thorough bibliographical footnotes.

297   Gulland, W. G. **Chinese Porcelain**. . . 2nd ed. London, Chapman & Hall, 1902. 2v. illus. index.
Older, serious history/handbook with good selection of illustrations of both museum pieces and pieces accessible to the collector. Bibliography, v. 1, pp. xiii-xiv, and v. 2, pp. xxxviii, lists basic reference works.

298   Hetherington, Arthur L. **The Pottery and Porcelain Factories of China; Their Geographical Distribution and Periods of Activity** . . . London, Paul, Trench, Trubner; New York, Dutton, 1921. 15p. map.

Useful list, by provinces, of the major factories, with dates of activity. Second list by dynasty. Map showing locations.

299   Hobson, Robert L. **Chinese Pottery and Porcelain; an Account of the Potter's Art in China from Primitive Times to the Present Day.** London and New York, Cassell, 1915. 2v. illus. index.

A good, serious history of Chinese ceramics through the Ch'ing dynasty. Illustrated with museum pieces. Chapters on motifs, decoration and forgeries. Bibliography, pp. xxvii-xxx, is an excellent list of the older literature. A standard history of Chinese ceramics.

300   Schmidt, Robert. **Chinesische Keramik von der Han-Zeit bis zum XIX Jahrhundert.** Frankfurt, Frankfurter-Verlag, 1924. 118p. illus. index.

Good pictorial history of Chinese ceramics from 202 B.C. to 1800, illustrated with museum pieces. Brief bibliography, p. 115, and further bibliography in the footnotes.

301   Zimmermann, Ernst. **Chinesisches Porzellan und die übrigen keramischen Erzeugnisse Chinas.** Leipzig, Klinkhardt & Biermann, 1923. 2v. illus. index.

Excellent older, serious handbook/history of Chinese ceramics, illustrated chiefly with museum pieces. Volume one, text; Volume two, plates. Good bibliography of the older literature, v. 1, pp. 325-29.

Japan and Korea

302   Gorham, Hazel H. **Japanese and Oriental Ceramics.** Rutland, Vt., Tuttle, 1970. 256p. illus. index. LC 70-130416.

First published under the title: *Japanese and Oriental Pottery.* Popular history of the ceramic arts in Japan and Korea, with an introductory chapter on the general history of Oriental ceramics. Sections on collecting, symbolism, inscriptions. Bibliography, pp. 237-41, lists books in English.

303   Honey, William B. **Corean Pottery.** London, Faber and Faber, 1957. 19p. (text), 96p. (illus.). index.

A good, popular history of pottery and porcelain in Korea from the earliest times to 1910. Illustrated with museum pieces. Bibliography, p. 17, lists basic books and periodical articles in all languages.

304   Kim, Chae-wŏn, and G. M. Gompertz, eds. **The Ceramic Art of Korea.** New York, Yoseloff, 1961. 222p. illus. LC 61-19038.

A good pictorial history of Korean ceramics from 57 B.C. to 1920. Brief introduction, which traces the outlines of Korean ceramics, is followed by an excellent collection of plates with good descriptive notes.

305   Koyama, Fujio. **The Heritage of Japanese Ceramics**. New York, Weatherhill, 1973. 256p. illus. index.
Good, popular history of Japanese ceramics from the earliest examples through the nineteenth century. Well illustrated. Brief bibliography of basic books in English and Japanese.

306   Mikami, Tsugio. **The Art of Japanese Ceramics**. New York, Weatherhill, 1972. 185p. illus. LC 77-162681.
Good, popular history/handbook of Japanese ceramics from prehistoric times to the late Edo period. Also has a chapter on the place of ceramics in Japanese life. Well illustrated with examples of museum quality.

307   Mitsuoka, Tadanari. **Ceramic Art of Japan**. 5th ed. Tokyo, Japan Travel Bureau, 1960. 184p. illus. LC 60-10373.
Popular history of Japanese ceramics from earliest times through the early twentieth century.

308   Munsterberg, Hugo. **The Ceramic Art of Japan: A Handbook for Collectors**. Rutland, Vt., Tuttle, 1964. 272p. illus. index. LC 63-20586.
Popular handbook of Japanese ceramics with chapters on periods, appreciation and collecting. Bibliography, pp. 265-66, lists books in all languages.

309   Stitt, Irene. **Japanese Ceramics of the Last 100 Years**. New York, Crown, 1974. 256p. illus. index.
Popular history of recent Japanese ceramics. No bibliography.

PORCELAIN

General Histories and Handbooks

310   Burton, William. **A General History of Porcelain** . . . London and New York, Cassell, 1921. 2v. illus. index.
Good, older history of world porcelain arranged by countries. Illustrated with museum pieces and some facsimiles of marks. Bibliography, v. 2, pp. 207-08, lists basic books chiefly in English.

311   Dillon, Edward. **Porcelain** . . . London, Methuen, 1904. 419p. illus. index.
Good, older history of world porcelain with list of marks.

312   Schmidt, Robert. **Porcelain as an Art and Mirror of Fashion** . . . London, Harrap, 1932. 336p. illus. index.
A popular history of porcelain with emphasis on its relationship to the cultural context. Introductory chapters, which treat the general history of Far Eastern and European porcelain, are followed by chapters on types and uses. Bibliography, pp. 311-17, is an annotated list of major books.

American Porcelain (U.S. and Canada)

Note: see also titles under "American Ceramics" above.

313   Schwartz, Marvin D., and Richard Wolfe. **A History of American Art
       Porcelain**. New York, Renaissance Editions, 1967. 93p. illus. LC 66-30197.
Popular history from the early eighteenth century to the present, covering painted
figurines, handpainted or relief modeled porcelain.

European Porcelain

General Works

314   Bacci, Mina. **European Porcelain**. London and New York, Hamlyn, 1969.
       157p. illus.
Popular history of European eighteenth century porcelain, well illustrated with color
plates of museum pieces.

315   Charles, Rollo. **Continental Porcelain of the Eighteenth Century**. London
       and Toronto, Benn, 1964. 198p. illus. index. LC 65-1933.
Popular history/handbook treating use, manufacture and style with survey of major
factories and their marks. Illustrated with examples in museums and collections in
Great Britain.

316   Danckert, Ludwig. **Manuel de la porcelaine européene. Le vade-mecum de
       l'amateur et du professionnel**. Paris, Office du Livre, 1973. 448p. illus.
French edition of *Handbuch des europäischen Porzellans* (Munich, 1954). Good
comprehensive dictionary of European porcelain marks arranged alphabetically by
initial or names; preceded by a dictionary of terms, places, and persons. Appendix
includes list of Sèvres ceramic artists. Good collection of plates showing representative pieces.

317   Ducret, Siegfried. **Porzellan der europäischen Manufacturen im 18.
       Jahrhundert**. Zürich, Silva, 1971. 136p. illus. index. LC 72-302796.
French translation: *La porcelaine des manufactures européenes du 18e siècle*. Good,
serious history of eighteenth century Continental porcelain by countries and centers.
Illustrated with major museum pieces.

318   Jedding, Hermann. **Europäisches Porzellan**. Munich, Keyser, 1972-73. 2v.
       illus. index.
Good, serious history/handbook of European porcelain, with well-chosen illustrations and lists of marks. Volume one covers to 1800 and Volume two from 1800 to
the present. Good, classified bibliographies at the end of each section.

319   Olivar-Daydi, Marcel. **La porcelana en Europa desde sus origines hasta principios del siglo XIX.** Barcelona, Barral, 1952-53. 2v. illus. LC 53-20258.
Good, serious history of European porcelain from its beginnings through the mid-nineteenth century. Bibliographies listing major books and periodical articles in all languages appear at the end of each section. Well-chosen illustrations of museum pieces.

320   Schnorr von Carolsfeld, Ludwig, and Erich Köllmann. **Porzellan der europäischen Fabriken.** 6th ed. Braunschweig, Klinkhardt & Biermann, 1974. 2v. illus. index. (Bibliothek für Kunst und Antiquitätenfreunde, Band 3)
Excellent, scholarly handbook of European eighteenth century porcelain, arranged by centers or factories. Introduction treats materials, techniques and history. Illustrated with museum pieces and pieces in major private collections. Good list of marks. Bibliography in the footnotes. A standard handbook of eighteenth century porcelain.

321   Hofmann, Friedrich H. **Das Porzellan der europäischen Manufakturen im XVIII Jahrhundert; eine Kunst- und Kulturgeschichte.** Berlin, Propyläen, 1932. 537p. illus. index.
An excellent, comprehensive history of European eighteenth century porcelain, illustrated with museum pieces. Sections deal with history, manufacture and technique. Short dictionary of major works. A standard history of European porcelain.

322   Rosa, Gilda. **La porcellana in Europa.** Milan, Bramante, 1966. 72p. (text), 369p. (illus.). index. LC 67-123302.
Good, serious illustrated history of European porcelain of the eighteenth and nineteenth centuries with especially good coverage of Italian porcelain. List of major works.

323   Wynter, Henry. **An Introduction to European Porcelain.** New York, Crowell, 1972. 255p. illus. index.
Well-illustrated popular survey of European porcelain of the eighteenth and nineteenth centuries. List of major marks and brief bibliography of basic books in all languages.

France

324   Alfassa, Paul, and Jacques Guérin. **Porcelaine française du XVIIe au milieu du XIXe siècle.** Paris, A. Lévy, 1931. 72p. illus.
Good, illustrated survey of French porcelain from the seventeenth to the middle of the nineteenth century. Bibliography, pp. 32-33, lists basic books and periodical articles.

325   Auscher, Ernest S. **A History and Description of French Porcelain**. London and New York, Cassell, 1905. 200p. illus. index.
Good, older popular history of French porcelain with section listing major marks. Bibliography, pp. 192-96, is a fairly complete list of the older literature.

326   Chavagnac, Xavier R. M., and Gaston A. Grollier. **Histoire des manufactures françaises de porcelaine** . . . Paris, Picard, 1906. 966p. illus. index.
Good, comprehensive history of French porcelain, arranged by place of manufacture. Illustrated with museum pieces and with numerous facsimiles of marks of manufacture. Well indexed, with separate index of manufacturers, decorators and artisans. A standard work on French porcelain.

327   Grollier, Charles de. **Manuel de l'amateur de porcelaines, manufactures françaises, suivi du répertoire alphabétique et systématique de toutes les marques connues**. Paris, A. Picard, 1922. 296p. illus.
Good, comprehensive dictionary of French porcelain marks, arranged alphabetically by initial letter and systematically by device. Bibliography of basic books, pp. xvii-xviii. A standard dictionary of French porcelain marks.

328   Honey, William B. **French Porcelain of the 18th Century**. London, Faber and Faber, 1950. 78p. illus. index.
Good, serious history/handbook of French eighteenth century porcelain arranged by centers and factories. Illustrated with museum pieces. Brief dictionary of marks, with facsimiles and a good chapter on forgeries. Brief bibliography, pp. 70-71, of books and catalogs in all languages.

329   Savage, George. **Seventeenth and Eighteenth Century French Porcelain**. New York, Macmillan, 1960. 243p. illus. index.
Popular history/handbook of French seventeenth and eighteenth century porcelain. Introductory chapter surveys the history of French decorative arts in the period; chapters follow on the major factories. A section on forgeries. Illustrated with examples in major British museums and collections. Bibliography, pp. 232-33, and appendix of marks.

330   Tilmans, Émile. **Porcelaines de France**. Paris, Éditions Mondes, 1952. 320p. illus. index.
Good, serious history of French porcelain from its beginnings through the first half of the present century. Arrangement is by centers and factories. Illustrated mostly with museum pieces. Good chapter on technique and manufacture, brief selection of marks and signatures and a good, classified bibliography, pp. 310-12, of books in all languages.

Germany, Austria and Switzerland

331   Savage, George. **18th Century German Porcelain**. London, Salisbury Square, 1958. 242p. illus. index.
Good, serious history/handbook arranged by centers, with chapter on collecting. Appendix of major marks in facsimiles. Illustrated with museum pieces and pieces accessible to collectors. Bibliography of basic books.

332   Schönberger, Arno. **Deutsches Porzellan**. Munich, Prestel, 1949. 36p.
         (text), 56 plates.
Good, illustrated survey of German eighteenth and early nineteenth century
porcelain, illustrated with major museum pieces.

333   Ware, George W. **German and Austrian Porcelain**. New York, Crown, 1963.
         244p. illus. index.
Good, popular history/handbook of German and Austrian porcelain of the
eighteenth, nineteenth and twentieth centuries. Chapters treat the history, production, and major factories. Useful chapter on collecting, a glossary, and a brief
bibliography, pp. 227-28, listing books in English and German. An excellent,
sensitively written introduction for the beginning collector and student.

Great Britain

334   Bemrose, G. **Nineteenth Century English Pottery and Porcelain**. London,
         Faber and Faber, 1952. 57p. (text), 100 plates. LC 52-3066.
Good, serious history illustrated with museum pieces and pieces accessible to the
collector. Bibliography of basic books and periodical articles, pp. 51-52.

335   Charleston, R. J., ed. **English Porcelain**. London, Benn, 1965. 183p. illus.
         index.
Collection of serious essays on major English ceramic manufactories directed to the
serious collector. Well illustrated. Bibliographies at the end of the chapter-essays.

336   Godden, Geoffrey. **British Porcelain: An Illustrated Guide**. New York,
         Potter, 1974. 456p. illus.
Good, serious handbook/history of British porcelain from the 1740s to the present.
Well illustrated with both key museum pieces and pieces accessible to the collector.
Bibliography of basic books, catalogs and periodical articles.

337   Savage, George. **18th Century English Porcelain**. London, Salisbury Square,
         1952. 435p. illus. index.
A good, serious history/handbook of English eighteenth century porcelain for the
student and collector. Part one treats the art and technique of eighteenth century
English porcelains; Part two, the biographies of the chief makers; and Part three,
the history of the major factories. Brief index of marks. Illustrated with pieces
within reach of the average collector.

Italy

338   Lane, Arthur. **Italian Porcelain**. London, Faber and Faber, 1954. 79p. illus.
         index.
Good, serious survey history of Italian porcelain through 1820. General arrangement
is by factories or centers. Has brief dictionary of marks with facsimiles. Illustrated

with museum pieces. Bibliography, pp. 74-75, is a brief but balanced classified list of books in all languages.

339   Morazzoni, Giuseppe. **Le porcellane italiane**. 2nd ed. Milan, Görlich, 1960. 2v. illus.

Good, scholarly history/handbook of Italian porcelain from its beginnings to the end of the nineteenth century, with arrangement by regions. Volume one is the text; Volume two contains the plates, illustrating pieces in museums and private collections. Brief, general bibliography with further bibliographical references in the footnotes. A standard work on Italian porcelain.

Netherlands

340   Schrijver, Elka. **Hollands porselein**. Bussum, Van Dishoeck, 1966. 85p. illus. index. LC 68-93565.

Good, popular handbook of Dutch eighteenth and nineteenth century porcelain illustrated with pieces accessible to the collector and with list of major marks. Bibliography of basic books and periodical articles, pp. 81-82.

341   Sypesteyn, Catharinus Henri C.A. van. **Het Oud-Hollandsch Porselein**. Hilversum, J. W. Ebert, 1933. 77p. illus. index.

Good, serious handbook of Dutch eighteenth and nineteenth century porcelain with good lists of marks.

342   Rust, W. J. **Nederlands Porselein**. Amsterdam, De Lange, 1952. 178p. illus.

A good, popular history of Dutch porcelain from its beginnings to the present. Illustrated with museum pieces and pieces in private collections. French résumé. Bibliography, pp. 167-68, lists basic books, most of them in Dutch.

Eastern European Countries

343   Csányi, Károly. **Geschichte der ungarischen Keramik, des Porzellans und ihre Marken**. Budapest, Verlag des Fonds für Bildende Künste, 1954. 153p. illus. index. LC 55-33362.

Good, serious handbook of Hungarian porcelain, arranged by place.

344   Poche, Emanuel. **Bohemian Porcelain**. Prague, Artia, n.d. 70p. (text), 160p. (plates).

Popular history of porcelain in Bohemia from its beginnings to the end of the nineteenth century. Illustrated with museum pieces. Brief bibliography, p. 71, lists books and catalogs. Short dictionary of marks.

345 Lukomsij, Georgii. **Russisches Porzellan 1744-1923**. Berlin, E. Wasmuth, 1924. 24p. illus.
Good, illustrated survey of Russian porcelain, featuring selected museum pieces. No bibliography.

346 Ryszard, Stanislaw R. **Porzellan vom Barock zum Empire**. Warsaw, Arkady, 1964. 311p. illus. index.
Good, serious history/handbook of Polish porcelain of the eighteenth and early nineteenth centuries, with list of major marks. Bibliography, pp. 122-24, gives good coverage of the basic Slavic literature.

347 Rozembergh, A. **Les marques de la porcelaine russe: Periode impériale**. Paris, Champion, 1926. 31p. (text), 76p. (plates).
Handbook of marks on Russian porcelain from 1750 to 1850, with a brief introductory history. Illustrated with museum pieces. No bibliography.

Oriental Porcelain

348 Feddersen, Martin. **Japanisches Porzellan; ein Brevier**. Braunschweig, Klinkhardt & Biermann, 1960. 48p. illus.
Brief survey of Japanese porcelain from its beginnings in the seventeenth century to the mid-nineteenth century, illustrated with major museum pieces. Brief bibliography of basic books in all languages.

349 Feddersen, Martin. **Chinese Porcelain**. Braunschweig, Klinkhardt & Biermann, 1956. 46p. illus. index. LC A57-6597.
Good, illustrated survey of Chinese porcelain from the earliest examples to circa 1915.

350 Jenyns, Soame. **Japanese Porcelain**. London, Faber and Faber, 1973. 252p. illus. index.
Serious history of Japanese porcelain of the seventeenth, eighteenth and early nineteenth centuries, with emphasis on ware exported to the West. Arranged by types. Bibliography, pp. 321-23, lists books in Japanese as well as in Western languages. An excellent general history for the collector and student.

351 Jenyns, Soame. **Late Chinese Porcelain. The Ch'ing Dynasty (1644-1912)**. London, Faber and Faber, 1951. 104p. illus. index.
A good, serious history of Chinese porcelain during the Ch'ing dynasty, illustrated with pieces in museums and private collections. Appendix of marks. Bibliography, pp. 100-102, lists major books and periodical articles in all languages.

352 Zimmermann, Ernst. **Chinesisches Porzellan. Seine Geschichte, Kunst, und Technik**. Leipzig, Klinkhardt & Biermann, 1913. 2v. illus. index.
Scholarly history of Chinese porcelain from 581 A.D. to 1912, arranged by dynasties. Chapter on technique. Illustrated with museum pieces. Appendix with dating marks.

Good, classified bibliography, pp. 208-10, and further bibliography in the footnotes. An older standard history of Chinese porcelain, though still very useful.

POTTERY, FAIENCE, MAJOLICA, STONEWARE

General Histories and Handbooks

353   Caiger-Smith, Alan. **Tin-Glaze Pottery in Europe and the Islamic World. The Tradition of 1000 Years in Maiolica, Faience and Delftware.** London, Faber and Faber, 1973. 128p. illus. index.
Popular history of tin-glaze pottery from the ninth century to the present. Good selection of plates illustrating museum pieces with descriptive notes. Brief bibliography of basic books.

354   Savage, George. **Pottery Through the Ages.** London, Cassell, 1963. 246p. illus. index. LC 64-6041.
Popular history of world pottery from ancient Egypt to the end of the nineteenth century. Illustrated with museum quality examples. Brief bibliographies are given at end of sections.

355   Weiss, Gustav. **Ullstein Fayencebuch. Eine Kunst- und Technikgeschichte der Fayencen mit Markenverzeichnis.** Frankfurt/Main and Berlin, Ullstein, 1970. 319p. illus. index. LC 77-569251.
Excellent, serious history/handbook of European faience, with emphasis on the history of manufacture and technique. Well illustrated with museum pieces. Good, condensed list of major works. Bibliography of basic books in all languages.

American Pottery, etc. (U.S. and Canada)

356   Henzke, Lucille. **American Art Pottery.** Camden, N.J., T. Nelson, 1970. 336p. illus. index. LC 70-113171.
Popular survey history of American nineteenth century ceramic figurines, tiles, and hand-painted pottery. Arranged by companies and provided with lists of artists' marks and signatures.

357   Kovel, Ralph M., and Terry H. Kovel. **The Kovels' Collector's Guide to American Art Pottery.** New York, Crown, 1974. 320p. illus. index.
Popular encyclopedia of American firms making art pottery from circa 1875 to the present, with facsimiles of marks and signatures. Numerous illustrations of collectibles.

358   Webster, Donald B. **Decorated Stoneware Pottery of North America.** Rutland, Vt., Tuttle, 1971. 232p. illus. index. LC 71-134032.
Good, popular history/handbook covering painted and incised pottery in the United States and Canada from Colonial times to the end of the nineteenth century. Illustrated with pieces accessible to the collector. Bibliography of basic books and periodical articles.

359   Webster, Donald B. **Early Canadian Pottery**. Greenwich, Conn., New York
        Graphic Society, 1971. 256p. illus. index. LC 75-162722.
Serious history of Canadian earthenware before 1900, with emphasis on techniques
of manufacture. Bibliography, pp. 249-50, lists most important books.

European Pottery, etc.

General Works

360   Penkala, Maria. **European Pottery, 5000 Marks on Maiolica, Faience and
        Stoneware**. 2nd ed. Rutland, Vt., Tuttle, 1969. 472p. illus. index.
        LC 69-19602.
Dictionary of 5,780 marks on European pottery, arranged by countries; contains
brief introductory histories and facsimile reproductions. Examples illustrated are
those most likely to be encountered by the average collector.

France

361   Chompret, Jean, Jean Bloch, Jacques Guérin, and Paul Alfossa. **Répertoire
        de la faïence française**. Paris, S. Lapina, 1933-35. 2v. illus. index.
Excellent serious history/handbook of French faience, featuring essays on various
major manufactures written by leading French specialists. Volume one comprises
plates originally published in five separate volumes. Volume two is text.

362   Curtil, Henri. **Marques et signatures de la faïence française**. Paris, Massin,
        1969. 152p. illus. LC 71-550456.
Pocket-sized dictionary of French faience marks, illustrated with facsimiles.

363   Fourest, Henry P. **L'oeuvre des faïenciers français du XVIe à la fin du
        XVIIIe siècle**. Paris, Hachette, 1966. 332p. illus. LC 67-79023.
A good, popular and well-illustrated history of French faience from the sixteenth
through the eighteenth century. Illustrated with museum pieces. Bibliography,
pp. 328-29, lists major books and periodical articles.

364   Giacommoti, Jeanne. **French Faïence**. New York, Universe, 1963. 266p.
        illus. index. LC 63-18339.
Serious, well-illustrated history/handbook of French faience through the nineteenth
century, with a chapter on folk faience. Arrangement is by regions; a brief introductory essay for each region is followed by a catalog of plates, with good descriptive
notes. Brief dictionary of marks with facsimiles. Illustrated with museum pieces.
Bibliography, p. 258, is a brief list of books in all languages.

365   Lane, Arthur. **French Faience**. 2nd ed. New York, Praeger, 1970. 49p. illus. index. LC 75-133087.
A good, brief but factual survey history of French faience of the seventeenth and eighteenth centuries. Illustrated with pieces in museums and major private collections.

366   Lesur, Adrien. **Les poteries et les faïences françaises**. 2nd ed. ed. Paris, Tardy, 1957-61. 5v. illus. index. LC A58-2072 rev.
Good, serious history/handbook of French pottery and faience, arranged by regions and centers of production. Well illustrated with museum pieces and pieces accessible to the collector, plus a good lists of marks.

367   Tilmans, Émile. **Faïence de France**. Paris, Éditions Mondes, 1954. 326p. illus. index.
Popular handbook/history of French faience from the fifteenth to the twentieth centuries. Includes a glossary of terms, short list of marks with facsimiles and a brief list of books (chiefly in French), pp. 307-08. Illustrated with major pieces of museum quality.

Germany, Austria and Switzerland

368   Hüseler, Konrad. **Deutsche Fayencen, ein Handbuch der Fabriken, ihrer Meister und Werke**. Stuttgart, Hiersemann, 1956-58. 3v. illus. index.
Good, scholarly history/handbook of German faience. Volume one is a comprehensive history of the various factories with a chapter on technique. Volume two is an art history of German seventeenth and eighteenth century faience, with biographies of the major painters, sections on dating, collecting, faience sculpture, role of color, and models. Volume three provides a comprehensive corpus of plates, a biographical dictionary and a dictionary of marks. Excellent classified bibliography, v. 3, pp. 435-41, listing books and periodical articles. A standard handbook on German faience.

369   Meyer-Heisig, Erich. **Deutsche Bauerntöpferei**. Munich, Prestel, 1955. 159p. illus.
A good, serious handbook of German folk ceramics. Illustrated with museum pieces, the work has chapters on technique, history and major regions of folk ceramic production in Germany, Alsace, Austria, and Switzerland. Excellent notes to the text with definitions of terms and techniques, lists of museums and bibliographical commentaries. General bibliography, pp. 69-71, is a good list of books and periodical articles in all languages. A standard work on the subject.

370   Stoehr, August. **Deutsche Fayencen und Deutsches Steingut. Ein Handbuch für Sammler und Liebhaber**. Berlin, Schmidt, 1920. 596p. illus. index. (Bibliothek fur Kunst- und Antiquitätensammler, Band 20)
Good, scholarly handbook/history of German faience. Chapters on technique, general history and development, and the major regions and centers of faience production. Good, special bibliographies at the beginning of each section or chapter. Though old, a standard handbook of German faience.

Great Britain

371   Godden, Geoffrey. **British Pottery**. New York, Potter, 1975. 452p. illus. index.

Good, serious history of British pottery from the Victorian period to circa 1930. Well illustrated with key museum pieces and pieces accessible to the collector. Bibliography of basic books and periodical articles.

372   Hughes, George B. **English and Scottish Earthenware, 1660-1860**. New York, Macmillan, 1961. 238p. illus. index. LC 61-1648.

Popular history illustrated with museum pieces and pieces accessible to the collector. Bibliography of basic works.

373   Lewis, Griselda. **A Collector's History of English Pottery**. New York, Viking, 1969. 221p. illus. index. LC 78-80264.

Popular history of English ceramics from the stone age to the present, illustrated with museum pieces and pieces accessible to the average collector. No bibliography.

Italy

374   Ballardini, Gaetano. **Corpus della maiolicha italiana**. Rome, Libreria dello Stato, 1933-35. 2v. illus. index. (Bollettino d'Arte, Pubblicazione Annuale, N. 1)

Scholarly history of Italian majolica to 1535, confined to dated examples. Illustrated with museum pieces. Bibliography in the footnotes. Volume I: Le maioliche datate fino al 1530. Volume II: Le maioliche datate dal 1531 al 1535. The standard history of early Italian majolica.

375   Ballardini, Gaetano. **La maiolicha italiana dalle origini alla fine del Cinquecento**. Florence, Babèra, Alfoni e Venturi, 1938. 64p. illus. index.

Pictorial history of Italian majolica from the Middle Ages to the end of the seventeenth century. No bibliography.

376   Brosio, Valentino. **Porcellane e maioliche italiane dell' Ottocento**. Milan, Vallardi, 1960. 139p. illus. index. LC A61-3713.

Popular history of Italian eighteenth century porcelain and faience. The brief introductory text is followed by a good collection of plates illustrating museum pieces. Brief bibliography of basic works in Italian.

377   Chompret, J. **Répertoire de la majolique italienne**. Paris, Éditions Nomis, 1949. 227p. illus. index.

A good, serious history of Italian majolica from the fifteenth century through the eighteenth century. Arranged according to major centers and illustrated with museum pieces. Brief bibliography, p. 210, of works consulted and further bibliography in the footnotes.

378   Conti, Giovanni. **L'arte della maiolica in Italia.** Milan, Bramante, 1973.
        387p. illus.
A good, scholarly survey history of Italian majolica from its beginnings to the end
of the nineteenth century. Well illustrated with pieces in museums and major private
collections. Arranged by centuries; brief introductory essays are followed by an
outline of events in the manufacture of majolica and an excellent catalog of plates.
Provides a good but unclassified bibliography, pp. 379-81, listing both books and
periodical articles. Further bibliography in the footnotes.

379   Falke, Otto von. **Majolike.** 2nd ed. Berlin, G. Reimer, 1907. 208p. illus.
        index. First edition published in 1896.
Good, serious history of Italian majolica of the fifteenth and sixteenth centuries,
with emphasis on examples in the Berlin Kunstgewerbe Museum. A classic,
pioneering work.

380   Liverani, Giovanni. **Five Centuries of Italian Majolica.** New York, McGraw-
        Hill, 1960. 258p. illus. index. LC 59-13206.
Good, serious history of Italian majolica with excellent selection of plates. Brief
bibliography of basic books and periodical articles.

381   Rackham, Bernard. **Italian Maiolica.** New York, Pitman, 1952. 35p. (text),
        96p. (illus). illus. index.
Good, popular history of Italian tin-glazed pottery from the fifteenth century to
1800. Illustrated with examples in British museums and great private collections.
Bibliography, pp. 32-33, is a brief list of books in all languages.

Netherlands

382   Havard, Henry. **La céramique hollandaise. Histoire des faïences de Delft,
        Haarlem, Rotterdam, Arnhem, Utrecht, etc. et des porcelaines de Weesp,
        Loosdrecht, Amsterdam et la Haye.** Amsterdam, Vivat, 1909. 2v. illus.
        index.
Comprehensive history/handbook of Dutch ceramics from prehistoric times to the
end of the eighteenth century. Volume two is a biographical dictionary of makers
with facsimiles of their marks. Illustrated with museum pieces. An old, standard
history/handbook by one of the great pioneering specialists in ceramics history.

383   Jonge, C. H. de. **Oud-Nederlandsche Majolica en Delftsch Aardewerke.**
        Amsterdam, Scheltema, 1947. 445p. illus. index.
Good, scholarly history of Dutch faience from 1500 to 1800. Illustrated with
museum pieces. Bibliography, pp. 428-31, is a good classified list of books and
periodical articles in all languages. Further reference to specialized literature in
the footnotes.

384   Neurdenburg, Elisabeth, and Bernard Rackham. **Old Dutch Pottery and Tiles**. London, Benn, 1923. 155p. illus. index.
Serious, but in part out-of-date, history of Dutch pottery including tiles from the earliest times to the end of the eighteenth century. Chapters treat techniques and major centers and makers. Brief list of marks. Bibliography, pp. 147-48, lists books and periodical articles.

385   Rackham, Bernard. **Early Netherlands Maiolica**. London, Bles, 1926. 136p. illus. index.
Serious history of Dutch earthenware, including tiles, of the sixteenth century. Chapter on seventeenth century pottery in Holland and England. Illustrated with museum pieces and illustrations of pottery in contemporary paintings. Bibliography, pp. 131-32, lists basic books and periodical articles.

Portugal

386   Santos, Reynaldo dos. **Faiança portuguesa**. Porto, Galaica, 1960. illus. index. LC 61-43631.
Pictorial history of Portuguese faience of the sixteenth and seventeenth centuries. Popular text, illustrated with museum pieces. French résumé.

Scandinavia

387   Frohne, J. W. **Danske fajancer** . . . Copenhagen, Schultz, 1911. 157p. illus. index.
Scholarly history of Danish faience to 1820. Well documented and illustrated with museum pieces. Some marks; bibliography in footnotes.

388   Uldall, Kai. **Gammel Dansk Fajence**. Copenhagen, Thaning & Appels, 1961. 300p. illus. index.
Excellent, serious history/handbook of Danish faience arranged by centers and factories. Illustrated with museum pieces. List of marks and good bibliographic footnotes.

Australian Pottery, etc.

389   Hood, Kenneth. **Australian Pottery**. South Melbourne, Macmillan, 1972. 173p. illus. index. LC 73-163201.
Popular illustrated survey of pottery produced by the European settlers in Australia from the eighteenth century to the present.

CHAPTER SIX

CLOCKS, WATCHES AND AUTOMATA

BIBLIOGRAPHIES

390   Baillie, Granville H. **Clocks and Watches; an Historical Bibliography.**
       London, N. A. G. Press, 1951. 414p. illus. index.
Good, chronologically arranged and annotated bibliography of books and periodical
articles on all aspects of mechanical timepieces up to the year 1800. Subject and
author index.

391   Tardy [firm]. **Bibliographie générale de la mesure du temps.** Paris, Tardy,
       1947. 352p. LC A49-1170.
Good, comprehensive bibliography of books and periodical articles in Western
languages on all aspects of the measuring of time, including clocks and watches.

DICTIONARIES AND ENCYCLOPEDIAS

General

392   Baillie, Granville H. **Watchmakers and Clockmakers of the World.** 2nd ed.
       London, N. A. G. Press, 1947. 388p. illus.
Good dictionary of some 35,000 watch and clock makers active to 1825. Brief
biographical entries also give initials and monograms used by the makers. No
bibliography.

393   Bruton, Eric. **Dictionary of Clocks and Watches.** New York, Crown, 1963.
       201p. illus.
Popular dictionary covering all aspects of clocks and watches including terms, major
makers, famous clocks, types of timepieces and parts of mechanism. Illustrated with
line drawings and plates of museum pieces. Bibliography, pp. 199-201, is a good
annotated guide to basic books in English.

394   Kiegeland, Burkhardt, ed. **Bruckmann's Uhrenlexikon.** Munich, Bruckmann,
       1974. 250p. illus.
Excellent, serious dictionary covering all aspects of world clocks and watches, with
special emphasis on material of interest to the collector and historian. Covers
mechanisms, materials, styles and forms and major makers. Well illustrated with
major museum pieces.

395   Lloyd, H. Alan. **The Collector's Dictionary of Clocks.** South Brunswick,
       N.J., A. S. Barnes, 1965. 214p. illus. LC 65-24848.
Good, popular dictionary of world clocks and watches, with emphasis on artistic
and mechanical aspects. Includes automata. Entries cover types of mechanisms,
forms of clocks, major clockmakers and watchmakers, styles and countries. Bibliography of basic books in all languages, pp. 204-06.

National Dictionaries of Clock and Watchmakers

France

396   Tardy [firm]. **Dictionnaire des horlogers français** . . . Paris, Tardy, 1971-72.
       2v. illus. LC 72-302813.
Good, serious dictionary of French clock and watch makers from the late Middle
Ages to the present, illustrated with major signed pieces and facsimiles of marks.

Italy

397   Morpurgo, Enrico. **Dizionario degli orologiài italiani.** Rome, "La Clessidra,"
       1950. 239p. illus.
Good, comprehensive dictionary of Italian clock and watchmakers from 1300 to
1880. Good, classified bibliography of books and major periodical articles,
pp. 213-18.

Netherlands

398   Morpurgo, Enrico. **Nederlands klokken- en horlogemakers vanaf 1300.**
       Amsterdam, Scheltema & Holkema, 1970. 152p. illus. index. LC 78-
       504861.
Good, serious dictionary of Dutch clock and watch makers from the late Middle
Ages to the present. Illustrated with major signed pieces; has facsimiles of marks.

Russia

399   Chenakal, Valentin L. **Watchmakers and Clockmakers in Russia, 1400 to
       1850.** London, Antiquarian Horological Society, 1972. 64p. illus.
       (Antiquarian Horological Society Monographs, 6)
Good dictionary of Russian watchmakers and clockmakers, with selected list of
plates of major pieces.

Spain

400   Basanta Campos, José L. **Relojeros de España: Diccionario bio-bibliográfico.**
        Pontevedra, Paredes, 1972. 151p. illus. LC 73-327348.
Good, serious dictionary of Spanish clock and watch makers from the late Middle
Ages to the present, illustrated with major signed pieces and facsimiles of marks.

Sweden

401   Sidenbladh, Elis T. **Urmakarei Sverige under äldre tider, anteckningar.** 2nd
        ed. Stockholm, Nordiska Museet, 1947. 256p. illus.
Good, comprehensive dictionary of Swedish clockmakers and watchmakers illustrated
with pieces in the Nordiska Museet in Stockholm. Bibliography of basic books, pp.
15-17.

GENERAL HISTORIES AND HANDBOOKS

402   Baillie, Granville H. **Watches; Their History, Decoration and Mechanism.**
        London, Methuen, 1929. 383p. illus. index.
Good, popular history that pays attention to decoration as well as mechanism.
Includes Oriental watches. Useful summary in the form of a chronology of the
development of watches. No bibliography.

403   Bassermann-Jordan, Ernst von. **Alte Uhren und ihre Meister.** Leipzig,
        W. Diebener, 1926. 179p. illus. index.
Good, serious history of Western clocks and watches from the Middle Ages to the
end of the nineteenth century. Brief bibliography of basic books. Superseded by the
author's *The Book of Old Clocks and Watches* (404).

404   Bassermann-Jordan, Ernst von. **The Book of Old Clocks and Watches.** 4th
        ed. fully revised by Hans von Bertele. New York, Crown, 1964. 522p. illus.
        index. LC 63-2111.
Translation of: *Uhren: Ein Handbuch für Sammler und Liebhaber* (Braunschweig,
1961). Excellent, scholarly history/handbook with chapters on the conception,
division and measurement of time, history of timepiece mechanisms and detailed
chapters on the development of particular parts. Includes water clocks and sand
glasses. Well illustrated; plates with good descriptive captions. Good classified
bibliography, pp. 497-503, of books and periodical articles in all languages. A
standard work.

405   Britten, Frederick J. **Britten's Old Clocks and Watches and Their Makers:
        A Historical and Descriptive Account of the Different Styles of Clocks
        and Watches of the Past in England and Abroad** . . . 8th ed. edited by
        Cecil Clutton. New York, Dutton, 1973. 532p. illus. index. LC 73-82531.
Excellent, serious history of Western clocks and watches from the earliest examples
in the late Middle Ages to the present. Arranged by centuries, countries, and

technical and decorative types. Appendices with glossary of terms, extensive list of makers and their marks and thorough bibliography of books and periodical articles in all languages with addenda to the eighth edition, pp. 326-31. A standard work on clocks and watches.

406   Bruton, Eric. **Clocks & Watches**. Feltham, Hamlyn, 1968. 140p. illus. index.
Popular history from prehistoric and ancient sundials and water clocks to present-day watches. Although emphasis is on technology, there are many well-chosen illustrations of artistic pieces. No bibliography.

407   Bruton, Eric. **Clocks and Watches, 1400-1900**. New York, Praeger, 1967.
       208p. illus. index. LC 67-14706.
Good, serious history of Western clocks and watches, with chapter on collecting. Appendices provide list of major collections, brief bibliography of basic books and list of major makers.

408   Cipolla, Carlo M. **Clocks and Cultures, 1300-1700**. London, Collins, 1967.
       192p. illus. index. LC 67-77490.
Unorthodox social history of clocks with emphasis on the relationship between clocks and time measurement and broad cultural changes. General bibliography, pp. 166-181.

409   Clutton, Cecil, and George Daniels. **Watches**. New York, Viking, 1965.
       159p. illus. index. LC 65-15108.
Good, serious history of European and American watches from 1500 to 1900, with equal emphasis on case decoration and mechanisms. Biographical dictionary of major watch makers. No bibliography.

410   Cuss, T. P. Camerer. **The Country Life Book of Watches**. London, Country
       Life, 1967. 128p. illus. index.
Good, serious history of watches from 1500 to 1900, well illustrated with artistically and technologically important pieces. No bibliography.

411   Fleet, Simon. **Clocks**. New York, Putnam, 1961. 128p. illus. LC 61-12199.
Popular illustrated survey of clocks from antiquity to the present. No bibliography.

412   Gélis, Edouard. **L'horlogerie ancienne; histoire, décor et technique**. Paris,
       Gründ, 1950. 254p. illus. index. LC 51-27388.
Good, popular history of Western clocks and watches from the late Middle Ages to the end of the eighteenth century, illustrated with museum pieces. Good general bibliography, pp. 241-44.

413   Guye, Samuel, and Henri Michel. **Time & Space; Measuring Instruments
       from the 15th to the 19th Century**. New York, Praeger, 1971. 289p.
       illus. index. LC 77-111070.
Good, serious history of Western clocks, watches and scientific measuring instruments. Excellent plates of museum pieces with good descriptive captions. No bibliography.

414   Lloyd, H. Alan. **Some Outstanding Clocks over Seven Hundred Years, 1250-1950.** London, Hill, 1958. 160p. illus. index.
Good, popular history that concentrates on major pieces, with particular emphasis on their technical features. Glossary of terms. Well illustrated with plates and technical drawings. No bibliography.

415   Tyler, Eric J. **European Clocks.** New York, Hawthorn, 1969. 258p. illus. index. LC 69-12962.
Popular history from the earliest examples to the present. Glossary of technical terms and brief bibliography of basic books. Good guide to museums and public collections in Europe.

416   Willsberger, Johann. **Zauberhafte Gehäuse der Zeit. Die schönen Uhren aus 6 Jahrhunderten.** Dusseldorf, Econ-Verlag, 1974. 180p. illus.
Good, illustrated survey of European clocks and watches chosen for the artistic significance of their cases.

NATIONAL HISTORIES

France

417   Edley, Winthrop. **French Clocks.** New York, Walker, 1967. 83p. illus. LC 67-23091.
Popular history from the sixteenth century to 1789, with chapter on collecting. No bibliography.

418   Tardy [firm]. **La pendule française, des origines à nos jours.** 3rd ed. Paris, Tardy, 1967. 2v. illus. index. LC 68-90858.
Good, serious history of French clocks from the late Middle Ages to the present. Well illustrated with both major museum pieces and examples accessible to the collector. Contents: 1e ptie., De l'horloge gothique à la pendule Louis XV; 2e ptie., Du Louis XVI à nos jours. Bibliographies at the end of each chapter.

Great Britain

419   Bird, Anthony. **English House Clocks, 1600-1850: an Historical Survey and Guide for Collectors and Dealers.** Newton Abbot, David and Charles, 1973. 313p. illus. index. LC 73-162361.
Good, well-illustrated handbook with emphasis on case forms. Illustrated with pieces accessible to the collector.

420   Cescinsky, Herbert, and Malcomb R. Webster. **English Domestic Clocks.** Feltham, England, and New York, Spring, 1969. 354p. illus. index. LC 70-579806.
Good, serious handbook/history of English clocks from the seventeenth century to the middle of the nineteenth century. Directed to the collector. Emphasis on both case and mechanism. Illustrated with pieces accessible to the collector.

421   Daniels, George. **English and American Watches**. London and New York, Abelard-Schuman, 1967. 128p. illus. index. LC 66-15599.
Good, popular history covering the period from the seventeenth century to the present. Appendices with technical descriptions of major mechanical features and list of major makers with biographical information.

422   Goaman, Muriel. **English Clocks**. London, Connoisseur, 1967. 119p. illus. index. LC 67-87912.
Good, popular history of English domestic clocks from the sixteenth through the nineteenth century, with emphasis on pieces accessible to the collector.

423   Symonds, Robert W. **A History of English Clocks**. London and New York, Penguin, 1947. 79p. illus. LC A48-6164.
Brief, illustrated history of English domestic clocks from the sixteenth through the nineteenth century. Bibliography of basic books, p. 80.

Italy

424   Simoni, Antonio. **Orologi italiani dal Cinquecento all'Ottocento**. Milan, Vallardi, 1965. 172p. illus. index. LC 67-124548.
Good, popular history of Italian clocks of the sixteenth through the eighteenth centuries. Illustrated with museum pieces. Brief bibliography of basic books in Italian.

Netherlands

425   Sellink, J. L. **Dutch Antique Domestic Clocks, ca. 1670-1870, and Some Related Examples**. Leiden, Stenfert, 1973. 60p. (text), 300p. (illus.). index. LC 73-177830.
Good, illustrated history featuring examples of timepieces in the Oegstgeest Museum of Clocks. Bibliography of basic books, p. 365.

Switzerland

426   Jaquet, Eugène, and Alfred Chapuis. **Technique and History of the Swiss Watch**. London and New York, Spring, 1970. 272p. illus. index. LC 70-22401.
Good, serious history with equal emphasis on mechanism and artistic form. Excellent illustrations and technical drawings.

United States

427   Drepperd, Carl W. **American Clocks & Clockmakers**. 2nd ed. Boston,
        Branford, 1958. 312p. illus. index.
Good, serious history/handbook covering the period from Colonial times to the
early twentieth century. Illustrated with museum pieces and pieces accessible to
the collector. Good list of major clockmakers and watchmakers, pp. 196-293,
giving basic biographical data and marks. Brief bibliography of basic books and
articles, p. 312.

428   Palmer, Brooks. **The Book of American Clocks**. New York, Macmillan,
        1950. 318p. illus.
Popular, pictorial survey of American clocks from the earliest examples to the
present. Brief introductory essay provides a short history; this is followed by a
good selection of plates, glossary of terms and list of about 6,000 American
clockmakers. Bibliography, pp. 317-18, lists basic books.

429   Palmer, Brooks. **A Treasury of American Clocks**. New York, Macmillan,
        1967. 371p. illus. LC 67-28469.
Good, illustrated history of eighteenth and nineteenth century clocks arranged by
case types, with chapters on labels and museums. Good list of makers with biographical data and bibliographical references. Designed as a companion to the
author's earlier work, *The Book of American Clocks* (428).

430   Thomson, Richard. **Antique American Clocks & Watches**. Princeton, N.J.,
        Van Nostrand, 1968. 192p. illus. index. LC 68-29920.
Good, popular illustrated survey from Colonial times to the present, with good
attention to clock and watch cases. No bibliography.

AUTOMATA

431   Chapuis, Alfred, and Éduard Gélis. **Le monde des automates; étude
        historique et technique**. Paris, E. Gélis and Neuchâtel, A. Chapuis, 1928.
        2v. illus. index.
Excellent, scholarly history of automata of all kinds, with equal attention to
mechanisms and cases. Good classified bibliography, v. 2, pp. 333-41, of books
and periodical articles in all languages. A standard work on automata.

432   Droz, Edmond, and Alfred Chapuis. **Les automates; figures artificielles
        d'hommes et d'animaux**. Neuchâtel, Éditions du Griffon, 1949. 426p.
        illus. index.
Excellent, scholarly history of automata from ancient Egypt to the modern period.
Includes animated puppets and masks. Covers both Western and Oriental work.
Chapters one and two cover the development in ancient times; Chapter three,
large-scale horological automata; and Chapter four, gold and silver horological
automata. Appendix gives a list of the chief makers of automata. Good selection

of plates, with English sub-captions. Thorough bibliographical footnotes. A standard work.

433   Maurice, Klaus. **Von Uhren und Automaten.** Munich, Prestel, 1968. 96p.
      illus. (Bibliothek des Germanischen Nationalmuseum Nürnberg zur
      Deutschen Kunst- und Kulturgeschichte, Band 29)
Excellent, serious history of German horological automata of the fifteenth through the seventeenth centuries. Includes early clocks and decorative watches. Well illustrated with plates of major pieces, tools, original designs and works of art illustrating clocks and automata. Good bibliography, pp. 95-96, lists basic books and periodical articles.

CHAPTER SEVEN

COSTUME

BIBLIOGRAPHIES

434   Arnold, Janet, and Anthony Pegaret. **Costumes; a General Bibliography.**
London, Victoria and Albert Museum in Association with the Costume
Society, 1968. 49p.
A classified bibliography of about 400 books and periodicals for the beginning
student. The annotated entries cover exclusively Western dress from ancient times
to the present, with emphasis on English and French material. A good reference
tool for the beginner.

435   Berlin, Kunstbibliothek. **Katalog der Lipperheideschen Kostümbibliothek.**
Neubearbeitet von Eva Nienholdt und Gretel Wagner-Neumann. Berlin,
Mann, 1965. 2v. index.
Excellent, scholarly, classified and descriptively annotated bibliography of books
and periodicals in the Staatliche Kunstbibliothek in Berlin, a collection which was
the bequest of Baron Franz Joseph von Lipperheide. First published in 1896-1905.
Covers all aspects of world costume and includes many artistically valuable
illustrated books from the fifteenth through the nineteenth centuries. A collection
of costume books *nonpareil*, and a standard reference work in the field of costume
history.

436   Colas, René. **Bibliographie générale du costume et de la mode; description
des suites, recueils, séries, revues et livres français et étrangers relatifs au
costume civil, militaire et religieux, aux modes, aux coiffures et aux divers
accessoires de l'habillement** . . . Paris, Colas, 1933. 2v. Reprint: New York,
Hacker Art Books, 1963. LC 65-87490.
Good, comprehensive bibliography of 3,131 books and periodical articles in Western
European languages arranged alphabetically with author, title, and subject indexes.
Entries are descriptively annotated. Standard reference work, although difficult to
use because it is unclassified.

437   Hiler, Hilaire, and Meyer Hiler. **Bibliography of Costume, a Dictionary
Catalog of about Eight Thousand Books and Periodicals** . . . New York,
Wilson, 1939. 911p. Reprint: New York, B. Blom, 1967.
Excellent, classified and annotated bibliography of some 8,400 books and periodical
articles on all aspects of costume and adornment in all languages. Authors, editors,
illustrators, and titles together with subjects in one alphabet. Interesting introductory
essay, "Costumes and Ideologies." Easy-to-use source for older literature.

DICTIONARIES AND ENCYCLOPEDIAS

438   Huenefeld, Irene P. **International Directory of Historical Clothing.** Metuchen, N.J., Scarecrow, 1967. 175p. LC 67-10186.
Good, comprehensive directory of costume in museums, galleries, historical societies, libraries and churches in the United States, Canada and Europe. Divided geographically and well cross-referenced.

439   Kybalová, Ludmila, *et al.* **The Pictorial Encyclopedia of Fashion.** New York, Crown, 1968. 607p. illus. LC 70-415002.
Good, popular comprehensive history of world costume from the 4th millenium B.C. to the present. Well illustrated. Glossary of garments and accessories.

440   Leloir, Maurice. **Dictionnaire du costume et de ses accessoires, des armes et des étoffes, des origines à nos jours** . . . Paris, Gründ, 1951. 435p. illus.
Excellent, scholarly dictionary of over 2,000 entries covering all aspects of Western costume, including accessories and arms and armor. Entries vary in length from short definitions of terms to longer essays tracing the development of major pieces. Well illustrated. No bibliography. A standard dictionary of costume.

441   Monro, Isabel S., and Dorothy Cook. **Costume Index; a Subject Index to Plates and to Illustrated Texts** . . . New York, Wilson, 1937. 338p.

        ————————. **Supplement.** New York, Wilson, 1957. 210p.
Good, classified index to illustrations of costume in 615 titles (347 additional titles in the *Supplement*). Classification follows country, class of person, types and items of costume, further subdivided by period. List of books indexed also gives location of several major libraries. Does not include armor. A standard reference tool for the study of costume.

442   Picken, Mary B. **The Fashion Dictionary; Fabric, Sewing and Dress as Expressed in the Language of Fashion.** Rev. and enl. ed. New York, Funk & Wagnalls, 1973. 434p. illus. index. LC 72-83771.
Popular dictionary of short entries covering all aspects of costume, with special emphasis on construction, design and material. Illustrated with line drawings and plates reproducing actual pieces and works of art depicting costume. No bibliography.

443   Planché, James R. **A Cyclopedia of Costume or Dictionary of Dress** . . . London, Chatto and Windus, 1876-79. 2v. illus. index.
Good, older history/handbook of Western costume from 53 B.C. to circa 1700. Volume one is a dictionary of terms covering all aspects including arms and armor, ecclesiastical vestments and jewelry. Volume two is a general history, illustrated with line drawings, engravings and color plates and emphasizing the general historical context. A classic pioneering work, still a standard reference work in the history of costume.

444   Wilcox, Ruth T. **The Dictionary of Costume.** New York, Scribner's, 1969.
       406p. illus. LC 68-12503.
Comprehensive dictionary of world costume covering all aspects, including accessories, fabrics, colors and designers. Cross reference of foreign terms. Copiously
illustrated with line drawings. Bibliography, pp. 404-06, lists books and periodical
articles chiefly in English.

GENERAL HISTORIES AND HANDBOOKS

445   Allemagne, Henry René d'. **Les accessoires du costume et du mobilier
       depuis le treizième jusqu'au milieu du dix-neuvième siècle** . . . Paris,
       Schemit, 1928. 3v. illus.
Good, comprehensive history of costume accessories, objets d'art, eating utensils
and scientific instruments. Good selection of illustrations. Bibliography, v. 3,
pp. 565-67, lists books and periodical articles chiefly in French.

446   Arnold, Janet. **A Handbook of Costume.** London, Macmillan, 1973. 336p.
       illus.
Good, serious handbook for the study of costume. Consists of chapters on dating
costume by construction technique, conservation, storage and display, costume for
children and students, costume for the stage, classified bibliography of books on
costume and list of collections of costume in the British Isles. The bibliography
gives directions on how to use sources in the study of costume. A useful handbook
for collectors, curators and students of costume.

447   Boehn, Max von. **Modes and Manners** . . . London, Harrap; Philadelphia,
       Lippincott, 1932-36. 4v. illus. index. Reprint: New York, B. Blom, 1970.
       4v. in 2. LC 68-56493.
Serious history of Western European dress as a manifestation of the general cultural
development. Covers dress from the migrations to the end of the eighteenth century.
Text divided into chapters on history, the arts, and fashion. Excellent selection of
illustrations, many derived from works of art depicting costume.

448   Boehn, Max von. **Modes & Manners of the Nineteenth Century as
       Represented in Pictures and Engravings of the Time** . . . New York,
       Dutton, 1927. 4v. illus.
Continuation of the author's *Modes and Manners* . . . (447). Published as volumes
five through eight in the original German edition (*Die Mode. Menschen und Moden*,
first published in 1909; 6th ed. revised by Ursula von Kardorff; Munich, Bruckmann,
1963). Covers the period from 1790 to 1914. Its most valuable feature, the large
collection of reproductions of works of art depicting costume, is marred in this set
by a haphazard arrangement.

449   Boucher, François. **20,000 Years of Fashion: History of Costume and Personal Adornment.** New York, Abrams, 1967. 441p. illus. index. LC 66-12103.

Translation of *Histoire du costume en occident de l'antiquité à nos jours* (Paris, 1965). Excellent, scholarly history of Western costume from prehistoric times to 1964 covering all aspects except armor. Good coverage of accessories and jewelry. Excellent illustrations with notes of actual garments and works of art depicting costume. Useful maps, chronological tables, and glossary of terms. Specialized literature given at the end of each chapter plus general classified bibliography of books, periodical articles and catalogs, p. 423.

450   Braun-Ronsdorf, Margarete. **Mirror of Fashion; a History of European Costume, 1789-1929.** New York, McGraw-Hill, 1964. 270p. illus. index. LC 64-22191.

Excellent, serious history of European feminine high fashion, very well illustrated with plates and line drawings with informative notes and catalog. Bibliography, pp. 265, is an unclassified list chiefly of German books and periodical articles.

451   Bruhn, Wolfgang, and Max Tilke. **A Practical History of Costume; a Survey of Costume of All Periods and Peoples from Antiquity to Modern Times Including National Costume in Europe and Non-European Countries . . .** New York, Praeger, 1955. 74p. (text), 200 plates.

Good, illustrated survey of world costume including armor, military costume, ecclesiastical costume, folk and native costume. Brief introductory text followed by good collection of plates. Index to plates, pp. 73-74. No bibliography.

452   D'Assailly, Gisèle. **Ages of Elegance: Five Thousand Years of Fashion & Frivolity.** Paris, Hachette, 1968. 251p. illus.

Popular history of Western costume from the ancient world to the 1960s, with emphasis on the trends of high fashion. Excellent illustrations with index to sources. One-page bibliography of basic books.

453   Davenport, Millia. **The Book of Costume.** New York, Crown, 1948. 2v. illus. index. Reprinted 1962 in one volume.

Good, serious history of Western costume from ancient Egypt and Mesopotamia through the nineteenth century. Large corpus of illustrations, mostly of works of art depicting costumed figures. Appendix, pp. 935-945, is a bibliography and index of sources for the illustrations, a valuable feature of the book. Treats ecclesiastical and military dress and armor as well as accessories. Most useful as a chronologically arranged corpus of illustrations.

454   Evans, Mary. **Costume Throughout the Ages.** Rev. ed. Philadelphia and New York, Lippincott, 1950. 360p. illus. index.

Good, serious history of Western costume from antiquity to 1900. Arranged as a textbook, with summary of the time periods at the beginning of each chapter, topics for discussion and bibliographical references at the end of each chapter. Good general bibliography, pp. 318-29, lists books and periodical articles.

455   Gorsline, Douglas W. **What People Wore: a Visual History of Dress from Ancient Times to Twentieth-Century America** . . . New York, Viking, 1952. 266p. illus.

Good, popular history of Western dress with some Byzantine and Near Eastern costume. Covers military dress, including some armor. Extensive collection of illustrations, mostly line drawings adapted from art sources. Classified bibliography of books chiefly in English, pp. 249-56. Most useful for its illustrations.

456   Kelly, Francis M., and Randolph Schwabe. **Historic Costume, a Chronicle of Fashion in Western Europe, 1490-1790** . . . London, Batsford, 1925. 284p. illus. Reprint: New York, B. Blom, 1968. 305p. illus. index. LC 67-13332.

Good, older, serious handbook/history illustrated with line drawings and black and white plates with descriptive notes. Text provides good, concise survey of the major trends and influences. Glossary index. Chronological tables of English and French rulers and good, critically annotated bibliography, pp. 299-302, of the basic books and periodical articles published before 1925.

457   Kelly, Francis M., and Randolph Schwabe. **A Short History of Costume and Armour** . . . London, Batsford, 1931. 2v. illus. index. Reprint: Newton Abbot, David & Charles, 1972. 261p. illus. index. LC 73-163461.

Good, serious history of Western costume and armor from 1066 to 1800, with emphasis on English material. Useful diagrams of armor, glossary of terms, and good (for the older literature) general bibliography of books, periodical articles and catalogs.

458   Köhler, Karl. **History of Costume.** New York, Watt, 1928. 463p. illus. index. Reprinted: New York, Dover, 1963. LC 63-16328.

Good but brief, serious history of Western costume from antiquity to circa 1870. Well illustrated with plates and line drawings some with useful construction details. Bibliography, pp. 457-58, is a limited list, chiefly of older German books.

459   Köhler, Karl. **Praktische Kostümkunde in 600 Bildern und Schnitten** . . . Munich, Bruckmann, 1926. 2v. illus.

Good, illustrated survey of costume from antiquity to 1870, which includes illustrations of patterns of historical costumes. Bibliography, pp. 545-46, lists basic books chiefly in German.

460   König, René, and Peter W. Schuppisser. **Die Mode in der menschlichen Gesellschaft.** Zürich, Modebuch-Verlag, 1958. 527p. illus.

Good, general history of Western costume from antiquity to the present, well illustrated with drawings and photographs drawn from original costume designs and contemporary art works. Emphasis on stylistic development. Good treatment of major fashion designers of the twentieth century. Bibliography, pp. 524-27, is a classified list of books and periodical articles mostly in German.

461   Laver, James. **Costume.** New York, Hawthorn Books, 1964. 136p. illus.
       index. LC 64-13277.
Popular history of Western costume from ancient Egypt to the twentieth century,
with chapters on Byzantine and Near Eastern dress. Good illustrations, mainly of
art works or line drawings adapted from contemporary art works. No bibliography.

462   Laver, James, ed. **Costume of the Western World; the Tudors to Louis XIII.**
       London, Harrap; New York, Harper, 1952. 390p. illus.
Serious history of Western European costume from 1485 to 1650, consisting of
chapter essays on the major periods written by various experts, followed by descriptive notes to the plates. Excellent selection of plates, mostly drawn from contemporary works of art. Bibliographies at the end of each chapter vary from six to more
than thirty entries. Originally published as six separate monographs.

463   Laver, James. **Costume Through the Ages.** New York, Simon and Schuster,
       1963. 144p. illus. LC 64-13341.
Popular pictorial survey of European costume from the first century A.D. to circa
1930, illustrated with line drawings, many drawn from contemporary works of art.
Includes some accessories and hair styles.

464   Leloir, Maurice. **Histoire du costume de l'antiquité à 1914.** Paris, Ernst,
       1933-49. v. 8-12. illus. index.
Good, comprehensive history of Western costume covering accessories, hairstyles
and jewelry as well as all major classes of costume. Volume 8 treats 1610-43;
volume 9, 1643-78; volume 10, 1678-1725; volume 11, 1725-74; volume 12,
1775-95. Volumes 1-7 never appeared. Bibliographies of books, catalogs, and
periodical articles are given at the end of each volume. Well illustrated with many
useful plates showing costumed figures in contemporary settings.

465   Lester, Katherine M., and Bess V. Oerke. **Illustrated History of Those Frills
       and Furbelows of Fashion Which Have Come to Be Known as: Accessories
       of Dress.** Peoria, Ill., Manual Arts Press, 1940. 587p. illus. index.
Good, serious history of clothing accessories in the West from prehistoric Bronze
Age to the early twentieth century, arranged by class or type of accessory. Fine
collection of illustrations with informative captions. Bibliographies at the end of
each chapter and general bibliography, chiefly of books in English, pp. 577-79.

466   Norris, Herbert. **Costume & Fashion** . . . London, Dent, 1931-40. 3v. in 4.
       illus. index.
Contents: Vol. 1: Evolution of European Dress through the Earlier Ages; Vol. 2:
Senlac to Bosworth, 1066-1485; Vol. 3, Book 1: The Tudors, 1485-1547; Vol. 3,
Book 2: The Tudors, 1547-1603. Good, serious history of Western costume with
emphasis on the social context. Well illustrated. Each chapter has an historical
introduction. Volume two has chapter on heraldry and feudalism. No bibliography.

467   Payne, Blanche. **History of Costume, from the Ancient Egyptians to the Twentieth Century.** New York, Harper & Row, 1965. 607p. illus. index. LC 65-10419.

Good, serious history of European costume including hair styles, accessories and some jewelry. Well illustrated with drawings, plates and pattern drafts for garment construction. Sources for illustrations given in captions. Bibliographical footnotes and general bibliography, pp. 591-95.

468   Racinet, Albert C. A. **Le costume historique** . . . Paris, Firmin-Didot, 1888. 6v. illus.

Good, older, scholarly history of world costume from ancient times to the nineteenth century. Volume one provides an introduction and catalog of the plates, tables of historical personalities, bibliography (pp. 113-24), glossary of terms, and geographical and ethnographical indexes. Volume two covers ancient Egyptian, Greek, Roman and Germanic, African and American Indian dress. Volume three treats Oriental dress; Volume four, Western medieval, including armor, through seventeenth century; Volume five, European dress of the eighteenth century; Volume six, nineteenth century European dress. Illustrations include some drawings of garment construction. A classic pioneering work.

469   Rudofsky, Bernard. **The Unfashionable Human Body.** New York, Doubleday, 1974. 287p. illus. index. LC 74-160871.

Popular history of world costume with emphasis on the oddities and eccentricities of fashions and the aesthetics of human adornment. Good selection of illustrations, mostly from contemporary art works. No bibliography.

470   Stibbert, Frederic. **Civil and Military Clothing in Europe: From the First to the Eighteenth Century.** New York, B. Blom, 1968. 217p. illus. LC 68-16212.

Originally published in Italian (Bergamo, 1914). Good, scholarly history/handbook consisting of brief introductory text followed by excellent corpus of drawings adapted from art sources displaying special attention to details. Thorough coverage of armor. One-page bibliography of basic books in English, French, German and Italian. Excellent source of illustrations.

471   Truman, Nevil. **Historic Costuming** . . . 2nd ed. with additional chapters by Ruth Green. London, Pitman, 1966. 170p. illus. index.

Originally published in 1936. Popular history/handbook of Western costume from ancient Greece and Rome to circa 1965, covering male and female dress and occasional treatment of clerical and military dress. Illustrated chiefly with line drawings. Most useful for English costume. No bibliography.

ANCIENT AND MEDIEVAL COSTUME

472   Abrahams, Ethel B. **Greek Dress: A Study of the Costumes Worn in Ancient Greece from Pre-Hellenic Times to the Hellenistic Age.** London, J. Murray, 1908. 134p. illus. index.

Older, serious history based on the author's M.A. thesis. Illustrated with line drawings and a few plates of works of art depicting costumed figures. Bibliographical footnotes.

473   Brooke, Iris. **Western European Costume, Thirteenth to Seventeenth Century & Its Relationship to the Theatre.** London, Harrap, 1939. 151p. illus.
Popular history/handbook illustrated with line drawings with descriptive notes. No bibliography.

474   Evans, Joan. **Dress in Medieval France.** Oxford, Clarendon, 1952. 94p. (text), 84p. (plates). index.
Good, serious history ranging from 1060 to 1515 and including clerical and military dress. Good collection of plates with catalog. Bibliography, pp. 81-82, lists books and periodical articles in all languages.

475   Houston, Mary G. **Ancient Greek, Roman and Byzantine Costume and Decoration.** 2nd ed. London, Black, 1947. 182p. illus. Reprinted 1963.
Serious history/handbook illustrated with line drawings from ancient art, details of construction, and decoration. Bibliography, pp. 179-82, lists books and periodical articles.

476   Houston, Mary G. **Medieval Costume in England & France; the 13th, 14th and 15th Centuries.** London, Black, 1939. 228p. illus.
Serious history including armor and ecclesiastical costume. Illustrated chiefly with line drawings, some with patterns and details of textiles. Glossary of terms. Bibliography, pp. 227-28, is an unclassified list of books and periodical articles.

477   Laver, James. **Costume in Antiquity.** New York, Potter, 1964. 139p. illus. LC 64-24791.
Popular pictorial survey of ancient costume from Sumerian times through 500 A.D. Includes Bronze Age Europe. Brief introductory text is followed by line drawings derived from various art historical sources.

MODERN COSTUME
(19th and 20th Centuries)

478   Gernsheim, Alison. **Fashion and Reality, 1840-1914.** London, Faber, 1963. 104p. illus. index. LC 65-89180.
Good, serious history illustrated with contemporary photographs with descriptive notes. Text reflects the social context and traces the evolution of fashion trends. Bibliography, pp. 95-100, lists books and periodicals chiefly in English.

AMERICAN COSTUME
(U.S. and Canada)

479   Earle, Alice. **Two Centuries of Costume in America, MDCXX-MDCCCXX.** New York, Macmillan, 1903. 2v. illus. index. Reprint: New York, Dover, 1970. LC 70-118167.

Popular history, useful for its numerous illustrations. No bibliography.

480   McClellan, Elisabeth. **Historic Dress in America: 1607-1800.** New York, B. Blom, 1969. 407p. illus. index. LC 70-81515.

Reprint of 1917 edition. Popular history of early American costume, with a section on dress in Spanish and French settlements in Louisiana. Glossary of terms. Well illustrated. Bibliography of "authorities cited," pp. 405-07.

481   McClellan, Elisabeth. **History of American Costume, 1607-1870; with an Introductory Chapter on Dress in the Spanish and French Settlements in Florida and Louisiana** . . . New York, Tudor, 1937. 661p. illus. index. Reprinted 1942.

Good, serious history covering male and female dress, some military dress and occasionally children's dress. Illustrations have captions and notes. Extensive glossary. Bibliography, pp. 657-65, lists books and periodical articles.

482   Wilcox, R. Turner. **Five Centuries of American Costume.** New York, Scribner's, 1963. 207p. illus. LC 63-9768.

Good, popular history from the earliest settlers to the present, with chapters on American Indian costume. Each chapter is followed by a good selection of line drawings. Good, classified bibliography of books and periodical articles, pp. 203-07.

EUROPEAN COSTUME

France

483   Renan, Ary. **Le costume en France.** Paris, Librairie d'Éducation Nationale, n.d. 272p. illus. index.

Serious history of costume in France from the first century A.D. to 1800, illustrated with line drawings, most adapted from contemporary art sources. No bibliography.

Great Britain

484   Brooke, Iris. **English Costume of the Age of Elizabeth: the Sixteenth Century.** London, A. & C. Black, 1933. 87p. illus. Reprinted 1938.

Popular history of English costume of the sixteenth century. Illustrated with line and color drawings, chiefly by the author, that suffer from a penchant for over-dramatic poses. No bibliography.

485   Brooke, Iris. **English Costume of the Early Middle Ages: The Tenth to the Thirteenth Centuries.** London, A. & C. Black, 1936. Reprinted 1948. 86p. illus.
Popular history dealing chiefly with civil dress. Illustrated with drawings, many by the author. No bibliography.

486   Brooke, Iris. **English Costume of the Seventeenth Century.** London, A. & C. Black, 1934. 87p. illus.
Popular history generally of upper class dress illustrated with drawings by the author in black and white and color. No bibliography.

487   Brooke, Iris. **English Costume 1900-1950.** London, Methuen, 1951. 90p. illus.
Popular history illustrated with line drawings covering women's, men's and children's fashion. No bibliography.

488   Brooke, Iris. **A History of English Costume.** 4th ed. New York, Theatre Arts, 1972. 196p. illus. index. LC 72-85476.
Popular history covering English dress from 1066 to 1970. Illustrated with line drawings. No bibliography.

489   Buck, Anne. **Victorian Costume and Costume Accessories.** New York, Nelson, 1962. 215p. illus. index. LC 62-8330.
Good, serious history of English costume and accessories from 1837 to 1900 with emphasis on ladies' dress. Well illustrated with informative notes to the plates. Appendix provides list of principal museum collections. Good classified bibliography, pp. 208-09, of major books and periodical articles.

490   Calthrop, Dion C. **English Costume, 1066-1820.** London, A. & C. Black, 1963. 463p. illus. LC 60-50250 rev.
Popular history illustrated chiefly with line drawings of rather mediocre exactitude. No bibliography.

491   Cunnington, Cecil W. **A Dictionary of English Costume, 900-1900.** Philadelphia, Dufour, 1960. 281p. illus. index. LC 60-3271.
Good, serious dictionary covering all aspects of English costume including accessories. Illustrated with line drawings. Has separate glossary of terms including obsolete color designations.

492   Cunnington, Cecil W. **English Women's Clothing in the Present Century.** London, Faber, 1952. 312p. illus. index.
Good, popular history/handbook covering female dress in Great Britain from 1900 to 1950. Well illustrated with line drawings and reproductions of original fashion designs and illustrations. Descriptive captions often give the original prices of the pieces. Good glossary. No bibliography.

493   Cunnington, Cecil W., and Phillis Cunnington. **Handbook of English Costume in the Nineteenth Century.** Philadelphia, Dufour, 1959. 606p. illus. index. LC A60-8603. Reprinted: Boston, Plays, Inc., 1971. LC 72-78805.
Popular handbook illustrated with line drawings, some of which have descriptive captions. Good section on the construction of male and female dress, plus glossary of materials. Bibliography, pp. 576-81, lists books and periodical articles.

494   Cunnington, Cecil W., and Phillis Cunnington. **Handbook of English Costume in the Sixteenth Century.** New rev. ed. London, Faber, 1970. 244p. illus. index. LC 79-509836.
Popular history covering 1480 to 1600. Illustrated with line drawings that have descriptive captions. Glossary of terms and bibliography of books and periodical articles, pp. 206-09, used as sources for the illustrations.

495   Cunnington, Cecil W., and Phillis Cunnington. **Handbook of English Medieval Costume.** 2nd ed. London, Faber, 1969. 210p. illus. index. LC 73-442678.
Popular handbook/history of English costume, 800 to 1500. Glossary of terms. Sources of illustrations, pp. 179-85. Bibliography of basic books, pp. 176-78.

496   Dunbar, Joan T. **History of Highland Dress: A Definitive Study of Scottish Costume and Tartan, Both Civil and Military, Including Weapons.** Edinburgh and London, Oliver & Boyd, 1962. 248p. illus. index.
Good, serious history of Scottish dress from its origins in the eleventh century through the nineteenth century. Includes some arms. Excellent collection of illustrations with descriptive notes. One-page bibliography lists basic books and periodical articles.

497   Grange, Richard M. D. **A Short History of Scottish Dress.** New York, Macmillan, 1967. 120p. illus. index. LC 67-10516.
Popular history/handbook of Scottish dress from circa 1550 to 1822, with emphasis on tartans. Well illustrated with plates and line drawings; notes to the plates are provided. Bibliography, pp. 115-16, is a chronological list of basic books.

498   Yarwood, Doreen. **English Costume from the Second Century B.C. to 1950.** Rev. ed. London, Batsford, 1961. 290p. illus. index. LC 62-52405.
Popular history of English costume, with an introductory chapter on development of costume in antiquity. Large collection of line drawings with sources given. Bibliography, pp. xiii-xiv, lists books and periodical articles used as sources for the illustrations.

ORIENTAL COSTUME

499   Ayer, Jacqueline. **Oriental Costume.** London, Studio Vista, 1974. 192p. illus.
Popular history/handbook of the costume of India, China, Southeast Asia and Japan from the earliest times to the present. Numerous line drawings

and color plates with brief descriptive notes. Glossary of terms. No
bibliography.

500   Fairservis, Walter A. **Costumes of the East**. New York, Chatham, 1971.
       160p. illus. index. LC 77-159783.
Serious handbook of Oriental costume covering the Middle East, India, Southeast
Asia, China, Japan and Central Asia. Chapter on the meaning of costume in the
East. Well illustrated with line drawings and color plates of actual garments.
Bibliography, p. 154, lists books, catalogs and periodicals in English and other
Western languages.

501   Ghurye, Govind S. **Indian Costume**. 2nd ed. Bombay, Popular Prakashan,
       1966. 302p. illus. index. LC SA67-2291.
Good, scholarly history of East Indian costume from circa 320 B.C. to the twentieth
century, with an introduction relating Indian dress to ancient dress in the West.
Appendix with short essays on special items of dress. Good selection of illustrations
but poorly reproduced. Bibliographies at the end of each chapter.

502   Minnich, Helen B., and Shojiro Nomura. **Japanese Costume and the Makers
       of Its Elegant Tradition**. Rutland, Vt., Tuttle, 1963. 374p. illus. index.
       LC 62-15063.
Good, serious history/handbook covering 660 B.C. to the present, with emphasis on
court dress. Well illustrated and with informative notes. Noteworthy appendices,
including ones on brocade and on color and design in the Edo period. Extensive
glossary of costume and textile terms. Comparative chronological table of events
in China, India and the West. Good basic bibliography, pp. 361-64, of Japanese,
French and English books and catalogs.

503   Tilke, Max. **Oriental Costumes, Their Designs and Colors**. London, Paul,
       Trench, Trubner, 1923. 32p. (text), 128 plates.
Illustrated survey of Mid-Eastern and Far Eastern ethnic dress. Illustrations show
the garments lying flat (not worn by models), which is most useful for demonstrat-
ing how the pieces are made. No bibliography.

AFRICAN AND AUSTRALIAN COSTUME

504   Eicher, Joanne B. **African Dress; a Select and Annotated Bibliography of
       Subsaharan Countries**. East Lansing, Michigan State University Press, 1969.
       134p. illus. index. LC 73-731220.
Bibliography of 1,025 books and periodical articles covering all aspects, including
accessories and jewelry. Arranged geographically. Most entries have descriptive
annotations.

505   Flower, Cedric. **Duck & Cabbage Tree, a Pictorial History of Clothes in
       Australia, 1788-1914**. Sydney, Angus & Robertson, 1968. 157p. illus.
       index. LC 75-414017.

Popular history of Australian dress, with separate chapter on aboriginal clothing. Well illustrated, with descriptive captions. No bibliography.

506   Lazar, Vicky. **Costume and Fashion in South Africa 1652-1910; a Bibliography.** Cape Town, University of Cape Town, 1970. 30p. index. LC 79-573152.
Good, classified and descriptively annotated bibliography of books and periodical articles dealing with the costume of the European settlers in South Africa from 1652 to 1910. Does not include native African dress.

CHAPTER EIGHT

ENAMELS

BIBLIOGRAPHIES, DICTIONARIES AND ENCYCLOPEDIAS

507   Clouzot, Henri. **Dictionnaire des miniaturistes sur émail.** Paris, Morancé, 1925. 243p. illus.
Good, comprehensive dictionary of European enamel miniaturists, providing basic biographical data and reference to major pieces. Bibliography of basic books and periodical articles, pp. 13-20.

508   McClelland, Ellwood H. **Enamel Bibliography and Abstracts, 1928 to 1939, Inclusive, with Subject and Coauthor Indexes.** Columbus, Ohio, American Ceramic Society, 1944. 352p. index.
Comprehensive bibliography of books and periodical articles in all languages covering all aspects of enamels and enameling. Subject index. Although concerned chiefly with technical aspects, lists a good sampling of works on the history of art enameling. Entries are described in the form of brief abstracts.

509   Molinier, Émile. **Dictionnaire des émailleurs depuis le moyen âge jusqu'à la fin du XVIIIe siècle** . . . Paris, Rouam, 1885. 113p. illus.
Short-entry dictionary of enamelists working in Europe from the Middle Ages through the eighteenth century, with facsimiles of their marks and signatures.

GENERAL HISTORIES AND HANDBOOKS

510   Dawson, Edith B. **Enamels.** Chicago, McClurg, 1908. 207p. illus. index.
Popular survey of world enamels from antiquity to the twentieth century. Bibliography, pp. 199-201, lists basic books in English.

511   Day, Lewis F. **Enameling, a Comparative Account of the Development and Practice of the Art** . . . London, Batsford, 1907. 222p. illus. index.
Popular history of world enamels with emphasis on technical development.

WESTERN ENAMELS

512   Belli Barsali, Isa. **European Enamels.** London and New York, Hamlyn, 1969. 158p. illus. LC 71-454617.
Popular survey of European enamels from Byzantine times through the eighteenth century. Illustrated with museum pieces.

513   Burger, Willy. **Abendländische Schmelzarbeiten.** Berlin, Carl Schmidt, 1930. 222p. illus. index. (Bibliothek für Kunst-und Antiquitätensammler, XXXIII).
Scholarly history of Western enamels from antiquity through the eighteenth century, with emphasis on the Middle Ages. Illustrated with museum pieces. Classified bibliography, pp. 215-20, is a good list of major books and periodical articles.

514   Chamot, Mary. **English Medieval Enamels** . . . London, Benn, 1930. 49p. illus. index. (University College Monographs on English Medieval Art, II)
Serious history of English medieval enamels from the sixth century through the fifteenth century. Plates with descriptive catalog. Bibliography, pp. 19-20, lists basic books and periodical articles.

515   Cunynghame, Henry H. **European Enamels** . . . London, Methuen; New York, Putnam, 1906. 187p. illus. index.
Older, popular history of Western enamels from antiquity through the nineteenth century. No bibliography.

516   Falke, Otto von, and Heinrich Frauberger. **Deutsche Schmelzarbeiten des Mittelalters.** Frankfurt/Main, J. Baer, 1904. 151p. illus.
Good, serious history of German medieval enamels from Carolingian times to the fifteenth century, illustrated with pieces shown at the exhibition of Rhenish art held in Düsseldorf in 1902.

517   Garnier, Édouard. **Histoire de la verrerie et de l'émaillerie** . . . Tours, Mame, 1886. 573p. illus. index.
Old, comprehensive history of Western glass and enamels from antiquity through the eighteenth century. Occasional bibliographical footnotes.

518   Gauthier, Marie-Madeleine. **Émaux du moyen âge occidental.** Fribourg, Office du Livre, 1972. 443p. illus.
An excellent, serious history of Western medieval enamels from the seventh through the fifteenth centuries. Chapters treat the major periods with excellent notes to the plates and thorough, scholarly catalog of the major pieces illustrated in the text. Excellent bibliographies with catalog entries. Good chapter on technique, useful maps and excellent, classified bibliography, pp. 425-39, of books and periodical articles.

519   Hackenbroch, Yvonne. **Italienisches Email des frühen Mittelalters.** Basel, Holbein-Verlag, 1938. 68p. illus. index. (Ars Docta, Band II).
Scholarly history of Italian enamels of the seventh through the thirteenth centuries. Chapters have brief introductions preceding detailed catalogs of the major examples; each entry has an extensive bibliography. A standard history of early medieval Italian enamels.

520   Hildburgh, W. L. **Medieval Spanish Enamels**. Oxford, Oxford University
      Press, 1936. 146p. illus. index.
Scholarly study that traces the history of Spanish enamels from the seventh through
the thirteenth centuries. Bibliographical footnotes.

521   Juaristi Sagarzazu, Victoriano. **Esmaltes con especial mención de los
      españoles**. Barcelona, Labor, 1933. 286p. illus. index.
Good, serious history of Western European enamels from the early Middle Ages
through the nineteenth century with special emphasis on Spanish enamels. Bibliography of books and periodical articles, pp. 264-70.

522   Kondakov, Nikolai P. **Geschichte und Denkmäler des byzantinischen Emails**.
      Frankfurt/Main, n.p., 1892. 412p. illus.
Old, pioneering history of Byzantine enamels based on pieces in the former
Swenigorodskoi Collection. Bibliographical footnotes.

523   Molinier, Émile. **L'émaillerie**. Paris, Hachette, 1891. 347p. illus. index.
Older popular history of Western enamels from ancient Egypt through the
eighteenth century.

524   Wessel, Klaus. **Byzantine Enamels**. Greenwich, Conn., New York Graphic
      Society, 1967. 211p. illus. index.
Good, serious history from the fifth through the thirteenth century. Introductory
essay with bibliographical footnotes, followed by excellent selection of plates; the
detailed notes to the plates have bibliographical references.

ORIENTAL ENAMELS

525   Cosgrove, Maynard G. **The Enamels of China and Japan: Champlevé and
      Cloisonné**. New York, Dodd, Mead, 1974. 115p. illus. index.
Well-illustrated, popular survey with chapter on technique and manufacture.
Bibliography, pp. 108-12, lists basic books and periodical articles in all languages.

526   Garner, Harry M. **Chinese and Japanese Cloisonné Enamels**. 2nd ed.
      London, Faber and Faber, 1970. 120p. illus. index.
Good, serious history of Far Eastern cloisonné enamels from earliest times to the
end of the Ch'ing dynasty in China and to the end of the nineteenth century in
Japan. Illustrated with museum pieces. Bibliography, pp. 114-16, is a good classified
list of major books in Western languages.

CHAPTER NINE

FURNITURE

DICTIONARIES AND ENCYCLOPEDIAS

527 Aronson, Joseph. **The New Encyclopedia of Furniture.** 3rd ed. New York, Crown, 1967. 484p. illus. LC 65-24334 rev.
Comprehensive dictionary of furniture terms covering decoration, woods, construction, types and objects, periods and styles, and cabinetmakers. Well illustrated; has a glossary of designers and good general bibliography, pp. 476-79. Although a popular work, it is a most useful reference for the collector and general reader.

528 Gloag, John. **A Short Dictionary of Furniture; Containing 1,767 Terms Used in Britain and America.** New York, Holt, Rinehart & Winston, 1965. 565p. illus. LC 65-22445.
Dictionary of terms used in the history of American and British furniture, covering woods, decoration, construction, styles, types and schools. A separate section lists American and British furniture makers and designers and clock makers. Illustrated with line drawings. Useful for the general reader and collector.

529 Lockwood, Luke V. **The Furniture Collectors' Glossary** . . . New York, Walpole Society, 1913. 55p. illus. Reprint: New York, DaCapo, 1967. LC 67-27460.
Old, pioneering dictionary of terms used in cabinetmaking. Illustrated with line drawings.

GENERAL HISTORIES AND HANDBOOKS

530 Boger, Louise A. **The Complete Guide to Furniture Styles.** Enl. ed. New York, Scribner's, 1969. 520p. illus. LC 73-85267.
Popular survey history of Western furniture from ancient times to the present. Bibliography, pp. 506-08, is a selected list of books in English.

531 Comoli Sordelli, Angela. **Il mobile antico dal XIV al XVII sècolo.** Milan, Görlich, 1967. 192p. illus. LC 68-119681.
Popular history of Western furniture from the fourteenth century to the end of the seventeenth century. Emphasis is on Italian furniture and the pieces illustrated are chiefly in Italian museums and private collections.

532   Davis, Frank. **A Picture History of Furniture**. New York, Macmillan, 1959.
       160p. illus. index. LC 62-5441.
Popular pictorial survey of world furniture from earliest times through the mid-
twentieth century. In later centuries emphasis is on English work. Illustrated with
museum pieces and pieces in the trade.

533   Evers, J. W. **Geschiedenis van het meubel**. Utrecht, Uitgeverij Ons Huis.
       1962. 612p. illus. index. LC 66-54316.
Good, serious history of world furniture from ancient Egypt to the present with
emphasis on Western European styles. Well illustrated with museum pieces. Bibliography of basic books in all languages, pp. 609-10.

534   Gloag, John. **A Social History of Furniture Design, from B.C. 1300 to
       A.D. 1960**. New York, Crown, 1966. 202p. illus. index. LC 66-20207.
Popular history of Western furniture from ancient times to the present. Introductory
chapters deal with the relationship of furniture and social habits, materials and
methods of construction, and the role of decoration. Brief bibliography, p. 192,
of reference books.

535   Hayward, Helena, ed. **World Furniture; an Illustrated History**. New York,
       McGraw-Hill, 1965. 320p. illus. index. LC 65-18175.
An excellent, popular history of world furniture from ancient times through the
twentieth century. Consists of essays by specialists, thoroughly illustrated with
museum pieces, views of interiors of historic buildings, and contemporary paintings
and graphic arts. Provides a glossary of terms and good classified bibliography of
books in all languages, p. 312.

536   Hinckley, F. Lewis. **A Directory of Antique Furniture; the Authentic
       Classification of European and American Designs for Professionals and
       Connoisseurs**. New York, Crown, 1953. 355p. illus. LC 52-10776.
Serious handbook of European and American furniture from the sixteenth century
to about 1840.

Brief introductory text followed by an extensive group of illustrations. Examples,
arranged by country, are chiefly from private collections and of the type available
to the collector. A useful handbook for beginning and experienced collectors.

537   Mercer, Eric. **Furniture, 700-1700**. New York, Meredith, 1969. 183p.
       illus. index. LC 69-18425.
Good, popular history of Western furniture from the early Middle Ages to the end
of the seventeenth century, with emphasis on general cultural context of furniture
design. Well illustrated with plates of furniture and works of art showing contemporary function of furniture in various interiors. Bibliography, pp. 173-77, is a good
though unclassified bibliography of books in all languages.

538   Müller, Sigrid Flamand (Christensen). **Alte Möbel von Mittelalter bis zum Jugendstil.** 7th ed. Munich, Bruckmann, 1968. 211p. illus. index. LC 77-452915.
Excellent, serious history of Western furniture, from the late Middle Ages through the early twentieth century. Illustrated with major museum pieces. Bibliography of basic books in all languages, pp. 210-11.

539   Philip, Peter. **Furniture of the World.** New York, Galahad, 1974. 128p. illus. index.
Well-illustrated popular survey of world furniture from the earliest times to the present. Initial chapters treat materials and techniques and the evolution of furniture styles in East and West; these are followed by chapters tracing the development of the major types of furniture pieces. Illustrated with both museum pieces and pieces accessible to the collector.

540   Schmitz, Hermann. **The Encyclopedia of Furniture; an Outline History of Furniture Design in Egypt, Assyria, Persia, Greece, Rome, Italy, France, the Netherlands, Germany, England, Scandinavia, Spain, Russia and in the Near and Far East up to the Middle of the Nineteenth Century . . .** 2nd ed. London, Benn, 1956; New York, Praeger, 1957. 63p. (text), 320 plates.
Illustrated survey of world furniture from ancient Egypt to the middle of the nineteenth century. Brief introductory text is followed by good collection of plates with descriptive captions. No bibliography.

541   Verlet, Pierre. **Styles. Meubles, decórs, du moyen âge à nos jours.** Paris, Larousse, 1972. 2v. illus. index.
Serious history of world furniture and interior decoration consisting of essays by specialists on various national and period styles. Well illustrated with museum pieces and views of historic interiors. Includes a biographical dictionary of major designers and a bibliography, pp. 255-56, of basic books in all languages.

542   Wanscher, Ole. **The Art of Furniture: 5000 Years of Furniture and Interiors.** New York, Reinhold, 1967. 419p. illus. index. LC 66-25546.
A good, popular survey history of furniture and interior decoration from ancient Egypt to the present, including China and Japan. Illustrated with examples in museums and with views of contemporary interiors. Provides a good bibliography of books in all languages, pp. 411-414.

543   Windisch-Graetz, Franz. **Le meuble baroque et rococo.** Paris, Presses Universitaires de France, 1959. 50p. illus.
Translation of *Möbel Brevier, Barock und Rokoko* (Braunschweig, 1959). Brief illustrated survey of Western European furniture of the seventeenth and eighteenth century, featuring major museum pieces. Brief bibliography of basic reference books.

ANCIENT FURNITURE

544   Baker, Hollis S. **Furniture in the Ancient World: Origins and Evolution, 3100-475 B.C.** New York, Macmillan, 1966. 351p. illus. index. LC 66-23893.
Serious history of furniture in the ancient world from early Egypt through Archaic Greece. Also covers Mesopotamian, Syrian and Palestinian furniture. A thorough but readable text plus an appendix on techniques, excellent illustrations, and helpful chronologies in each chapter. Literature citations in the footnotes. Although not as scholarly, it complements Richter's history of ancient furniture (546).

545   Felletti Maj, Bianca M. **La casa e l'arredamento.** Rome, Colombo, 1940. 95p. illus. (Civiltà romana, 15).
Good, popular illustrated history of ancient Roman furniture and interior decoration. Bibliography, pp. 92-95, lists basic books and periodical articles in all languages.

546   Richter, Gisela M. A. **The Furniture of the Greeks, Etruscans and Romans.** London, Phaidon, 1966. 369p. illus. index.
Scholarly history of ancient furniture from Minoan and Mycenaean times through late Roman. Represents a complete rewriting of the author's earlier (1926) work, *Ancient Furniture*. Includes a chapter on techniques, excellent illustrations, and a short but well-selected bibliography of books in all languages, pp. 341-343. A standard work on ancient furniture.

547   Williams, Caroline L. Ransom. **Studies in Ancient Furniture: Couches and Beds of the Greeks, Etruscans and Romans.** Chicago, University of Chicago Press, 1905. 128p. illus. index.
Scholarly history of ancient furniture, with emphasis on couches and beds. Sections on sources, materials, and techniques. Illustrated with museum pieces and works of art, chiefly sculpture, showing ancient furniture. Bibliography, pp. 113-15, lists books and periodical articles in all languages. An older study still useful to the scholar for its plates and careful examination of sources.

AMERICAN FURNITURE
(U.S., Canada and Latin America)

548   Bjerkoe, Ethel H., and John A. Bjerkoe. **The Cabinetmakers of America . . .** Garden City, N.Y., Doubleday, 1957. 252p. illus.
Popular, but useful, dictionary of American cabinetmakers from Colonial times to the mid-twentieth century. Brief biographical entries give references to sources. Introduction traces the history of cabinetmaking in America. Bibliography, pp. 241-46, is a good list of books and some periodical articles.

549   Butler, Joseph. **American Furniture from the First Colonies to World War I.**
        London, Triune, 1973. 144p. illus.
Good, popular illustrated survey history. Well-chosen color plates of historic interiors
and museum pieces. Brief bibliography of basic books.

550   Carrillo y Gariel, Abelardo. **Evolucion del mueble en Mexico.** Mexico City,
        Instituto Nacional de Antropologia e Historia, 1957. 166p. illus. index.
        LC 65-66407.
Good, serious history of the development of Mexican furniture from the early
Colonial period through the nineteenth century. Bibliographical footnotes.

551   Comstock, Helen. **American Furniture: Seventeenth, Eighteenth and
        Nineteenth Century Styles.** New York, Viking, 1962. 336p. illus. index.
        LC 62-18074.
A good, serious history of American furniture from Jacobean (1640) through early
Victorian (1870) styles. Illustrated with examples in museums and historic sites.
Useful chart of style characteristics for each chapter. Good bibliography, pp. 319-24,
lists both books and periodical articles.

552   Duarte, Carlos F. **Muebles venezolanos; siglos XVI, XVII, y XVIII.** Caracas,
        Cuatro, 1966. 189p. illus. index. LC 77-277689.
A good, popular history of furniture in Venezuela from the sixteenth through the
eighteenth centuries, illustrated with pieces in private collections. Brief bibliography,
p. 183.

553   Grotz, George. **The New Antiques: Knowing and Buying Victorian
        Furniture.** Garden City, N.Y., Doubleday, 1964. 224p. illus. index.
        LC 64-11400.
Popular history/handbook of American Victorian furniture, covering styles from
1815 to 1910 for the beginning collector. Illustrated with line drawings. Although
the prices quoted are no longer current, the succinct classification and description
of nineteenth century furniture styles are useful.

554   Kirk, John T. **Early American Furniture: How to Recognize, Evaluate,
        Buy & Care for the Most Beautiful Pieces—High Style, Country, Primitive
        & Rustic.** New York, Knopf, 1970. 208p. illus. index. LC 71-111232.
Popular handbook on American furniture, with chapters on design, construction,
style, proportions, fakes, evaluation and collecting. For the beginning collector.

555   Miller, Edgar G. **American Antique Furniture, a Book for Amateurs . . .**
        New York, Barrows, 1937. 2v. illus. index. Reprint: New York, Dover,
        1966. 2v. illus. index. LC 66-20419.
Serious handbook of American furniture from earliest times to about 1840. Introductory chapters discuss styles and periods, problems of dating, fakes, restoration
and refinishing. Bulk of the work consists of a most valuable collection of plates,
with examples arranged by type; examples are of a level available to the average
collector. A standard reference tool for the collector of American period furniture.

556   Nagel, C. **American Furniture: 1615-1850.** New York, Chanticleer Press, 1949. 112p. illus. index.
Popular history illustrated with museum pieces and views of historic interiors. List of notable museum collections. Bibliography, p. 110, lists basic books.

557   Nutting, Wallace. **Furniture Treasury.** New York, Macmillan, 1968. 2v. in 1. illus. Reprint of 1948 edition.
Illustrated handbook of American furniture from the seventeenth century to the mid-nineteenth century. Brief text is followed by large number of black and white plates arranged by type of piece, mostly from private collections. Emphasizes those pieces available to the average collector. A standard reference work for collectors of early American furniture.

558   Ormsbee, Thomas H. **Early American Furniture Makers, a Social and Biographical Study** . . . New York, Crowell, 1930. 183p. illus. index.
Popular survey of American furniture to circa 1850, with chronological list of furniture and clockmakers. Bibliography, pp. 177-79, lists basic books and periodicals.

559   Ormsbee, Thomas H. **Field Guide to American Victorian Furniture.** Boston, Little, Brown, 1952. 428p. illus. LC 52-9095. Reprint: New York, Crown, n.d.
Good, popular history/handbook covering the period 1840 to 1880. Illustrated with line drawings of pieces accessible to the average collector. Arrangement is by type. Brief one-page bibliography of basic books.

560   Ormsbee, Thomas H. **Field Guide to Early American Furniture.** Boston, Little, Brown, 1951. 464p. illus. Reprint: New York, Crown, n.d.
Good, popular handbook/history covering American furniture from the early eighteenth century to circa 1850. Arranged by types, with a chapter on periods of American furniture. Useful dictionary of terms, list of furniture woods and types of hardware. One-page list of basic books. Illustrated with line drawings of pieces accessible to the average collector.

561   Otto, Celia J. **American Furniture of the Nineteenth Century.** New York, Viking, 1965. 229p. illus. index. LC 65-21483.
Popular survey history of American nineteenth century furniture. Chapters examine the development of furniture design styles by types—i.e., chairs, dressers, etc.— including musical instruments. Sensible, factual text.

562   Palardy, Jean. **The Early Furniture of French Canada.** 2nd ed. Toronto, Macmillan, 1965. 413p. illus. index. LC 65-22627.
Good, illustrated handbook for the beginning and experienced collector, covering Canadian furniture to the early nineteenth century. Arranged by types of furniture with a brief historical introduction. Provides an index to master wood-carvers, glossary and lexicon of French-Canadian furniture terms. Bibliography, pp. 405-06, lists books and periodical articles in all languages.

563   Sack, Albert. **Fine Points of Furniture: Early American.** New York, Crown, 1950. 303p. illus. Reprinted 1969.

Good handbook of American furniture through 1800. Introductory chapter on collecting is followed by a substantial corpus of illustrations, grouped by types and arranged according to levels of quality, with explanatory captions. Final section lists the most often encountered restorations, replacements and imperfections of various types of American period furniture. A useful handbook for both beginning and experienced collectors.

564   Santos, José de Almeida. **Mobiliário artístico brasileiro.** 2nd ed. São Paulo, Calecão Museu Paulista, 1963. 3v. illus. LC 64-6406 rev.

Comprehensive history/handbook of Brazilian furniture illustrated with museum pieces. Tomo I is an historical survey; Tomo II and Tomo III comprise a dictionary of terms, persons, places and types of Brazilian furniture. Some bibliography in the footnotes.

565   Taullard, A. **El mueble colonial sudamericano.** Buenos Aires, Ediciones Peuser, 1944. 286p. illus.

Good, serious history/handbook of Colonial South American furniture to the end of the nineteenth century. Introduction traces parallel developments in Spain and France. Concluding chapter traces the evolution of major furniture types. Illustrated with pieces in private collections. A standard handbook of South American furniture.

566   Williams, Henry L. **Country Furniture of Early America.** South Brunswick, N.J., A. S. Barnes, 1970. 138p. illus. index.

Popular handbook of American country furniture to circa 1850, arranged by types. Illustrations of pieces within reach of the average collector. Useful drawings of construction details.

EUROPEAN FURNITURE

General Works

567   Feulner, Adolf. **Kunstgeschichte des Möbels seit dem Altertum** . . . Berlin, Propyläen-Verlag, 1927. 654p. illus. index.

Scholarly history of Western furniture from the early Middle Ages to the early nineteenth century. Illustrated with museum-quality examples. Good annotated bibliography, pp. 613-17, lists books in all languages. A standard history of furniture.

568   Grandjean, Serge. **Empire Furniture, 1800 to 1825.** New York, Taplinger, 1966. 120p. illus. index. LC 66-11303.

History/handbook of Empire furniture, chiefly French, for the advanced collector. Good section on typical kinds of Empire style furniture. Well illustrated. Bibliography, pp. 112-14, lists books and some articles, chiefly in English.

569   **Great Styles of Furniture: English, Italian, French, Dutch, Spanish.** New
       York, Viking, 1963. 308p. illus. LC 63-18910.
Popular, illustrated handbook of most major European furniture styles. Brief
essays on the various countries are followed by good collection of plates, many
of interiors. No bibliography.

570   Ritz, Gislind. **Alte geschnitzte Bauernmöbel.** Munich, Callwey, 1974.
       200p. illus. index. (Bauernmöbel, Band III).
Excellent, serious history/handbook of European folk furniture with carved decoration arranged by countries and illustrated with major museum pieces. Companion
to the author's work on painted folk furniture.

571   Ritz, Gislind M. **The Art of Painted Furniture.** New York, Van Nostrand,
       Reinhold, 1971. 175p. illus. LC 76-150509.
Serious general history of painted furniture in Scandinavia, Central and Eastern
Europe, Italy, and Spain, with a brief chapter on Pennsylvania German painted
furniture. Well-illustrated, factual text and good classified bibliography, pp. 169-73,
of books and periodical articles in all languages. The best book on painted furniture
in English.

572   Schmidt, Robert. **Möbel** . . . 9th ed. Braunschweig, Klinkhardt & Biermann,
       1965. 307p. illus. index. LC 79-274946. (Bibliothek für Kunst- und
       Antiquitätenfreunde, Band 5.)
A good, serious history/handbook of European furniture from the early Middle Ages
through the Biedermeier period. Illustrated with pieces in museums. Bibliography,
pp. 299-301, lists books in all languages.

France

573   Béné-Petitclerc, Frédérique. **Ebenisten der Louis-XVI-Möbel.** Braunschweig,
       Klinkhardt & Biermann, 1968. 43p. illus. LC 72-581346.
Good, scholarly handbook of the chief furniture makers of Louis XVI period, with
facsimiles of their marks, biographical data and illustrations of signed pieces. Bibliographical footnotes.

574   Boulanger, Gisèle. **L'art de reconnaître les meubles régionaux.** Paris,
       Hachette, 1966. 511p. illus. LC 66-82710.
Popular guide to French provincial furniture, ceramics and pewter. Arranged by
region and well illustrated with views of period interiors and pieces within reach
of the average collector.

575   Félice, Roger de. **French Furniture of the Middle Ages and under Louis
       XIII** . . . London, Heinemann, 1923. 152p. illus. index.
A good but brief survey illustrated with museum pieces. Bibliography of basic
books, p. xvii, and glossary-index.

576   Félice, Roger de. **French Furniture under Louis XV.** London, Heinemann,
         1927. 132p. illus. index.
Popular survey illustrated with museum pieces. One-page bibliography of basic books
and glossary-index.

577   Félice, Roger de. **French Furniture under Louis XIV** ... London, Heine-
         mann, 1922. 147p. illus. index.
Popular survey illustrated with museum pieces. One-page list of basic books and
glossary-index.

578   Félice, Roger de. **French Furniture under Louis XVI and the Empire.**
         London, Heinemann, 1920. 142p. illus. index.
Popular survey illustrated with museum pieces. Glossary-index.

579   **French Cabinetmakers of the Eighteenth Century.** Paris, Hachette, 1965.
         341p. illus. LC 65-28468.
Well-illustrated, popular history of French nineteenth century furniture, with
emphasis on the general cultural context of furniture design and the personalities
of the major cabinetmakers. Good section on manufacturing techniques. Section
on marks and signatures of Parisian makers, with facsimiles. No bibliography.

580   Hinckley, F. Lewis. **A Directory of Antique French Furniture, 1735-1800.**
         New York, Crown, 1967. 220p. illus. index. LC 67-24767.
Pictorial survey of French furniture of the eighteenth and early nineteenth centuries.
Brief introductory essay, plus a good collection of plates arranged by region, a
register of furniture makers, and a vocabulary of French furniture terms. A short
bibliography, pp. 213-14, lists chiefly books published before 1950. For the
collector.

581   Longnon, Henri, and Frances W. Huard. **French Provincial Furniture.**
         Philadelphia and London, Lippincott, 1927. 166p. illus. index.
Popular history illustrated with museum pieces and plates of interiors.

582   Nicolay, Jean. **L'art et la manière des maîtres ébénistes français au XVIIIe**
         siècle. Paris, Le Prat, 1956-59. 2v. illus. index. LC 56-40968 rev.
A good, serious handbook of French eighteenth century cabinetmakers and furniture
designers. Volume one is a biographical dictionary with rather full *oeuvre* catalogs
of the major designers. Volume two provides a dictionary of marks and signatures,
with an index by initials, and a collection of documents on furniture manufacture
in eighteenth century Paris.

583   Ricci, Seymour de. **Louis XIV and Regency Furniture and Decoration.**
         New York, Helburn, 1929. 214p. illus.
Popular, illustrated handbook of French furniture of the Louis XIV and Regency
styles. Brief introductory essay is followed by a good corpus of illustrations of
interiors and pieces in private collections.

584   Salverte, François de. **Les ébénistes du XVIIIe siècle, leurs oeuvres et leurs marques.** 5th ed. Paris, De Nobèle, 1962. 365p. illus. index.
Comprehensive dictionary of French cabinetmakers and furniture designers of the eighteenth century, with facsimiles of their marks and signatures. Illustrated with museum pieces. Bibliographical references in the footnotes. A standard reference work.

585   Salvy, Claude. **Dictionnaire des meubles régionaux.** Paris, Hachette, 1971. 291p. illus. LC 72-301263.
Good, serious dictionary covering all aspects of French provincial furniture, with a separate section devoted to the symbolism found in furniture decoration by Olivier Beigbeder, pp. 271-87. Brief bibliography of basic books in French, p. 291.

586   Souchal, Geneviève. **French Eighteenth Century Furniture.** New York, Putnam, 1961. 128p. illus. LC 61-12202.
Popular survey with emphasis on the development of the major types and classes of furniture. Well illustrated with museum pieces (inadequately identified in the captions) and with works of eighteenth century French painting depicting furniture and its use.

587   Stany-Gauthier, Joseph. **La connaissance des meubles régionaux français; évolution, caractéristiques.** Paris, Moreau, 1952. 272p. illus. index. LC 53-30629.
Popular history/handbook of French provincial furniture illustrated with museum pieces and pieces accessible to the collector. Bibliography of basic reference works.

588   Stany-Gauthier, Joseph. **Le mobilier des vieilles provinces de France.** Paris, C. Massin, 1960. 220p. illus.
First published in 1933. Good, serious history/handbook of French provincial furniture arranged by province and then by type of piece. Includes Flemish furniture. Dictionary of terms. No bibliography.

589   Tardieu, Suzanne. **Meubles régionaux datés.** Paris, Fréal, 1950. 31p. illus. LC A51-5742.
Illustrated survey of French provincial furniture featuring dated examples. Bibliography of basic books and periodical articles in French, pp. 28-29.

590   Theunissen, André. **Meubles et sièges du XVIIIe siècle; menuisiers, ébénistes, marques, plans et ornementation de leurs oeuvres.** Paris, Éditions "Le Document," 1934. 194p. illus. index.
Good dictionary of French eighteenth century furniture makers, their marks and signatures. Illustrated with plates and line drawings of decorative details of museum-quality pieces. Useful plates of types of marble used in eighteenth century French furniture. A standard reference work on the subject.

591   Verlet, Pierre. **The Eighteenth Century in France: Society. Decoration. Furniture.** Rutland, Vt., Tuttle, 1967. 292p. illus. index.
A good, popular history of French nineteenth century furniture and furnishings, with emphasis on general cultural context and function. Very well illustrated with views of restored interiors and contemporary paintings and prints showing eighteenth century interiors.

592   Verlet, Pierre. **French Royal Furniture.** New York, C. Potter, 1963. 200p. illus. index. LC 64-20134.
Good, scholarly history of French furniture made in the eighteenth century for the French crown. Excellent chapter on the discovery and dispersal of French eighteenth century royal furniture. Thorough treatment of the major cabinetmakers and designers. Very useful glossary. Illustrated with forty pieces in American and British museums and collections; each plate is accompanied by good notes.

593   Verlet, Pierre. **Les meubles français au XVIIIe siècle.** Paris, L'Oeil du Connoisseur, 1956. 2v. illus.
Serious handbook/history of French eighteenth century furniture. Chapters on technique, schools, styles, types of furniture, collections and collectors. Provides a short dictionary of marks and signatures and a good annotated bibliography, pp. 95-98. Illustrated with pieces in museums and private collections. A standard work on French eighteenth century furniture.

594   Viaux, Jacqueline. **Bibliographie du meuble.** Paris, Société des Amis de la Bibliothèque Forney, 1966. 589p. index. LC 67-84648.
Comprehensive, classified bibliography of French secular furniture from the Middle Ages to 1966. Includes both books and periodical articles. Special sections on exhibitions, sales, and museum catalogs. A basic, scholarly work.

595   Viaux, Jacqueline. **French Furniture.** New York, Putnam, 1964. 200p. illus. index. LC 64-13023.
Good, serious history from the early Middle Ages to the present. Chapters are devoted to the major periods and style, and each has a good section on technique and ornament. Illustrated with museum pieces. Useful translator's glossary with definitions of major French furniture terms. No bibliography.

596   Watson, F. J. B. **Louis XVI Furniture.** New York, Philosophical Library, 1960. 162p. illus. index. LC 61-4064.
Serious history/handbook of French furniture during the reign of Louis XVI. Chapters on the development of style and forms, on techniques and materials, trade guilds and the influence of major designers. Illustrated with signed examples. Bibliography, p. 95, is an addendum to the bibliography in the author's catalog of Louis XVI furniture in the Wallace Collection.

Germany, Austria and Switzerland

597   Deneke, Bernward. **Bauernmöbel; ein Handbuch für Sammler und Liebhaber.**
       Munich, Keyser, 1969. 408p. illus. index. LC 70-459441.
Good, serious handbook/history of German folk furniture with a good selection of
illustrations and a chapter on collecting.

598   Falke, Otto van, and Hermann Schmitz, eds. **Deutsche Möbel vom**
       Mittelalter bis zum Anfang des 19. Jahrhunderts. Stuttgart, Hoffmann,
       1923-24. 3v. illus. (Bauformen-Bibliothek, Band XIV, XVIII, XX)
Good, serious illustrated history of German furniture from the early Middle Ages
through the early nineteenth century. Concise text outlines the major periods and
is followed by excellent corpus of illustrations of museum pieces and period
interiors. Contents: I. Band: *Vom Mittelalter bis zur Renaissance.* II. Band:
Deutsche Möbel des Barock und Rokoko. III. Band: *Deutsche Möbel des*
Klassizismus.

599   Himmelheber, Georg. **Biedermeier Furniture.** London, Faber and Faber,
       1973. 115p. illus. index.
Excellent, serious history/handbook of German and Austrian Biedermeier furniture.
Illustrated with examples in museums. Chapters on technique and upholstery.
Bibliography, pp. 104-105, lists chiefly books in German.

600   Kreisel, Heinrich, ed. **Die Kunst des deutschen Möbels. Möbel und**
       Vertäfelungen des deutschen Sprachraums von den Anfängen bis zur
       Jugendstil. Munich, Beck, 1970-74. 3v. illus. index. LC 68-121635.
Excellent scholarly history of furniture and paneling in German-speaking countries
from the early Middle Ages to end of Jugendstil (art nouveau). Illustrated with
pieces in museums. Text is arranged by periods, then by types, techniques and
centers. Excellent corpus of plates with accompanying descriptive captions. General
bibliography in third volume, pp. 280-323, is an excellent classified bibliography of
books and periodical articles in all languages. There are further bibliographical citations in the textual footnotes of the individual volumes. Does not include folk
furniture or works by German furniture makers in foreign countries. Contents:
Band 1: H. Kreisel, *Von den Anfängen bis zum Hochbarock.* 2nd ed., 1974. 396p.
illus. index. Band 2: H. Kreisel, *Spätbarock und Rokoko.* 1970. 475p. illus. index.
Band 3: G. Himmelheber, *Klassizismus, Historismus, Jugendstil.* 1973. 417p.
illus. index. The standard history of German furniture.

601   Möller, Lieselotte. **Der Wrangelschrank und die verwandten suddeutsche**
       Intarsienmöbel des 16. Jahrhunderts. Berlin, Deutscher Verein für
       Kunstwissenschaft, 1956. 194p. illus. index.
Excellent scholarly history of south German intarsia furniture of the second half of
the sixteenth century. Illustrated with museum pieces, with a thorough catalogue
raisonné. General bibliography, pp. 156-76, and specific bibliographical references
in the catalog entries. A standard work in the field of Mannerist furniture and
decorative arts.

602   Ritz, Joseph M., and Gislind Ritz. **Alte bemalte Bauernmöbel. Geschichte und Erscheinung, Technik und Pflege.** 5th ed. Munich, Callwey, 1968. 70p. illus. index. LC 68-133006. (Bauernmöbel, Band I).
Excellent, concise handbook of German folk furniture for the student and collector. Chapters on history, technique and care. Illustrated with both museum pieces and pieces within reach of the serious collector. Bibliography, pp. 68-70, is a good, classified list of books and periodical articles. Together with the other volume in the series (570), forms a standard work on European folk furniture.

603   Ritz, Joseph M. **Deutsche Bauermöbel.** Darmstadt, Schneekluth, 1953. 35p. illus. LC 55-28669.
Good, illustrated survey of German painted folk furniture of the eighteenth and nineteenth centuries. Good general bibliography, pp. 33-35.

604   Schade, Günter. **Deutsche Möbel aus Sieben Jahrhunderten.** Leipzig and Heidelberg, Schneider, 1966. 183p. illus. index. LC 67-75736.
A serious, survey history of German furniture from the early Middle Ages through Jugendstil. Illustrations of museum pieces. Includes a glossary of terms and a bibliography of books in German, pp. 176-78.

605   Schmidt, Leopold. **Bauernmöbel aus Süddeutschland, Österreich und der Schweiz.** Vienna and Hanover, Forum, 1967. 207p. illus. index. LC 68-92690.
Excellent, serious handbook of folk furniture in southern Germany, Austria and Switzerland. Arranged by regions, with illustrations of pieces within reach of the average collector. Bibliography, pp. 191-97, is a good classified list of books and periodical articles.

Great Britain

606   Ash, Douglas. **Dictionary of English Antique Furniture.** London, Muller, 1970. 164p. illus. LC 78-537012.
Good, concise dictionary treatment of English furniture designers, plus materials and ornamental motifs used in the manufacture of English furniture. Some line drawing illustrations. Brief bibliography, p. 164.

607   Aslin, Elizabeth. **Nineteenth Century English Furniture.** New York, Yoseloff, 1962. 93p. illus. index. LC 63-946.
A good, serious history of English furniture from early Victorian style through art nouveau. Illustrated with museum pieces, reproductions of period design drawings, and selected interiors. Good, classified bibliography, pp. 89-90, lists books and periodicals. Further bibliographical references in the text footnotes.

608   Brackett, Oliver. **English Furniture Illustrated.** London, Spring, 1958. 403p. illus. index. LC 59-48824.
Popular survey history of English furniture from the Gothic period through the nineteenth century. Brief introductory text with good corpus of illustrations and informative notes to the plates.

609   Cescinsky, Herbert. **English Furniture from Gothic to Sheraton.** New York, Crown, 1958. 406p. illus. index. Reprint: New York, Dover, 1968. LC 68-19173.

A good, concise survey history of English furniture and woodwork from the late Middle Ages through the late eighteenth century. Includes chapters on lacquer ware and needlepoint. Comprehensive but poor quality collection of plates of buildings, interiors, drawings, and pieces of furniture (many representative of examples accessible to the collector). An older work still useful to the collector because of its plentiful illustrations.

610   Cescinsky, Herbert, and Ernest R. Gribble. **Early English Furniture and Woodwork.** London, Routledge, 1922. illus. index.

An old and once standard history of English furniture and woodwork from the Middle Ages through the seventeenth century. Covers both interior and exterior wooden decoration. Many valuable illustrations of buildings that have been razed since the publication of the book.

611   Dean, Margery. **English Antique Furniture, 1450-1850.** New York, Universe, 1969. 109p. illus. LC 69-17308.

Brief popular survey history of English furniture with emphasis on examples available to the modest collector; lacks sufficient illustrations.

612   Edwards, Ralph. **The Shorter Dictionary of English Furniture; from the Middle Ages to the Late Georgian Period.** London, Country Life, 1964. 684p. illus. LC 66-43510.

One-volume condensation of the author's *The Dictionary of English Furniture* (627). A most useful reference work for English furniture and interior decoration, treating types of furniture and accessories, materials and techniques, and decoration. Also includes major British furniture designers and cabinetmakers. No bibliography. Illustrated with pieces in museums and private collections.

613   Edwards, Ralph, and Margaret Jourdain. **Georgian Cabinet-Makers.** 3rd ed. London, Country Life, 1955. 247p. illus. index.

Good, scholarly biographical dictionary of English eighteenth century cabinetmakers, arranged chronologically. Entries give basic biographical data with reference to inventories, sales records and other documentary sources. Section devoted to lesser-known and minor cabinetmakers, joiners and carvers. Bibliographical footnotes. Good collection of plates illustrating signed pieces.

614   Fastnedge, Ralph. **English Furniture Styles from 1500 to 1830.** Baltimore, Penguin, 1967. 321p. illus. index.

A good, serious general history of English furniture from late Gothic through Regency styles. Illustrated with plates and line drawings of museum-quality pieces. Good glossary and list of cabinetmakers and designers. Notes to the chapters refer to further literature.

615   Gloag, John. **English Furniture.** 5th ed. rev. and enl. London, A. & C. Black, 1965. 183p. illus. index. LC 65-4602.
Popular history of English furniture from 1500 to 1920 with chapter on the art of buying furniture. Illustrated with pieces in museums and private collections. No bibliography.

616   Gloag, John. **Guide to Furniture Styles: English and French, 1450 to 1850.** New York, Scribner's, 1972. 232p. illus. index. LC 72-162.
Popular survey history of English and French furniture from Gothic through early Victorian. Illustrated with line drawings. No bibliography.

617   Hayward, Charles H. **English Period Furniture.** Rev. and enl. ed. New York, Scribner's, 1971. 270p. illus. index. LC 77-155926.
A serious but concise general history of English furniture from Tudor through Empire styles with emphasis on construction and decorative details. Illustrated with black and white plates of documented pieces and line drawings of details of design and construction. Because of its emphasis on construction, it is a useful book for the collector and restorer.

618   Hughes, Therle. **Old English Furniture.** New York, Praeger, 1969. 201p. illus. index. LC 69-19858.
Handbook of English furniture for the beginning collector covering medieval through mid-eighteenth century creations. Includes long case clocks. Plates and line drawings illustrate examples within the reach of the average collector.

619   Jervis, Simon. **Victorian Furniture.** London, Ward Lock, 1968. 96p. illus. index.
Popular history of English furniture from circa 1850 to circa 1900. Illustrated with examples in museums. No bibliography.

620   Jourdain, Margaret. **English Decoration and Furniture of the Early Renaissance (1500-1650)** . . . London, Batsford, 1924. 305p. illus. index.
A good, but older, popular history of English furniture and interior design of the early Renaissance period. Well illustrated with many details of decoration.

621   Jourdain, Margaret. **English Decoration and Furniture of the Later XVIIIth Century (1760-1820), an Account of Its Development and Characteristic Forms.** London, Batsford, 1922. 269p. illus. index.
Good, serious history covering furniture and interior decoration. Well illustrated with numerous useful details.

622   Jourdain, Margaret. **English Interior Decoration 1500 to 1830.** London, Batsford, 1950. 84p. illus. index.
A condensed version of the author's four-volume history of the major periods of English furniture and interior design. A good, serious history; well illustrated with plates of interiors, pieces of furniture and details of decoration. Arranged by periods, then by features and types. Bibliographical references in the footnotes.

623   Joy, Edward. **Furniture.** New York, Hearst, 1972. 226p. illus. index.
Good, popular history of English furniture from circa 1200 to the present, with
references to Continental and American developments. Illustrated with line drawings and color plates. Short bibliography, p. 215, lists books in English.

624   Lenygon, Francis. **Furniture in England from 1660-1760.** 2nd ed. London,
        Batsford, 1927. 276p. illus. index.
A good, serious history of English furniture from 1660 to 1760. Chapters treat the
major period styles and furniture types. Well illustrated with pieces in private
collections and in the trade. Still a valuable reference work for the experienced
collector.

625   Macdonald-Taylor, Margaret S. **English Furniture from the Middle Ages
        to Modern Times.** New York, Putnam, 1966. 299p. illus. index. LC 66-
        14485.
Good, popular history/handbook with chapters on historical development and
major types. Also contains a chronological table and glossary of furniture terms.
Illustrations show both museum quality furniture and pieces accessible to the
collector. One-page bibliography of basic books.

626   Macquoid, Percy. **A History of English Furniture.** London, Lawrence &
        Bullen, 1904-08. 4v. illus. index. Reprint: New York, Dover, 1972.
        LC 76-158732.
Good, older history of English furniture from the sixteenth through early
eighteenth century, illustrated with museum pieces and pieces typical of those
accessible to the average collector. An older standard history.

627   Macquoid, Percy, and Ralph Edwards. **The Dictionary of English Furniture
        from the Middle Ages to the Late Georgian Period.** Rev. and enl. ed. by
        Ralph Edwards. London, Country Life, 1954. 3v. illus.
Good, comprehensive dictionary covering terms, techniques, ornament, objects and
types, periods and styles, cabinetmakers and designers. Well illustrated. No bibliography. For a good, condensed version see (612). A standard reference tool for
English furniture.

628   Musgrave, Clifford. **Regency Furniture, 1800 to 1830.** 2nd rev. ed. London,
        Faber and Faber, 1970. 157p. illus. index. LC 73-593790.
Popular history/handbook of English furniture from 1800 to 1830. Illustrated with
examples accessible to the average collector. Sections on types, processes and materials of Regency furniture.

629   Nickerson, David. **English Furniture.** London, Octopus, 1973. 96p. illus.
Popular illustrated survey of English furniture from the Middle Ages through the
nineteenth century. No bibliography.

630   Nickerson, David. **English Furniture of the Eighteenth Century**. New York, Putnam, 1963. 128p. illus. LC 63-15528.
Good, popular history concentrating on the styles of Chippendale, Adam, Hepplewhite and Sheraton. Well illustrated with museum pieces (inadequately identified in the captions) and with original furniture designs.

631   Penderei-Brodhurst, James G., and Edwin J. Layton. **A Glossary of English Furniture of the Historic Periods** . . . London, Murray, 1925. 196p. illus.
Popular dictionary covering terms, techniques, materials, decoration, and cabinetmakers and designers. No bibliography.

632   Stafford, Maureen. **British Furniture Through the Ages**. New York, Coward-McCann, 1966. 112p. illus. index. LC 66-10846.
Popular history from the late Gothic period to the present, illustrated with line drawings. No bibliography.

633   Symonds, Robert W. **Furniture Making in Seventeenth and Eighteenth Century England; an Outline for Collectors**. London, Connoisseur, 1955. 238p. illus. index.
Good, serious handbook/history with emphasis on style and construction. Well illustrated. Bibliographical footnotes.

634   Symonds, Robert W., and B. B. Whineray. **Victorian Furniture**. London, Country Life, 1962. 232p. illus. index. LC 63-2076.
Good, serious history of English Victorian furniture with chapter on techniques and materials. Well-chosen plates of museum pieces and original designs. No bibliography.

635   Wills, Geoffrey. **English Furniture, 1550-1760**. Garden City, N.Y., Doubleday, 1971. 256p. illus. index. LC 74-180909.

_____. **English Furniture, 1760-1900**. Garden City, N.Y., Doubleday, 1971. 256p. illus. index.
Popular survey history of English furniture from the time of Elizabeth I through the late Victorian period. Well illustrated with examples from museums and private collections.

636   Wolsey, Samuel W., and R. W. Luff. **Furniture in England: The Age of the Joiner**. New York, Praeger, 1969. 104p. illus. index. LC 69-17082.
Handbook for the beginning collector of English furniture dating 1550 to 1660. Chapters devoted to types of furniture follow a brief historical introduction. Glossary of terms. No bibliography.

Italy

637   Aprà, Nietta. **Il mobile barocco e barochetto italiano**. Novara, De Agostini, 1971. 64p. illus.
Popular illustrated survey of Italian seventeenth and eighteenth century furniture, illustrated with museum pieces and historic interiors.

638   Brosio, Valentino. **Il mobile italiano**. Rome, Editalia, 1971. 246p. illus. index. LC 72-877466.
Well-illustrated, popular survey of Italian furniture from the late Middle Ages to the present.

639   Brosio, Valentino. **Mobili italiani dell'Ottocento**. Milan, Vallardi, 1964. 157p. illus. LC 67-57010.
Popular illustrated survey of Italian nineteenth century furniture. Features museum pieces and historic interiors.

640   Cito-Filomarino, Anna M. **L'Ottocento: i mobili del tempo dei nonni dall'Impèro al Liberty**. Milan, Görlich, 1969. 255p. illus. index. LC 75-863251.
Popular history of Italian nineteenth century furniture well illustrated, with museum pieces and interiors. Brief bibliography of basic works chiefly in Italian.

641   Eberlein, Harold D., and Roger W. Ramsdell. **The Practical Book of Italian, Spanish and Portuguese Furniture**. Philadelphia and London, Lippincott, 1927. 354p. illus. index.
Popular history of furniture in Italy, Spain and Portugal from the early Renaissance to the beginning of the eighteenth century.

642   Ghelardini, Armando. **Il mobile italiano dal medioevo all'Ottocento**. Milan, Bramante, 1970. 154p. illus. index. LC 75-551229.
Popular illustrated survey of Italian furniture from the Middle Ages to the end of the eighteenth century.

643   Mannelli, Vinicio. **Il mobile regionale italiano**. Florence, Edam, 1964. 178p. illus. LC 67-58656.
Popular history/handbook of Italian regional furniture, arranged by regions and illustrated with pieces in private collections. Bibliography, pp. 177-78, lists books in all languages.

644   Mazzariol, Giuseppe. **Mobili italiani del Seicento e del Settecento**. Milan, Vallardi, 1963. 154p. illus. index. LC 66-80857.
Popular, illustrated survey of Italian furniture of the seventeenth and eighteenth centuries. Well illustrated with museum pieces and views of historic interiors.

645   Morazzoni, Giuseppe. **Il mobile neoclassico italiano.** Milan, Görlich, 1955.
       62p. (text), 335 plates.
Good, serious handbook of Italian neoclassical furniture arranged by place—i.e.,
Rome, Turin, Genoa, Parma, Florence, Naples, Milan and Venice. Illustrated with
examples in museums and private collections. Bibliographical references in the
footnotes.

646   Odom, William M. **A History of Italian Furniture, From the Fourteenth
       to the Early Nineteenth Century.** Garden City, N.Y., Doubleday, 1918-19.
       2v. illus. Reprint: New York, Archive Press, 1966. LC 67-10441.
Good, serious history illustrated with museum pieces and pieces in major private
collections. No bibliography. An older, standard history.

647   Pedrini, Augusto. **Italian Furniture: Interior Decoration of the Fifteenth
       and Sixteenth Centuries.** London, Tiranti, 1949. 24p. (text), 256 plates.
       index. LC 49-6923.
Popular, illustrated history with plates of museum pieces and historic interiors.
No bibliography.

648   Pignatti, Terisio. **Mobili italiani del Rinascimento.** 2nd ed. Milan, Vallardi,
       1962. 125p. illus. LC 72-201957.
Well-illustrated, popular survey of Italian furniture of the fifteenth and sixteenth
centuries.

649   Schottmüller, Frida. **Furniture and Interior Decoration of the Italian
       Renaissance . . .** New York, Brentano, 1921. 246p. illus.
Pictorial survey of Italian Renaissance furniture and interiors illustrating furniture
museum pieces and period interiors in both historic buildings and Renaissance
paintings. Brief introductory text followed by good collection of plates. Bibliographical footnotes.

Low Countries

650   Jonge, C. H. de, and Willem Vogelsang. **Holländische Möbel und Raumkunst
       von 1650-1780.** The Hague, Nijhoff, 1922. 185p. illus. index.
A good, serious illustrated history of Dutch furniture and interior decoration from
1650 to 1780. Introductory chapters discuss interiors as seen in paintings, historic
buildings and doll houses. Remaining chapters treat the principal types of furniture
and rooms. Provides good corpus of illustrations, mainly of museum quality pieces.
Bibliographical references in the footnotes.

651   Pearse, Geoffrey E. **Eighteenth Century Furniture in South Africa.** Pretoria,
       Van Schaik, 1960. 193p. illus. LC 61-41481.
A good, serious handbook of eighteenth century furniture made in South Africa.
Historical introduction traces the background of furniture design in seventeenth
and eighteenth century Holland and England, followed by sections on developments

in the Cape. Chapters on South African silver, china and glass. Also covers clocks. Illustrated with measured drawings and plates of pieces in museums and private collections. Bibliography, p. 193, lists basic books.

652   Singleton, Esther. **Dutch and Flemish Furniture.** New York, McClure, Phillips, 1907. 338p. illus. index.
Popular history of furniture in the Low Countries from the Middle Ages through the mid-nineteenth century, with emphasis on the place of furniture in the general history of interior design. Has a good chapter on the Dutch home and its furnishings with documented inventories. Illustrated with pieces in museums, interiors in historic buildings and contemporary paintings and prints. A work still useful in this field.

653   Vogelsang, Willem. **Le meuble hollandais au Musée National d'Amsterdam.** Amsterdam, Van Rijkom, 1910. 13p. (text), 64 plates.
Good, illustrated survey of Dutch furniture from the Middle Ages through the early nineteenth century, illustrated with examples in the National Museum in Amsterdam. No bibliography.

Scandinavia

654   Andrén, Erik. **Möbelstilarna; en handbok i den svenska möbel-och inredningskonstens historia.** Stockholm, Saxon and Lindström, 1961. 279p. illus. index. LC 62-44178.
Good, serious history of Swedish furniture and interior decoration from the Middle Ages to the present. Good plates of museum pieces and interiors. Bibliography of basic works.

655   Clemmensen, Tove. **Danske møbler; stiludviklingen fra renaessance til klunketid.** 3rd ed. Copenhagen, Thaning and Appel, 1960. 97p. illus. LC 62-48467.
Popular history of Danish furniture from the Renaissance through the Empire style. Illustrated with museum pieces. Bibliography, pp. 96-97, lists chiefly books in Danish.

656   Erixon, Sigurd. **Folklig möbelkultur i svenska bygder.** Stockholm, Nordisk, 1938. 288p. illus.
Good, serious handbook of Swedish folk furniture arranged by type. Well illustrated with museum pieces and pieces accessible to the average collector. Bibliography, pp. 285-86, is a good list of books and periodical articles in all languages.

657   Fischer, Erik. **Svenska möbler i bild.** Stockholm, Natur och Kultur, 1950. 272p. illus.
Popular, well-illustrated history of Swedish furniture from the early Middle Ages through the early nineteenth century. Illustrated with museum quality pieces; captions are in Danish and German.

658   Henschen Ingvar, Ingegerd. **Svenska möbellexikon**. Malmö, Norden, 1961-62. 3v. illus. LC 62-46920.

Good, comprehensive dictionary of Swedish furniture. Covers all aspects, including makers, types, styles, and decoration. Well illustrated with museum pieces. Bibliographical references for the larger entries.

659   Steensberg, Axel. **Danske Bondemøbler**. Copenhagen, Hassings, 1949. 47p. (text), 456 plates. index.

Good, serious handbook of Danish furniture consisting of a brief historical introduction followed by a good collection of plates that illustrate museum pieces; descriptive captions. No bibliography.

Spain and Portugal

660   Burr, Grace H. **Hispanic Furniture**. 2nd rev. and enl. ed. New York, Archive, 1964. 231p. illus. index. LC 64-22364.

First published in 1941. Popular history of Spanish furniture from the Gothic period through the eighteenth century. Includes Spanish colonial furniture plus a good chapter on the important collection of Spanish furniture in the New York Hispanic Society. Bibliography, pp. 215-19, lists books and periodical articles in all languages.

661   Byne, Arthur, and Mildred Byne. **Spanish Interiors and Furniture** . . . New York, Helburn, 1921-22. 4v. illus. index. Reprint: New York, Dover, 1969. 330p. (plates only). LC 70-97502.

Popular, illustrated survey of Spanish interior decoration and furniture. A useful collection of plates, especially those depicting historic interiors.

662   Doménech, Rafael, and Luis Pérez Bueno. **Antique Spanish Furniture**. New York, Archive, 1965. 142p. illus. index. LC 64-25672.

Reprint of 1921 Spanish edition. Popular, bilingual history of Spanish furniture from the fourteenth through the seventeenth century, consisting of a brief introduction and notes to plates illustrating examples in museums and private collections.

663   Feduchi, Luis M. **Spanish Furniture**. New York, Tudor, 1969. 313p. illus.

Multilingual popular history of Spanish furniture covering the tenth century to the early twentieth century. Illustrated with examples in Spanish museums and historic restorations. Brief bibliography, mostly of Spanish books.

664   Guimarães, Alfredo, and Albano Sardoeira. **Mobiliário artistico português**. Porto, M. Abreu, 1924-35. 2v. illus. index.

Good, serious history of Portuguese furniture from the Middle Ages to the end of the nineteenth century. Bibliography, v. 1, pp. 107-08, lists basic books, catalogs and periodical articles.

665   Lozoya, Juan C. **Muebles de estilo español; desde el gótico hasta el siglo XIX con el mueble popular.** Barcelona, Gili, 1962. 451p. illus. LC 65-88720.
Popular history of Spanish furniture from the Gothic period to the end of the nineteenth century. Arranged by periods, it consists of short chapters followed by line drawings. Brief list of books in all languages, p. 451.

666   Pinto Cardoso, Augusto. **Cadeiras portuguesas.** Lisbon, n.p., 1952. 121p. (text), 131p. (illus.).
Serious history of Portuguese furniture from its medieval origins to the early decades of the nineteenth century. Plates of museum quality pieces are accompanied with descriptive notes. Short list of books, p. 119, plus reference to more specialized literature in footnotes.

667   Sandão, Arthur de. **O móvel pintado em Portugal.** Porto, Livraria Civilização, 1966. 249p. illus. index. LC 67-5803.
Good, popular history of Portuguese painted furniture from the eighteenth century to the present. Most is folk furniture. Summary in French, English and German. Bibliography, pp. 221-28, lists books and periodical articles in Portuguese.

ORIENTAL FURNITURE

668   Dupont, Maurice, and O. Roche. **Les meubles de la Chine.** Paris, A. Calavas, 1925. 6p. (text), 54 plates. Reprinted 1950.
Illustrated history of Chinese furniture. Brief introductory essay is followed by plates of major examples chiefly in French museums. No bibliography.

669   Ecke, Gustave. **Chinese Domestic Furniture.** Rutland, Vt., Tuttle, 1962. 49p. (text), 161p. (illus.). LC 62-21540.
Brief but serious study of Chinese domestic furniture, based chiefly on construction methods. Well illustrated with plates and detailed line drawings.

670   Ellsworth, Robert H. **Chinese Furniture. Hardwood Examples of the Ming and Early Ch'ing Dynasties.** New York, Random House, 1971. 299p. illus. index. LC 71-85592.
Good, serious handbook with chapter on the historical background, conservation and restoration. Covers metal mounts. Good bibliography, pp. 297-99, of books and periodical articles in all languages.

671   Kates, George N. **Chinese Household Furniture.** New York, Harper, 1948. 125p. illus. Reprint: New York, Dover, 1962.
A good, popular survey of the development of Chinese domestic furniture. Initial chapters treat Eastern and Western attitudes to Chinese furniture, problems of dating, materials and techniques, and the general historical development; followed by chapters on the major types of Chinese domestic furniture. Good descriptive notes to the plates. Bibliography, p. 125, lists chief publications in Western languages.

CHAPTER TEN

GLASS

BIBLIOGRAPHIES

672   "Check List of Recently Published Articles and Books on Glass," in:
       Journal of Glass Studies, v. 1 (1959)– .
Annual classified bibliography of books and articles on all aspects of the history and
technology of glass. Items omitted in earlier issues are included in later issues.
Includes museum and exhibition catalogs. A standard reference tool for all serious
study of glass.

673   Duncan, George S. **Bibliography of Glass**. Sheffield and London, Dawson
       of Pallmall, 1960. 544p. LC 59-9650.
Classified bibliography of about 20,000 titles consisting of books and periodical
articles on all aspects of glass and glass painting.

DICTIONARIES AND ENCYCLOPEDIAS

674   Elville, E. M. **The Collector's Dictionary of Glass**. London, Country Life,
       1961. 194p. illus. LC 62-2440.
This dictionary of glass was designed for collectors. Covers persons, styles, periods,
techniques, nations and types of old glass. Brief unclassified bibliography of books
in English, pp. 193-94.

GENERAL HISTORIES AND HANDBOOKS

675   Bernt, Walther. **Altes Glas**. Munich, Prestel, 1950. 63p. illus. LC 55-33395.
Good, popular handbook of antique Western glass with useful index of auction
catalogs which illustrate old glass. No bibliography.

676   Buckley, Wilfred. **European Glass** . . . Boston, Houghton Mifflin, 1926.
       96p. illus. index.
Older popular history of European glass from ancient Egypt through the nineteenth
century. The sources of pieces illustrated in the plates are not noted.

677   Dillon, Edward. **Glass**. London, Methuen; New York, Putnam, 1907. 373p.
       illus. index.
Older popular history of world glass from ancient times to the beginning of the
twentieth century. Brief, selected bibliography, pp. xxii-xxviii.

678   Fuchs, Ludwig F. **Die Glaskunst im Wandel der Jahrtausende.** Darmstadt, Schneekluth, 1956. 40p. illus. (Wohnkunst und Hausrat, Einst and Jetzt, 23)
Popular illustrated survey of European glass from the late Middle Ages through the nineteenth century.

679   Gros-Galliner, Gabriella. **Glass: A Guide for Collectors.** New York, Stein & Day, 1970. 175p. illus. index. LC 78-126973.
Popular history of glass and glassmaking from ancient Egypt to the present, with a chapter on technique. List of museums and glossary of terms. Bibliography, pp. 163-66, lists books and periodical articles in all languages.

680   Haynes, Edward B. **Glass Through the Ages.** Rev. ed. Baltimore, Penguin, 1964. 309p. illus. index. LC 64-55875.
A good, popular history of Western glass from circa 500 B.C. through the early nineteenth century. Illustrated with museum pieces. Special chapter on English eighteenth century glass. No bibliography.

681   Kämpfer, Fritz, and Klaus G. Beyer. **Glass: A World History of 4000 Years of Fine Glass-Making.** Greenwich, Conn., New York Graphic Society, 1967. 314p. illus. LC 67-70992.
Well-illustrated history of world glass from ancient Egypt to the present. Brief historical essay is followed by plates with descriptive captions and good, comprehensive notes that include bibliographical references. Provides a good glossary of terms, techniques, types and glass artists; many of the entries have bibliographical references. An excellent survey history of glass.

682   Mariacher, Giovanni. **Glass from Antiquity to the Renaissance.** London, Hamlyn, 1970. 157p. illus. LC 71-884683.
Popular illustrated survey with good color plates of museum pieces. No bibliography.

683   Savage, George. **Glass.** New York, Putnam, 1965. 128p. illus. LC 65-12438. Reprinted: London, Octopus, 1972.
Popular history of glass from ancient Egypt to the mid-nineteenth century, including Oriental glass. Well illustrated. No bibliography.

684   Schlosser, Ignaz. **Das Alte Glas. Ein Handbuch für Sammler und Liebhaber.** 2nd ed. Braunschweig, Klinkhardt & Biermann, 1965. 388p. illus. index. (Bibliothek für Kunst- und Antiquitätenfreunde, 36).
A good, serious history of world glass from ancient Egypt to the mid-twentieth century, directed to the serious collector. Provides a glossary of terms, a chapter on collecting and restoring glass and a good, classified bibliography of books and periodical articles.

685   Weiss, Gustav. **The Book of Glass.** New York, Praeger, 1971. 353p. illus. index-glossary. LC 78-107151.
Excellent, serious history of Western and Islamic glass from the Bronze Age to the present with section on the history of the techniques of glassmaking.

Well illustrated with museum pieces. Supplied with good maps, useful chronological charts of major makers and charts showing the development of major types of glass. Thorough but unclassified list of books and periodical articles in all languages, pp. 346-49.

ANCIENT AND BYZANTINE GLASS

686   Eisen, Gustav. **Glass, Its Origin, History, Chronology, Technic and Classification to the Sixteenth Century** . . . New York, Rudge, 1927. 2v. illus. index.
Serious history of glass from ancient Egypt through the Middle Ages, illustrated with museum pieces and pieces in private collections. Good, classified bibliography, pp. 751-61.

687   Kisa, Anton. **Das Glas im Altertum.** Leipzig, Hiersemann, 1908. 3v. illus. index.
Comprehensive, scholarly handbook/history of glass from ancient Egypt through late Roman times. Provides a good chapter on technique and a useful appendix of marks and stamps. Illustrated with museum pieces. A pioneering work in the history of glass, still essential to any serious study of ancient glass.

688   Neuburg, Frederic. **Ancient Glass.** Toronto, University of Toronto Press, 1962. 110p. illus. index. LC 63-5593.
A good, serious historical survey of glass from ancient Egypt through the fourth century A.D. Illustrated with museum pieces; descriptive captions to the plates. Provides useful chronological table, maps, and a good, classified bibliography of books and articles, pp. 106-107.

689   Philippe, Joseph. **Le monde byzantin dans l'histoire de la verrerie (V^e–XVIe siècle).** Bologna, Patron, 1970. 248p. illus. index. LC 72-553225.
Good, scholarly history of Byzantine glass from the fifth through the fifteenth centuries, with emphasis on the role of glass and glass production in the general culture. Illustrated with museum pieces, line drawings and views of glass in Byzantine painting and mosaics. Provided with many useful maps and plans of excavations and extensive bibliographical coverage in the footnotes.

MODERN GLASS
(19th and 20th Centuries)

690   Daniel, Dorothy. **Cut and Engraved Glass, 1771-1905.** 6th ed. New York, M. Barrow, 1950. 441p. illus. index.
A thorough history, treating types and time periods in chapters. Useful remarks on distinguishing American from Irish or English glass. Includes a glossary of terms, facsimiles of trademarks, a chart of glasshouses and a good, classified bibliography, pp. 420-29.

691   Grover, Ray, and Lee Grover. **Carved and Decorated European Art Glass.**
         Rutland, Vt., Tuttle, 1970. 244p. illus. index. LC 71-94025.
Handbook of carved and decorated art glass of the second half of the nineteenth
and early twentieth centuries arranged by countries, types and makers. Brief
bibliography of books in English.

692   Janneau, Guillaume. **Modern Glass.** London, The Studio; New York,
         W. E. Rudge, 1931. 184p. illus. index. LC 32-1528.
Good, popular history of European glass from the late nineteenth century through
the 1920s. Good select bibliography by Arnold Fleming, pp. 54-56.

693   Lee, Ruth W. **Nineteenth-Century Art Glass.** New York, Barrows, 1952.
         128p. illus. LC 52-10057.
Popular illustrated survey of American nineteenth century glass, with emphasis on
Victorian pressed and pattern glass.

694   Lee, Ruth W. **Victorian Glass, Specialties of the Nineteenth Century.**
         13th ed. Wellesley Hills, Mass., Lee, 1944. 608p. illus. index.
Popular handbook of American pressed and pattern glass. Directed toward the
collector. Useful index list of patterns and designs.

695   Pazaurek, Gustav E. **Gläser der Empire und Biedermeierzeit.** Leipzig,
         Klinkhardt & Biermann, 1923. 412p. illus. index. (Monographien des
         Kunstgewerbes XIII/XV).
Good, scholarly history of Western European glass in the first half of the nineteenth
century, with emphasis on the German-speaking countries. Illustrated with museum
pieces. Bibliographical footnotes.

696   Pazaurek, Gustav E. **Kunstgläser der Gegenwart.** Leipzig, Klinkhardt &
         Biermann, 1925. 264p. illus. index. (Monographien des Kunstgewerbes,
         Band XIX/XX).
Scholarly history of European glass in the first quarter of the twentieth century.
Chapters on technique, types, major artists and manufacturers. Bibliographical
footnotes.

697   Pazaurek, Gustav E. **Moderne Gläser.** Leipzig, Seemann, 1910. 133p. illus.
         index.
Good, popular survey of Western European glass of the late nineteenth century,
including art nouveau. No bibliography.

698   Polak, Ada B. **Modern Glass.** New York, Yoseloff, 1962. 94p. illus.
         index. LC 62-10191.
Good, serious history of Western glass from 1875 to 1960, illustrated with museum
pieces. Appendix with signatures. Bibliography, pp. 89-90, is a brief list of basic
books.

699   Revi, Albert C. **Nineteenth Century Glass: Its Genesis and Development.**
       Rev. ed. London and Camden, N.J., T. Nelson, 1967. 301p. illus. index.
       LC 67-103761.
Popular history of nineteenth century glass by types and kinds of glassware.
Illustrated with works in the author's collection and some museum pieces. Glossary
of terms but no bibliography.

AMERICAN GLASS

(U.S. and Canada)

Note: see also no. 715

700   Knittle, Rhea M. **Early American Glass.** London and New York, Appleton,
       1927. 496p. illus. index. Reprint: Garden City, N.Y., Garden City Pub.
       Co., 1948. LC 48-10807.
Good, popular history of glass in the United States from early Colonial times
through the mid-nineteenth century. Bibliography of basic books and periodical
articles, pp. 449-53.

701   Lindsey, Bessie M. **American Historical Glass** . . . Rutland, Vt., Tuttle,
       1966. 541p. illus. index. LC 67-11934.
Popular history of American glass from Colonial times to mid-twentieth century,
with emphasis on commemorative pieces. No bibliography.

702   McKearin, George S., and Helen McKearin. **American Glass.** New York,
       Crown, 1941. 622p. illus. index.
Useful, popular history/handbook of American glass from Colonial times through
the nineteenth century. Chapters on techniques, types, major periods and centers
of glass production. Illustrated with pieces accessible to the average collector.
Bibliography, pp. 615-17, lists books and periodical articles.

703   McKearin, Helen, and George S. McKearin. **Two Hundred Years of
       American Blown Glass** . . . Rev. ed. New York, 1966. 382p. illus. index.
       LC 66-5563.
Popular history of American blown glass from Colonial times to the mid-nineteenth
century. Good collection of plates, with detailed descriptive notes. Bibliography,
pp. 361-66, lists books and periodical articles.

704   Revi, Albert C. **American Cut and Engraved Glass.** New York, Nelson,
       1965. 497p. illus. index.
Popular history from the late nineteenth century to the 1930s, arranged by manufacturing firms. Introduction traces the general development. Gives facsimiles of
trademarks and labels. Brief bibliography.

705   Revi, Albert C. **American Pressed Glass and Figure Bottles.** New York, Nelson, 1964. 446p. illus. index. LC 64-14510.
Popular history arranged by manufacturing firms with an introduction on the development of the industry. Treats the subject from circa 1825 to the 1930s. Brief bibliography of basic books.

706   Schwartz, Marvin D. **Collector's Guide to Antique American Glass.** Garden City, N.Y., Doubleday, 1969. 150p. illus. index. LC 68-27138.
Good, popular history/handbook of American glass through art nouveau, with chapters on European backgrounds, technique, folk glass, and cut, pressed and art glass. No bibliography.

707   Stevens, Gerald F. **Canadian Glass c. 1825-1925.** Toronto, Ryerson, 1967. 262p. illus. index. LC 68-77094.
Good, serious history/handbook of Canadian blown, cut and art glass. Illustrated with museum pieces and pieces accessible to the collector. Bibliography of basic books, pp. 257-58.

708   Van Tassel, Valentine. **American Glass.** New York, Gramercy, 1950. 128p. illus. index.
Popular history of all types of glass from Colonial times through art nouveau. Chapters on technique and collecting. Glossary of terms.

709   Unitt, Doris J., and Peter Unitt. **Treasury of Canadian Glass.** 2nd ed. Peterborough, Ont., Clock House, 1969. 280p. illus. index. LC 75-480391.
Popular handbook of Canadian pressed, blown and cut glass from the eighteenth century to the present. Directed to the average collector. Brief bibliography of books and periodical articles, p. 275.

710   Watkins, Lura. **American Glass and Glassmaking.** New York, Chanticleer, 1950. 104p. illus.
Popular history from early Colonial times to the present. List of important public collections and brief bibliography of basic books.

EUROPEAN GLASS

General Works

711   Davis, Frank. **Continental Glass.** New York, Praeger, 1972. 144p. illus. index. LC 79-180728.
Popular history from ancient Rome to the present. Illustrated with museum pieces and pieces within reach of the average collector. Short bibliography of books in English.

712   Mariacher, Giovanni. **L'arte del vetro**. Milan, Mondadori, 1954. 183p. illus.
       LC 54-41008.
Popular illustrated survey of European glass from antiquity to the present. Bibliography of basic books in all languages, pp. 185-87.

713   Middlemas, Keith. **Antique Glass in Color**. Garden City, N.Y., Doubleday, 1971. 120p. illus.
Popular survey of European glass from the fifteenth century through art nouveau, with particularly nice color photographs.

714   Moore, Hannah H. **Old Glass, European and American**. New York, Tudor, 1935. 394p. illus. index.
First published in 1924. Good, older, popular history arranged by major centers of production. List of American glass factories, pp. 369-82. No bibliography.

715   Schmidt, R. **Das Glas**. 2nd ed. Berlin, Leipzig, de Gruyter, 1922. 419p. illus. index.
A good, serious handbook/history of Western glass from antiquity through the eighteenth century, with special emphasis on German glass. Illustrated with museum pieces. Bibliography, pp. 408-409, lists basic books in all languages. Once a standard history of glass, now somewhat out of date.

716   Schrijver, Elka. **Glass and Crystal**. New York, Universe, 1964. 2v. illus. index. LC 64-10342.
Good, popular history of Western glass from ancient Egypt to the present. Volume I: from earliest times to 1850; Volume II: from mid-nineteenth century to present. Brief bibliography of books in all languages at the end of each volume.

717   Steenberg, Elisa, and Bo Simmingsköld. **Glas**. Stockholm, Natur och Kultur, 1958. 434p. illus. index. LC 58-46941.
Good, serious history of European glass, with emphasis on Scandinavia. First part treats the history, and the second part covers the technique of antique and modern glass. Bibliography of basic books, pp. 427-29.

718   Wilkinson, O. N. **Old Glass: Manufacture, Styles, Uses**. New York, Philosophical Society, 1968. 200p. illus. index. LC 68-6826.
Popular history of Western glass from antiquity to the present, with emphasis on manufacture technology. Basic bibliography given at end of each chapter and general list of books in English, pp. 187-89.

France and Belgium

719   Barrelet, James. **La verrerie en France**. Paris, Larousse, 1953. 207p. illus.
Good, serious history of glass in France from Gallo-Roman times to the present. Includes a glossary, maps, and dictionaries of artists and centers of glass production. Good, classified bibliography, pp. 189-92, of books and periodical articles.

720   Chambon, Raymond. **L'histoire de la verrerie en Belgique.** Brussels,
       Librairie Encyclopedique, 1955. 331p. illus. index.
Good, scholarly history of glass in Belgium from the second century A.D. to the
present. Illustrations of museum pieces with accompanying descriptive catalog.
Good, comprehensive bibliography, pp. 261-81, of books and periodical articles.
A standard work on Belgian glass.

721   Rosenthal, Léon. **La verrerie française depuis cinquante ans.** Paris and
       Brussels, G. Van Oest, 1927. 47p. illus.
Illustrated survey of French glass from 1875 to 1925. Bibliography, pp. 41-43, lists
basic books and some periodical articles in French.

Germany, Austria and Switzerland, with Czechoslovakia

722   Hetteš, Karel. **Glass in Czechoslovakia.** Prague, SNTL, 1958. 64p. illus.
Popular history from the fourteenth century to the present. Includes glass mosaic.

723   Rademacher, Franz. **Die deutschen Gläser des Mittelalters.** 2nd ed. Berlin,
       Verlag für Kunstwissenschaft, 1963. 151p. illus.
A good, scholarly history of German medieval glass, covering hollow glass from the
seventh through the sixteenth centuries with sections on technique and sources.
Thorough bibliographical footnotes. Illustrated with museum pieces. A standard
work in the field of medieval glass.

724   Schade, Günter. **Deutsches Glas von der Anfängen bis zum Biedermeier.**
       Leipzig, Koehler & Amelang, 1968. 219p. illus. LC 71-381541.
Good, serious history of German glass from late Roman times to circa 1800.
Illustrated with museum pieces and provided with bibliographical footnotes.

Great Britain

725   Crompton, Sidney, ed. **English Glass.** New York, Hawthorn, 1968. 255p.
       illus. index.
Good collection of serious essays by various specialists on English glass from the
Middle Ages through the nineteenth century. Bibliography of basic books, pp. 86-87.

726   Davis, Frank. **Early 18th-Century English Glass.** Feltham (England),
       Hamlyn, 1971. 63p. illus.
Popular handbook covering English glass from 1700 to about 1745. Arranged by
types and illustrated with pieces within reach of the advanced collector.

727   Davis, Derek C. **English and Irish Antique Glass.** New York, Praeger, 1965.
       151p. illus. index. LC 65-22886.
Good history/handbook treating the subject from the sixteenth century to the
present, with emphasis on the development of types and uses of glass. Appendixes
on terminology, dates, glasshouses, paperweights, and collections. Bibliography,
pp. 145-46, lists basic books in English.

728   Hughes, George B. **English Glass for the Collector, 1660-1860.** New York,
       Praeger, 1968. 251p. illus. index.
Popular history of English glass arranged by types and aimed at both beginning and
experienced collectors. Illustrated with pieces in museums and private collections.
Bibliography, p. 251, is a brief list of basic books.

729   Hughes, George B. **English, Scottish and Irish Table Glass from the 16th**
       Century to 1820. Boston, Boston Book and Art Shop, 1956. 410p. illus.
       index.
Popular history arranged according to types of glass. Illustrated with museum pieces
and pieces accessible to the average collector. Glossary of terms and selected bibliography of books in English.

730   Thorpe, William A. **English Glass.** 3rd ed. London, A. & C. Black, 1961.
       304p. illus. index. LC 65-592.
Popular history treating the Early Middle Ages to the present, with emphasis on the
general cultural context. Brief unclassified list of books in English.

731   Thorpe, William A. **A History of English and Irish Glass.** London, Medici
       Society; Boston, Hale, Cushman & Flint, 1929. 2v. illus. index.
Good, popular history of glass in Great Britain and Ireland from the thirteenth
century to the second quarter of the nineteenth century. Illustrated with museum
pieces and pieces accessible to the average collector. Appendix on special types of
glassware, glossary of terms, and good classified bibliography of books and periodical
articles, pp. 341-49.

732   Warren, Phelps. **Irish Glass: The Age of Exuberance.** New York, Scribner's,
       1970. 155p. illus. index. LC 72-15256.
Good, serious history of Irish glass from 1745 to circa 1835, with chapters on
English glass of 1571-1745, major factories, and types. Illustrations chiefly of
museum pieces. Bibliographical footnotes and general bibliography, pp. 150-51,
of books and periodical articles.

733   Webber, Norman W. **Collecting Glass.** New York, Arco, 1973. 196p. illus.
       index.
A good history/handbook concentrating on British glass from the late seventeenth
century to the early twentieth century. Written with the collector in mind, it makes
reference to American offshoots of British glass. Discusses types and decoration as
they differ from decade to decade. Outline drawings of stem features, foot forms
and bowl shapes. Glossary of terms, and list of basic books in English, p. 184.

734   Wills, Geoffrey. **Antique Glass for Pleasure and Investment**. New York, Drake, 1972. 174p. illus. index.
Good, popular history/handbook of English glass from the sixteenth through the nineteenth century, with chapter on Irish glass. Good chapter on manufacture and decoration. Glossary of terms. No bibliography.

735   Wills, Geoffrey. **English and Irish Glass**. London, Guinness, 1968. 16 signatures of 16pp. illus. index.
Popular handbook/history of English and Irish glass from the Renaissance to the present arranged by types of objects (i.e., decanters, chandeliers, etc.). Brief bibliography of basic works.

Italy

736   Mariacher, Giovanni. **Italian Blown Glass from Ancient Rome to Venice**. New York, McGraw-Hill, 1961. 245p. illus. index. LC 61-15890.
Sumptuously illustrated history of Italian blown glass from ancient Roman examples to the present. Brief text outlines the historical development; followed by excellent plates of museum pieces with descriptive captions. Good, classified bibliography of books and periodical articles, pp. 61-62.

737   Mariacher, Giovanni. **Vetri italiani del cinquecento**. Milan, Vallardi, 1959. 91p. illus. LC 62-26183.
Good, popular illustrated survey of Italian glass of the sixteenth century illustrated with museum pieces. Brief bibliography of basic works in Italian.

Scandinavia

738   Jexlev, Thelma. **Dansk glas i renaessancetid 1556-1650**. Copenhagen, Nyt Nordisk, 1970. 189p. illus. index. LC 74-577288.
Good, serious history of Danish Renaissance glass, with emphasis on engraved and enameled vessels. Bibliographical footnotes.

739   Larsen, Alfred, Peter Riismøller, and Mogens Schlüter. **Dansk Glas, 1825-1925**. Copenhagen, Nyt Nordisk, 1963. 412p. illus. LC 63-59927.
Scholarly handbook/history of Danish glass from 1825 to 1925. Separate sections by the three authors deal with technique, industrial background and art history. Illustrated with museum pieces, which have descriptive notes. Provided with an excellent glossary of terminology. Brief bibliography of basic books, p. 376.

740   Polak, Ada B. **Gammelt Norsk Glas**. Oslo, Gyldendal Norsk, 1953. 353p. illus. index.
Good, scholarly history of glass in Norway from 1741 to 1852, with a summary in English. Good collection of plates of museum pieces with descriptive catalog. Includes lighting fixtures of glass. Bibliography, pp. 348-50, lists books and periodical articles. Standard work on antique Norwegian glass.

741   Seitz, Heribert. **Aldre svenska glas med graverad dekor . . .** Stockholm, Norstedt, 1936. 231p. illus. index.
Good, serious history of Swedish engraved and decorated glass from the early eighteenth century to the present. English summary and good bibliography of books and periodical articles, pp. 218-223.

742   Steenberg, Elisa. **Swedish Glass.** New York, Barrows, 1950. 168p. illus.
Good, popular survey of Swedish glass from the late Middle Ages to the present.

Spain

743   Frothingham, Alice W. **Spanish Glass.** London, Faber and Faber, 1963; New York, Yoseloff, 1964. 96p. illus. index. LC 64-3365.
A good, serious history of glass in Spain and Portugal from the Romanesque to the early nineteenth century. Illustrated with museum pieces. Bibliography, pp. 90-92, lists books and periodical articles.

744   Perez Bueno, Luiz. **Vidros y vidrieras.** Barcelona, A. Martin, 1942. 277p. illus. index. LC 44-24083.
Good, serious history of Spanish glass from the Middle Ages through the nineteenth century. Bibliographies at the end of each chapter.

ORIENTAL GLASS

745   Blair, Dorothy. **A History of Glass in Japan.** New York, Corning Museum of Art, 1973. 479p. illus. index. LC 72-87011-196-5.
Excellent, scholarly history of glass in Japan from the Jomon period to the early twentieth century. Illustrated chiefly with museum pieces. Descriptive notes to the plates include bibliographical references. Useful maps and chronological tables plus excellent classified bibliography of books and articles, pp. 461-69.

746   Lamm, Carl J. **Mittelalterliche Gläser und Steinschnittarbeiten aus dem Nahen Osten.** Berlin, Reimer-Vohsen, 1929-30. 2v. illus. index.
(Forschungen zur Islamischen Kunst, V)
Excellent, scholarly history/study of Near Eastern glass of the twelfth through the fifteenth centuries. Volume one is text; Volume two is plates. Illustrations of museum pieces with good notes to the plates. Bibliography, pp. 522-49, is an incomparably comprehensive list of books and periodical articles. A standard history of later Islamic glass.

CHAPTER ELEVEN

IVORY

GENERAL HISTORIES AND HANDBOOKS

747   Beihoff, Norbert J. **Ivory Sculpture through the Ages.** Milwaukee, Public
       Museum, 1961. 93p. illus. index. LC 61-59507.
Popular history of world ivory carving with emphasis on use and manufacture. Brief
reading list of basic books in English.

748   Kunz, George F. **Ivory and the Elephant in Art, in Archaeology and in
       Science.** Garden City, N.Y., Doubleday, 1916. 527p. illus. index.
Popular history of ivory carving from prehistoric times through the nineteenth
century. Includes Oriental ivories. Much useful information on trade, manufacture
and technique. List of ivory carvers. Bibliographical footnotes.

749   Tardy [firm]. **Les ivoires, évolution décorative du Ier siècle à nos jours.**
       Paris, Tardy, 1966. 319p. illus. index. LC 67-71291. (Collection Tardy,
       v. 112)
Good, illustrated handbook of world ivory carving. Contents: première partie:
Europe et Byzance, sujets religieux; deuxième partie: sujets profanes; troisième
partie: Islam, Inde-Ceylon, Chine, Japon, Afrique. Concluding chapter: Les faux
gothiques. Appendices with list of ivory carvers and dictionary of netsuke marks.
Bibliography, pp. 279-80, lists basic books in all languages. Most useful for quick
identification of ivories.

750   Wills, Geoffrey. **Ivory.** South Brunswick, N.J., A. S. Barnes, 1969. 94p.
       illus. index. LC 68-27235.
Popular survey history of ivory carving in both East and West from ancient Egypt
to the present, with chapter on care of ivory. Brief bibliographical note.

WESTERN IVORY

751   Beckwith, John. **Ivory Carvings in Early Medieval England.** London,
       Harvey, Miller and Medcalf, 1972. 168p. illus. index. LC 73-158589.
Good, serious history of British ivories from the seventh through the twelfth
centuries. Introductory text is followed by an excellent scholarly catalog of
major examples, each entry with a thorough bibliography.

752   Beigbeder, Olivier. **Ivory**. New York, Putnam, 1965. 128p. illus.
       LC 64-16768.
Popular survey history of European ivories from prehistoric times to the end of the
eighteenth century, including Byzantine ivories. Illustrated with museum pieces. No
bibliography.

753   Carrà, Massimo. **Ivories of the West**. Feltham, England, Hamlyn, 1970.
       159p. illus. LC 77-861323.
Popular history of ivory carving in the West from prehistoric times through the
baroque. Good selection of color plates. No bibliography.

754   Cust, Anna Maria. **The Ivory Workers of the Middle Ages**. London, Bell,
       1902. 170p. illus. index.
Popular history from the Early Christian period through the Gothic, including
Byzantine ivories. "List of places where important examples of ivories can be
found." Brief bibliography of basic books, pp. xvii-xix.

755   Goldschmidt, Adolf, and Kurt Weitzmann. **Die byzantinischen
       Elfenbeinskulpturen des X.-XIII. Jahrhunderts**. Berlin, Cassirer, 1930-34.
       2v. illus.
Excellent scholarly history/handbook of Byzantine ivory carving from the tenth
through the thirteenth century. Volume one covers caskets; volume two, reliefs.
Each volume provides a summary history that discusses dating, provenance, and
technique in addition to a critical descriptive catalog of the plates, each entry
with a thorough bibliography. Fully indexed. Standard history of Byzantine
ivories.

756   Goldschmidt, Adolf. **Die Elfenbeinskulpturen aus der romanischen Zeit,
       XI.-XII. Jahrhundert**. Berlin, Deutscher Verlag für Kunstwissenschaft,
       1923-26. 2v. illus. index. (Die Elfenbeinskulpturen, Band 3-4)
Excellent, scholarly handbook/history of Western European ivories of the Ottonian
and Romanesque periods. Chapters treat the major schools and centers; each has an
introductory essay followed by a detailed catalog of the major pieces, with exhaustive bibliographies. The entire work is thoroughly indexed by name, place and
iconographic themes. Together with (757), a standard work on medieval ivories.

757   Goldschmidt, Adolf. **Die Elfenbeinskulpturen aus der Zeit der Karolingischen
       und Sächsischen Kaiser, VIII.-XI. Jahrhundert**. Berlin, Deutscher Verlag
       für Kunstwissenschaft, 1914-18. 2v. illus. index. Reprint: Berlin, Deutscher
       Verlag für Kunstwissenschaft, 1969-70. LC 72-365274 (Die Elfenbein-
       skulpturen, Band 1-2)
Excellent, scholarly handbook/history of Carolingian ivories. Chapters treat the
major schools and centers; each chapter has an introductory essay followed by a
detailed catalog of the major pieces. Catalog entries have exhaustive bibliographies
of the older literature, and the entire work is thoroughly indexed by name, place
and iconographic themes. The standard work of Carolingian ivories; together with
Volumes 3 and 4 of the series (756), this forms the standard scholarly study of
early medieval ivories.

758   Koechlin, Raymond. **Les ivoires gothiques français.** Paris, Picard, 1924.
       2v. plus folder of plates.
Good, scholarly history of French ivories from the thirteenth through the fifteenth
century. Covers both sacred and secular ivories. Introductory chapter treats technique, manufacture, and patronage. Volume one, text; volume two, critical catalog
of the plates with separate bibliographies for each entry. Appendix with list of
dated examples. Bibliographical footnotes. A standard handbook of French gothic
ivories.

759   Longhurst, M. H. **English Ivories.** London, Putnam, 1926. 123p. illus.
       index.
Older, serious history from pre-Conquest times through the nineteenth century,
with descriptive catalog accompanying the well-chosen plates. Brief annotated list
of basic books and extensive bibliographical footnotes.

760   Maskell, Alfred. **Ivories.** London, Methuen; New York, Putnam, 1905.
       551p. illus. index. Reprint: Rutland, Vt., Tuttle, 1966. LC 66-20572.
Older, popular survey of Western ivories from prehistoric times through the
nineteenth century. Chapters cover major countries, periods and types of ivories.
Bibliography, pp. 539-45, is still a useful list of the older literature.

761   Molinier, E. **Ivoires.** Paris, Librairie Centrale des Beaux-Arts, 1896. 245p.
       illus. (Histoire général des arts appliqués à l'industrie, I)
Early, pioneering history of Western ivory carving from the fifth century A.D.
through the eighteenth century. Bibliographical footnotes.

762   Natanson, John. **Early Christian Ivories.** London, Tiranti, 1953. 34p. illus.
Good, popular history of Early Christian ivories of the fourth through the sixth
centuries, with a chapter on style and iconography. Black and white plates of
major examples with descriptive notes. Brief list of major books, p. 23.

763   Natanson, John. **Gothic Ivories of the Thirteenth and Fourteenth
       Centuries.** London, Tiranti, 1951. 40p. illus.
Good, popular history of Western European ivories of the thirteenth and fourteenth
centuries, with chapters on iconography and polychroming. Black and white illustrations of major examples, with descriptive notes. Brief list of major books, p. 31.

764   Pelka, Otto. **Elfenbein.** 2nd ed. Berlin, Schmidt, 1923. 419p. illus. index.
       (Bibliothek für Kunst- und Antiquitäten Sammler, XVII)
Good, older scholarly history of Western ivory carving from ancient Egypt through
the eighteenth century, with a chapter of materials and techniques. Brief bibliography of basic works in all languages.

765   Philippovich, Eugen von. **Elfenbein.** Braunschweig, Klinkhardt & Biermann,
       1961. 353p. illus. index. (Bibliothek für Kunst- und Antiquitätenfreunde,
       XVII).
Excellent, scholarly history/handbook of Western ivories from ancient Egypt to the
twentieth century, with chapters on materials and techniques, major periods and

countries, fakes, photographing ivories, their care and restoration. Especially useful section on types of ivory carving (e.g., crucifixes, portrait medallions, etc.). Bibliography, pp. 347-49, lists major books and periodical articles in all languages.

ORIENTAL IVORY
(including Netsuke)

766   Brockhaus, Albert. **Netsuke. Versuch einer Geschichte der Japanischen Schnitzkunst.** Leipzig, Brockhaus, 1905. 482p. illus. index.
Good, comprehensive history/handbook covering netsuke to 1853. Part one treats technique; part two, history; and part three provides a list with biographical data, and marks of major netsuke carvers. Bibliography, pp. 71-76, lists basic books in all languages. An abridged translation was published as *Netsuke* by Albert Brockhous [sic] (New York, Duffield, 1924).

767   Bushell, Raymond. **Collectors' Netsuke.** New York, Walker-Weatherhill, 1971. 199p. illus. index. LC 70-139687.
Good, popular history of netsuke from the early eighteenth century to the present. Chapters treat the work of individual artists. Glossary of terms. No bibliography.

768   Bushell, Raymond. **An Introduction to Netsuke.** Rutland, Vt., Tuttle, 1971. 80p. illus.
Popular history consisting of a brief introduction followed by thirty plates with descriptive captions. No bibliography.

769   Bushell, Raymond. **The Wonderful World of Netsuke.** Rutland, Vt., Tuttle, 1964. 71p. illus. LC 64-24948.
Popular pictorial survey of 160 pieces, chiefly from the nineteenth century. Brief introductory text precedes plates, which have descriptive captions.

770   Kühnel, Ernst. **Die islamischen Elfenbeinskulpturen. VIII.-XIII. Jahrhunderts.** Berlin, Deutscher Verlag für Kunstwissenschaft, 1971. 103p. illus. LC 73-327439.
Continuation of Adolf Goldschmidt, *Die Elfenbeinskulpturen* (see no. 755). Excellent, scholarly history/handbook of Islamic ivories from the eighth through the thirteenth century. Part one provides a summary history; part two is a critical catalog of the plates, each entry with thorough bibliography. Appendix with list of sources. Standard work on Islamic ivory carving.

771   Laufer, Berthold. **Ivory in China.** Chicago, Field Museum of Natural History, 1925. 78p. illus.
Serious history/handbook of Chinese ivory carving with emphasis on trade, manufacture and use. Brief bibliography of basic books in English.

772   Ryerson, Egerton. **The Netsuke of Japan Illustrating Legends, History, Folklore & Custom.** London, Bell, 1958. 131p. illus. index.
Good, popular handbook with emphasis on the subject matter. Glossary of Japanese terms. Bibliography, pp. 125-26, lists basic books in English and Japanese.

CHAPTER TWELVE

JEWELRY

GENERAL HISTORIES AND HANDBOOKS

773   Barth, Hermann. **Das Geschmeide; Schmuck- und Edelsteinkunde.** Berlin, A. Schall, 1903. 2v. illus. index.
Good, serious older history/handbook of Western jewelry. Volume one provides a history from antiquity through the nineteenth century; volume two is a good handbook of jewelry-making and lapidary techniques. Bibliographical footnotes.

774   Biehn, Heinz. **Juwelen und Preziosen.** Munich, Prestel, 1965. 415p. illus. index. LC 66-80680.
Good, serious history of precious gems from the early Middle Ages to the present with chapters on collectors, famous gifts and commemorations. Bibliography, pp. 410-15, is a good list of books and periodical articles in all languages.

775   Bott, Gerhard. **Ullstein Juwelenbuch, Abendländische Schmuck von der Antike bis zu Gegenwart.** Berlin, Frankfurt, and Vienna, Ullstein, 1972. 305p. illus. index. LC 73-33552.
Good, popular survey of Western jewelry from antiquity to the present. Well illustrated with major museum pieces and works of art illustrating the wearing of jewelry in various periods.

776   Gregorietti, Giovanni. **Jewelry Through the Ages.** New York, Crescent, 1969. 319p. illus. LC 74-83809.
Popular survey history of world jewelry from prehistoric times to the present. Introductory chapters treat the history of gold and gems. Well illustrated with museum pieces, original designs and works of art depicting jewelry. Bibliography, pp. 314-16, is a chronological list of basic books in all languages.

777   Mason, Anita. **An Illustrated Dictionary of Jewellery.** New York, Harper & Row, 1974. 390p. illus. LC 73-11590.
Alphabetical dictionary of terms including tools and techniques, precious and non-precious gemstones and metals, history of jewelry from ancient times to the present, and biographical entries for a number of notable jewelers and jewelry-making firms. Illustrated with line drawings.

ANCIENT JEWELRY

778   Aldred, Cyril. **Jewels of the Pharaohs; Egyptian Jewelry of the Dynastic Period**. New York, Praeger, 1971. 256p. illus. index. LC 72-108266.
Good, serious history of Ancient Egyptian jewelry from 3100 to 330 B.C., illustrated chiefly with pieces in the Egyptian National Museum in Cairo. Bibliography, pp. 246-49, lists basic books in all languages.

779   Becatti, Giovanni. **Oreficerie antiche dalle minoiche alle barbariche**. Rome, Istituto Poligrafico dello Stato, 1955. 255p. illus. index.
Good, scholarly history of ancient jewelry from Minoan times through the seventh century A.D. Thorough catalog. Illustrated with museum pieces. Extensive bibliographical footnotes in the text and separate bibliographies in the catalog entries.

780   Coraelli, Filippo. **Greek and Roman Jewellery**. Feltham, England, Hamlyn, 1970. 157p. illus. LC 72-193344.
Popular, illustrated survey of ancient Greek and Roman jewelry, with emphasis on major museum pieces. No bibliography.

781   Higgins, Reynold A. **Greek and Roman Jewellery**. London, Methuen, 1961. 236p. illus. index. LC 63-4648.
Excellent, scholarly handbook/history of ancient Greek and Roman jewelry from 2500 B.C. to 400 A.D. Illustrated with museum pieces. Excellent, classified bibliography, pp. 193-223, of books and periodical articles in all languages.

782   Jessup, Ronald F. **Anglo-Saxon Jewellery**. New York, Praeger, 1953. 148p. illus. index. LC 52-13579.
Good, illustrated survey of early medieval jewelry from the British Isles, with emphasis on material dating before the ninth century.

783   Rosenthal, Renate. **Jewellery in Ancient Times**. London, Cassell, 1973. 96p. illus. index.
Popular, illustrated survey from ancient Egypt through the early Middle Ages. No bibliography.

784   Wilkinson, Alex. **Ancient Egyptian Jewellery**. London, Methuen, 1971. 266p. illus. index. LC 79-874376.
Good, serious history of dynastic Egyptian jewelry, with chapter on technique and materials. Partially annotated bibliography, pp. li-lvi, of basic books and periodical articles.

WESTERN JEWELRY

General Histories and Handbooks

785   Bradford, Ernle D. **Four Centuries of European Jewellery**. New York,
       Philosophical Library, 1935. 226p. illus. index. LC 53-7921. Reissued:
       London, Spring, 1967. LC 68-113002.
Good, popular history of European jewelry from the Renaissance to the early
twentieth century, with emphasis on British material. Brief bibliography of basic
books and exhibition catalogs, pp. 219-20.

786   Evans, Joan. **History of Jewellery, 1100-1870**. 2nd ed. Boston, Book and
       Art, 1970. 224p. illus. index. LC 72-124160.
Excellent serious history of European jewelry from the early Middle Ages to 1870,
arranged by periods. Illustrated with museum pieces. Bibliography, pp. 204-14, is a
thorough but unclassified list of books and periodical articles in all languages. A
standard history of Western jewelry.

787   Frégnac, Claude. **Jewelry from the Renaissance to Art Nouveau**. New York,
       Putnam, 1965. 128p. illus. index. LC 65-12434. Reissued: London,
       Octopus, 1973. 97p.
Popular, illustrated survey featuring major museum pieces and illustrations of
jewelry worn in contemporaneous works of art. No bibliography.

788   Gere, Charlotte. **Victorian Jewellery Design**. Chicago, Regnery, 1973.
       285p. illus. index. LC 72-11941.
Popular history with chapters on technique and special types of Victorian jewelry.
Useful section of biographical notes of major jewelers. Brief bibliography of basic
books.

789   Giltay-Nijssen, L. **Jewelry**. New York, Universe, 1964. 112p. illus. index.
       LC 64-10345.
Good, popular history/handbook of Western jewelry from the Middle Ages to the
present, with chapters on technique and collecting. Brief bibliography of basic
books.

790   Smith, Harold C. **Jewellery**. London, Methuen; New York, Putnam, 1908.
       409p. illus. index. Reprint: Wakefield, E. P. Publishing, 1973.
Popular history of Western jewelry from ancient Egypt through the nineteenth
century, with chapters on peasant jewelry and forgeries. Arrangement is by periods
and countries. Bibliography, pp. 371-79, is a useful list of the older literature.

791   Steingräber, Erich. **Antique Jewelry**. New York, Praeger; London, Thames,
       1957. 191p. illus. index.
Excellent, serious history of European jewelry from 800 to 1900. Illustrated are
museum pieces, works of art depicting jewelry, and original designs. Introduction
has useful list of gemstones with their properties and types of cut. Bibliography,
pp. 187-91, is an unclassified list of books in all languages.

National Histories and Handbooks

France

792   Vever, Henri. **La bijouterie française au XIX siècle.** Paris, H. Floury, 1908. 3v. illus. index.
Comprehensive history of French jewelry of the nineteenth century. Illustrated with museum pieces and works of art depicting French nineteenth century jewelry. Bibliographical footnotes. An older standard history.

Great Britain

793   Armstrong, Nancy. **Jewellery: An Historical Survey of British Styles and Jewels.** London, Lutterworth, 1973. 304p. illus. index.
Good, serious history of British jewelry from the Middle Ages to the present. Illustrated with major museum pieces and pieces accessible to the collector. Bibliography, pp. 273-75, is a good list of basic books.

794   Bradford, Ernle D. S. **English Victorian Jewellery.** New ed. London, Spring, 1967. 141p. illus. index. LC 68-111095.
Good, serious history/handbook of English jewelry of the second half of the nineteenth century. Chapters cover the eighteenth and early nineteenth century background, early and high Victorian styles, types and techniques. Illustrated with museum pieces and pieces accessible to the average collector. Glossary of terms and brief list of basic books in English, pp. 133-34.

795   Evans, Joan. **English Jewellery from the Fifth Century A.D. to 1800.** New York, Dutton, 1921. 168p. illus. index.
Good, serious history of British jewelry from Anglo-Saxon and Celtic times through the eighteenth century. Illustrated with museum pieces. Bibliographical footnotes.

796   Flower, Margaret C. **Victorian Jewellery.** Rev. ed. South Brunswick, N.J., A. S. Barnes, 1973. 271p. illus. index. LC 72-6463.
Good, serious history of English jewelry from 1837 to circa 1900, with chapter on collecting, glossary of terms and list of major jewelers of the period. Illustrated with museum pieces and pieces within reach of the average collector. Bibliography, pp. 259-60, lists basic books in all languages.

Italy

797   Rossi, Filippo. **Italian Jewelled Arts.** London and New York, Abrams, 1958. 233p. illus. index. LC 58-3307.
Good, serious history of Italian jewelry and goldsmithery decorated with gems from the early Middle Ages through the nineteenth century. Bibliographical footnotes and general bibliography of basic books, p. 223.

Netherlands

798   Gans, M. H. **Juwelen en mensen; de geschiedenis van het bijou van 1400 tot 1900, voornamelijk naar Nederlandse bronnen.** Amsterdam, de Bussy, 1961. 479p. illus. index. LC 66-55674.
Excellent, serious history of European jewelry from the late Middle Ages to 1900, with emphasis on developments in the Netherlands. Bibliographical footnotes.

Spain

799   Muller, Priscilla E. **Jewels in Spain, 1500-1800.** New York, New York Hispanic Society, 1972. 195p. illus. index.
Excellent scholarly history of Spanish jewelry from 1500 to 1800. Well illustrated with museum pieces, original designs and contemporaneous works of art showing pieces of jewelry. Extensive bibliographical footnotes, plus the bibliography, pp. 181-84, which is a thorough but unclassified list of books and articles in all languages.

ORIENTAL JEWELRY

800   Eudel, Paul. **Dictionnaire des bijoux de l'Afrique du Nord.** Paris, E. Leroux, 1906. 242p. illus.
Comprehensive dictionary covering all aspects of the jewelry and goldsmithery of Morocco, Algeria and Tunisia. Covers objects, countries, centers, styles and techniques.

801   Maxwell-Hyslop, K. R. **Western Asiatic Jewellery, c. 3000-612 B.C.** London, Methuen, 1971. 286p. illus. index. LC 75-874454.
Excellent serious history of ancient Near Eastern jewelry, treating Mesopotamia, Iran, Anatolia and the region of the Black Sea. Good classified bibliography of books and periodical articles, pp. 271-73.

CAMEOS AND INTAGLIOS

802   Davenport, Cyril J. H. **Cameos.** London, Seeley; New York, Macmillan, 1900. 66p. illus. index.
Older, popular history of cameos from antiquity to the end of the nineteenth century, with chapter on materials and techniques. No bibliography.

803   Furtwängler, Adolf. **Die antiken Gemmen. Geschichte der Steinschneidekunst im classischen Altertum.** Leipzig and Berlin, Giesecke & Devrient, 1900. 3v. illus. index. Reprint: Amsterdam and Osnabruck, Hakkert and Zeller, 1965.
Excellent scholarly history/handbook of ancient Greek and Roman glyptics. Volume one is plates; Volume two is a catalog of the illustrated examples; and Volume three

is a history. Bibliographical footnotes. A pioneering and standard history of engraved gems of antiquity.

804   Gebhart, Hans. **Gemmen und Kameen**. Berlin, R. C. Schmidt, 1925.
         232p. illus. index. (Bibliothek für Kunst- und Antiquitä ten Sammler, Bd. XXVII).
Good, serious history/handbook of Western engraved gems and cameos from antiquity through the nineteenth century. List of artists' marks and signatures, pp. 187-225. Bibliography, pp. 226-28, is a good guide to the major works of the older literature.

805   Kris, Ernst. **Die Meister und Meisterwerke der Steinschneidekunst in der italienischen Renaissance**. Vienna, Schroll, 1929. 2v. illus. index.
Good, scholarly history of engraved gems of the Italian Renaissance. Volume one, text with bibliographical footnotes; Volume two, good selection of plates. A standard work on Renaissance glyptics.

806   Lippold, Georg. **Gemmen und Kameen des Altertums und der Neuzeit**.
         Stuttgart, J. Hoffmann, 1922. 190p. illus. index.
Good, serious history of Western engraved gems and cameos from antiquity through the eighteenth century. Bibliography of basic books, p. 187.

807   Osborne, Duffield. **Engraved Gems, Signets, Talismans and Ornamental Intaglios, Ancient and Modern** . . . New York, Holt, 1912. 424p. illus. index.
Good, older, serious history of engraved gems from antiquity through the nineteenth century, with chapters on subject matter (e.g., emblemata and devices), technique and materials. No bibliography.

CHAPTER THIRTEEN

LACQUER

808   Feddersen, Martin. **Chinesische Lackarbeiten; ein Brevier.** Braunschweig,
        Klinkhardt & Biermann, 1958. 46p. illus. LC A58-6098.
Brief illustrated survey of Chinese lacquer, including furniture from the third
century B.C. through the middle of the nineteenth century. Brief bibliography
of basic books and periodical articles.

809   Herberts, Kurt. **Oriental Lacquer: Art and Technique.** New York, Abrams,
        1962. 513p. illus. index. LC 66-22168.
Good, serious history/handbook of Chinese and Japanese lacquer, including furniture. Well illustrated with museum pieces and pieces accessible to collectors. Useful
"Notes on Japanese Lacquer Artists," pp. 394-500. Good classified bibliography of
books and articles in Oriental and Western languages, pp. 502-13.

810   Holzhausen, Walter. **Lackkunst in Europa: Ein Handbuch für Sammler
        und Liebhaber.** Braunschweig, Klinkhardt & Biermann, 1959. 320p.
        illus. index. (Bibliothek für Kunst- und Antiquitätenfreunde, Band 38)
Excellent, serious history/handbook of Western lacquer covering both furniture
and smaller objects. Good selection of illustrations. Bibliography of basic books
in all languages, p. 307, and further literature in the footnotes.

811   Huth, Hans. **Lacquer of the West: The History of a Craft and Industry,
        1550-1950.** Chicago and London, University of Chicago Press, 1971.
        158p. (text), 364 plates. index. LC 73-130185.
Excellent, scholarly history arranged by century and country. Covers furniture
and small objects. Chapter on the lacquer industry at Spa in Belgium. Thorough
bibliographical footnotes and good, chronological list of basic books in all
languages, pp. 136-38. A standard work on European lacquer.

812   Jahss, Melvin, and Betty Jahss. **Inro and Other Miniature Forms of
        Japanese Lacquer Art.** Rutland, Vt., Tuttle, 1971. 488p. illus. index.
        LC 76-109406.
Good, serious history/handbook of Japanese lacquer with emphasis on inro. Chapters on the history and technique of Japanese lacquer, subject matter and lacquer
artists with seals and signatures. Glossary and bibliography of basic works in
Japanese and Western languages.

813   Luzzato-Bilitz, Oscar. **Oriental Lacquer.** London and New York, Hamlyn, 1969. 158p. illus.
Popular, illustrated survey of Far Eastern lacquer, including furniture, from fourth century B.C. through the nineteenth century. Color plates of major museum pieces. No bibliography.

814   Yu-kuan, Lee. **Oriental Lacquer Art.** New York, Weatherhill, 1972. 394p. illus. LC 74-157275.
Good, serious history/handbook of Chinese, Japanese and Korean lacquer covering furniture and smaller objects. Chapters on technique, identification, and history (by dynasties). Appendices with source texts. No bibliography.

CHAPTER FOURTEEN

LEATHER AND BOOKBINDING

815   Adam, Paul. **Der Bucheinband; seine Technik und seine Geschichte.**
       Leipzig, Seemann, 1890. 268p. illus. index. (Seemanns Kunsthandbücher, 6)
An excellent, older scholarly history/handbook, arranged in two parts. Part I treats
the technique of book making, including binding and decoration. Part II discusses
the decorated bindings of the Middle Ages and Renaissance. Bibliography, pp. 262-63.

816   Bogeng, Gustav A. E. **Der Bucheinband.** Halle a. S., Knapp, 1913. 382p.
       illus. index.
An excellent, older scholarly history of bookbinding from the Middle Ages to the
twentieth century. Illustrations are a few line drawings. Bibliography, pp. 345-67.
Classic, pioneering work on the history of bookbinding.

817   Brassington, William Salt, ed. **A History of the Art of Bookbinding.**
       London, Elliot Stock, 1894. 277p. illus. index.
Early general history from "records of prehistoric man" to the late nineteenth
century. No bibliography.

818   Cundall, Joseph, ed. **On Bookbinding, Ancient and Modern.** London, Bell,
       1881. 132p. illus. index.
Older general history from Egyptian times through the nineteenth century.

819   Devauchelle, Roger. **La reliure en France de ses origines à nos jours.** Paris,
       Rousseau-Girard, 1959-61. 3v. illus. index.
Good, serious history of French binding to the present. Vol. 1: from earliest
Egyptian books to the end of the seventeenth century, with French bindings
exclusively after the Renaissance. Vol. 2: French bindings of 1700-1850. Vol. 3:
French bindings from 1850 to about 1950. Each volume is indexed separately
and has its own bibliography.

820   Diehl, Edith. **Bookbinding, Its Background and Technique.** New York,
       Rhinehart, 1946. 2v. illus. index.
Good, serious history/handbook treating the history of the craft, with special
attention to technical aspects. Vol. 1 is a history of binding from antiquity to the
early twentieth century, with discussions of format, signatures, types of book
cases, decoration of book edges, and conservation. Vol. 2 is devoted to the technical aspects of the craft of binding. Volumes are separately indexed and each has
a glossary of terms. Bibliography, Vol. 1, pp. 205-219.

821   Gall, Günther. **Leder im europäischen Kunsthandwerk. Ein Handbuch für Sammler und Liebhaber.** Braunschweig, Klinkhardt & Biermann, 1965. 406p. illus. index. (Bibliographie für Kunst- und Antiquitätenfreunde, 44)
Excellent, serious history/handbook of the art of leatherwork from antiquity to the twentieth century, with emphasis on the craft before 1600. Arranged by period and country or center. No bibliography.

822   Gruel, Léon. **Manuel historique et bibliographique de l'amateur de reliures.** Paris, Gruel & Engelmann, 1887. 186p. illus. index.

_____. **Part Two.** Paris, Gruel & Leclerc, 1905. 186p. illus. index.
A general history of fine binding treating the origin of formats and styles of decoration from the Middle Ages through the eighteenth century. A dictionary of binders, patrons, collectors, and terms of bookbinding forms a major part of both works. Part two begins with a section on bookbinding oddities. Bibliography, pp. 179-86, Part One.

823   Helwig, Hellmuth. **Das deutsche Buchbinder-Handwerk. Handwerks- und Kulturgeschichte.** Stuttgart, Hiersemann, 1962-65. 2v. illus. index.
Excellent, scholarly history/handbook on German bookbinding from the early Middle Ages to the 1960s. Chiefly a social history, the craft is traced from the cloister to the modern workshop, with sections on guilds, the apprentice, journeyman, and master. Large compendium of sayings, songs, superstitions and beliefs by and about binders and their art. No bibliography as such, but extensive references to literature throughout the text and list of frequently cited sources in Vol. 1, pp. xvii-xx, and Vol. 2, pp. xviii-xxiii. Standard work on German bookbinding.

824   Helwig, Hellmuth. **Einführung in die Einbandkunde.** Stuttgart, Hiersemann, 1970. 278p. illus. index.
An excellent, scholarly history/handbook with particular emphasis on bibliographic coverage. Sections treat technique and types of binding, history of binding decoration from Carolingian times to the mid-nineteenth century, great collections of bindings, fakes, research and methods of research, the cataloging of bindings, reproduction bindings, conservation and restoration. Suggestions for library care of fine bindings, samples of descriptive cataloging, and a polyglot glossary are included as appendices. Illustration is limited to a few line drawings. Exhaustive classified and annotated bibliography, pp. 184-97.

825   Helwig, Hellmuth. **Handbuch der Einbandkunde.** n.p., Maximilian-Gesellschaft, 1953-55. 3v. illus. index.
Excellent, scholarly history/handbook distinguished by its exhaustive bibliographic coverage. Vol. 1 treats the history of binding and binding decoration, its significance, and value; the state of the literature; conservation and cataloging of bindings; aspects of connoisseurship. Vol. 2 contains a biobibliography of European bookbinders to about 1850, and a topo-bibliography of binderies arranged by country and century. Vol. 3 is an exhaustive index by name and place. A standard handbook on bookbinding.

826   Kyriss, Ernst. **Verzierte gotische Einbände im alten deutschen Sprachgebiet.**
      Stuttgart, Hettler, 1951. 160p. index.

      _____. Tafelband 1., 1953
      _____. Tafelband 2., 1956
      _____. Tafelband 3., 1958
Scholarly catalogue raisonée of mainly fifteenth and sixteenth century bindings
produced in German-speaking countries. Grouped according to locations, binders,
initials, armorials, and workshops. The three volumes of plates illustrate the catalog
in sequence. An important scholarly reference checklist and catalog.

827   Larsen, Sofus, and Anker Kyster, eds. **Danish Eighteenth Century Bindings,
      1730-1780.** Copenhagen, Levin & Munksgaard, 1930. 53p. (text), 101
      plates. illus.
Good general history with emphasis on eight renowned Danish binders of the
eighteenth century. Excellent plates, with good details. No bibliography.

828   Loubier, Hans. **Der Bucheinband von seinen Anfang bis zum Ende des 18.
      Jahrhunderts.** 2nd rev. and enl. ed. Leipzig, Klinkhardt & Biermann, 1926.
      272p. illus. index. (Monographien des Kunstgewerbes, 21/22)
Excellent, serious history of binding from antiquity to about 1800. Introduction,
on the technical aspects of the craft, is followed by a chronological history of the
art. A standard work.

829   McLean, Ruari. **Victorian Publishers' Book-Bindings in Cloth and Leather.**
      London, Gordon Fraser, 1974. 160p. illus. index.
Popular pictorial survey of English commercial Victorian bookbindings. Very brief
text and many good illustrations.

830   Marius Michel [firm]. **La reliure française. Depuis l'invention de l'imprimerie
      jusqu'à la fin du XVIIIe siècle.** Paris, Morgand & Fatout, 1880. 144p. illus.
Older, popular history by a prominent binding firm of the late nineteenth century.
General text and lavish illustrations of the most important French bindings.

831   Mejer, Wolfgang. **Bibliographie der Buchbinderei-Literatur.** Leipzig,
      Hiersemann, 1925. 208p. index.

      _____, and Hermann Herbst. **Bibliographie der Buchbinderei-
      Literatur, 1924-1932.** Leipzig, 1933.
Excellent retrospective, classified bibliography of 2,691 items. Includes books and
selected major articles from the major journals of bookbinding. The supplement
is more exhaustive in coverage for the years 1924-32. Indexed by author and key
word.

832   Michon, Louis-Marie. **La reliure française.** Paris, Larousse, 1951. illus.
      index.
Good, serious history from the ninth and tenth centuries to contemporary French
bindings. Emphasis is almost wholly stylistic. Bibliography, p. 140.

833   Prideaux, Sarah T. **An Historical Sketch of Bookbinding**. London,
       Lawrence & Bullen, 1893. 303p. index.
Older general history of bookbinding from the Carolingian period to the mid-
nineteenth century. Sections on related themes, among them book-edge decoration
and early documents on bookbinding. No illustrations. Bibliography, pp. 253-94.

834   Schreiber, Heinrich. **Einführung in die Einbandkunde**. Leipzig, Hiersemann,
       1932. 277p. index.
Excellent, scholarly history/handbook handicapped only by the lack of illustrations.
Aspects treated include the phenomena of bookbinding, the literature of bookbinding (an excellent formal bibliography for this chapter appears an an appendix,
pp. 256-59), the many facets of technique, forms of bookbinding materials, decoration by type and nationality, and the state of research to that date. Appendices
include models for descriptive cataloging of a bookbinding, and a polyglot glossary
of bookbinding terms. A standard, classic work on bookbinding.

835   Steenbock, Frauke. **Der kirchliche Practheinband im frühen Mittelalter,
       von den Anfängen bis zum Beginn der Gotik**. Berlin, Deutscher Verlag
       für Kunstwissenschaft, 1965. 238p. (text), 176 plates. illus. index.
Excellent, scholarly history of the great sumptuous bindings made for church use
in the early Middle Ages. Book covers are discussed by types, by symbolism, relation
to liturgy, and other specialized approaches. The bulk of the work is an excellent
scholarly catalog of 127 bindings from the fifth to the thirteenth century, each
entry with literature for the binding discussed. Bibliography, pp. 233-37.

836   Thoinan, Ernest (pseud.). **Les reliures français (1500-1800)**. Paris, Paul,
       Huard, Guillemin, 1893. 416p. illus.
An older serious history of bookbinding in France, chiefly Paris, treated as social
history and history of styles by Antoine Ernest Roquet. The first section is a history
of the profession in Paris; the second is a stylistic history of French bindings. Includes
biographical dictionary with some facsimiles of signatures and labels.

837   Waterer, John William. **Leather Craftsmanship**. London, Bell; New York,
       Praeger, 1968. 121p. illus. index. LC 68-25991.
General survey of the art of leatherwork, arranged in two parts. Part 1 discusses the
properties and preparation of leather; Part 2 encompasses the craftsmanship aspects
by technique: molding, lamination, without reinforcement, and with decoration.
Articles covered include bookbindings, shoes, upholstery, saddles, armor, and cases
from the Iron Age to the present. Bibliography, pp. 117-18.

838   Waterer, John W. **Leather in Life, Art and Industry**. London, Faber and
       Faber, 1946. 320p. illus. index.
Good general history of leather work, mainly in Britain, with a large section devoted
to leather industry and products of the twentieth century. Historical survey traces
leather crafting from prehistory to the late nineteenth century, covering trade guilds
and the various professions in leather work: saddlers, tanners, skinners, etc. Chapters
on the properties and processing of leather. Items made of leather are treated in

chapters on footwear, gloves, clothing, accessories, upholstery, bookbinding, and cases. Bibliography, pp. 305-07.

839   Weisweiler, Max. **Der islamische Bucheinband des Mittelalters.** Wiesbaden, Harrassowitz, 1962. 193p. (text), 42 plates. (Beiträge zum Buch- und Bibliothekswesen, 10)

Excellent, scholarly history/handbook treating all aspects of technique and decoration. Includes an index of stamping designs and a scholarly catalog of manuscripts and bindings in six major collections. Extensive literature citations in the catalog.

CHAPTER FIFTEEN

MEDALS AND SEALS

840   Armand, Alfred. **Les médailleurs italiens des quinzième et seizième siècles** ...
        2nd ed. Paris, Plon, 1883-87. 3v. illus. index.
Comprehensive handbook of Italian medals of the fifteenth and sixteenth centuries.
The 2,600 medals are divided into two parts: pieces by known medallists, and
anonymous pieces. Entries give full descriptions including references to reproductions and location of unpublished medals. Volume three contains a supplement to
both parts and indexes. A classic work that is still a standard reference tool.

841   Babelon, Jean. **Dauernder Erz. Das Menchenbild auf Münzen und Medaillen
        von der Antike bis zur Renaissance.** Vienna and Munich, Schroll, 1958.
        38p. (text), 96 plates.
Good, popular illustrated survey of numismatic and medallion portraiture from
antiquity through the Renaissance. Well illustrated. No bibliography.

842   Berchem, Egon von. **Siegel.** 2nd ed. Berlin, R. C. Schmidt, 1923. 222p.
        illus. index. (Bibliothek für Kunst- und Antiquitätensammler, Bd. II)
Good, scholarly history/handbook of German seals from the Middle Ages to the
nineteenth century. Classified bibliography of basic books, pp. 209-19, and list
of major collections.

843   Birch, Walter de Gray. **Seals.** London and New York, Methuen, 1907. 327p.
        illus. index.
Older, serious history of Western seals from ancient Egypt and Rome to the end of
the nineteenth century. Emphasis is on British seals of medieval and modern times.
Glossary of heraldic terms applicable to the study of seals. No bibliography.

844   Brugmans, Hajo. **Corpus sigillorum neerlandicorum. De nederlandsche
        zegels tot 1300** ... The Hague, Nijhoff, 1937-40. 3v. illus. index.
Excellent, scholarly handbook/history of the seals of the Netherlands dating after
1300. Thorough bibliographical footnotes. A standard work on Dutch seals.

845   Ewald, Wilhelm. **Siegelkunde.** Munich and Berlin, Oldenbourg, 1914. 244p.
        illus. index. (Handbuch der mittelalterlichen und neueren Geschichte,
        v.4, 1)
Good, scholarly handbook of Western seals from the early Middle Ages through the
nineteenth century. Bibliography, pp. 1-20, lists basic books chiefly in German.

846   Fabriczy, Cornelius von. **Italian Medals.** New York, Dutton, 1904. 223p.
       illus. index.
Older, popular history/handbook of Italian fifteenth and sixteenth century medals.
No bibliography.

847   Forrer, Leonard. **Biographical Dictionary of Medallists; Coin, Gem, and
       Seal-engravers, Mint-masters, etc.** . . . London, Spink, 1902-30. 8v. illus.
       index.
Good, comprehensive dictionary with references to bibliographical sources at end
of most entries. General bibliography, v. 1, pp. xxxix-xlviii, and v. 8, p. 368.
Volumes 7 and 8 are supplements.

848   Friedländer, Julius. **Die italienischen Schaumünzen des fünfzehnten
       Jahrhunderts (1430-1530). Ein Beitrag zur Kunstgeschichte** . . . Berlin,
       Weidmann, 1882. 223p. illus. index.
Good, scholarly history of Italian Renaissance medals. Bibliographical footnotes.
Early classic work.

849   Gandilhon, René. **Bibliographie de la sigilloraphie française.** Paris,
       Imprimerie nationale, 1955. 187p.
Good, comprehensive bibliography of books and periodical articles on all aspects of
French seals published before 1954.

850   Grandjean, Poul-B. **Dansk sigillografi.** Copenhagen, Schultz, 1944. 374p.
       illus. index.
Excellent, scholarly history/handbook of Danish seals from the early Middle Ages
through the nineteenth century. Bibliography, pp. 333-43, is a good classified list
of books and periodical literature. A standard handbook on Danish seals.

851   Grierson, Philip. **Coins and Medals: A Short Bibliography.** London,
       G. Philip, 1954. 88p.
Useful, classified bibliography of basic books, chiefly in English, on coins and
medals of the Western world.

852   Grotemeyer, Paul. **"Da ich het die gestalt." Deutsche Bildnismedaillen
       des 16. Jahrhunderts.** Munich, Prestel, 1957. 56p. illus. (Bibliothek des
       Germanischen National-Museums Nürnberg zur deutschen Kunst- und
       Kulturgeschichte, Band 7)
Good, serious history of German medals of the sixteenth century. Well illustrated.
Useful collection of excerpts from contemporary documents. Extensive biblio-
graphical footnotes.

853   Habich, Georg, ed. **Die deutschen Schaümunzen des XVI. Jahrhunderts** . . .
       Munich, Bruckmann, 1929-34. 5v. illus. index.
Excellent, but incomplete, scholarly handbook of German medals of the sixteenth
century. Arrangement is by masters and schools. Well illustrated and with extensive
bibliographical references. A standard work on German medals.

854   Habich, Georg. **Die Medaillen der italienischen Renaissance** . . . Stuttgart
        and Berlin, Deutsche Verlags-Anstalt, 1923. 168p. illus. index.
An excellent, older history of Italian fifteenth and sixteenth century medals, with
good selection of plates. Thoroughly indexed both by artist and by iconography.
Six-item bibliography of basic works.

855   Hill, George F. **A Corpus of Italian Medals of the Renaissance before
        Cellini** . . . London, British Museum, 1930. 2v. illus.
Good, comprehensive handbook of Italian medals, 1390 to 1530. Volume one,
text; volume 2, plates. Bibliography, v. 1, pp. xii-xiv, lists basic works in all
languages.

856   Hill, George F. **Medals of the Renaissance.** Oxford, Clarendon Press,
        1920. 204p. illus. index.
Good, but somewhat out-of-date, history of Italian, German, French, English and
Netherlandish medals of the fifteenth and sixteenth centuries. Bibliography,
pp. 174-82, is a good classified list of basic works.

857   Kittel, Erich. **Siegel.** Braunschweig, Klinkhardt & Biermann, 1970.
        530p. illus. index. LC 76-545573. (Bibliothek für Kunst- und
        Antiquitätenfreunde, Band II)
Excellent, serious handbook/history of Western seals from antiquity through the
nineteenth century. Illustrated with museum pieces. Chapter on collecting and
technique. Excellent classified bibliography of books and periodical articles in
all languages, pp. 466-509.

858   Lenormant, François. **Monnaies et médailles.** Nouv. éd. Paris, Quantin,
        1885. 328p. illus. index.
Reissue of the first edition, 1883. Good, older serious history of European medals
and art coinage, with emphasis on French and Italian medals.

859   Roman, Joseph H. **Manuel de sigillographie française.** Paris, Picard, 1912.
        401p. illus. index.
Good, but older, scholarly history/handbook of the seals of France from the
early Middle Ages through the nineteenth century. Bibliographical footnotes.

CHAPTER SIXTEEN

METALWORK

GENERAL HISTORIES AND HANDBOOKS

860   Branigan, Keith. **Aegean Metalwork of the Early and Middle Bronze Age.**
       Oxford, Clarendon, 1974. 216p. illus. index.
Good, scholarly history covering from 3000 to 1700 B.C. Thorough bibliographic
footnotes.

861   Clouzot, Henri. **Les arts du métal** . . . Paris, Laurens, 1934. 524p. illus.
       index.
Good, comprehensive history of metalwork from ancient times to the twentieth
century. Covers precious metals, iron, bronze, pewter, brass and copper. Includes
armor. Illustrated with museum pieces. Good bibliography, pp. 485-94, lists books
and periodical articles. An older, standard history.

862   Clouzot, Henri. **Le travail du métal.** Paris, Rieder, 1921. 116p. illus.
Popular history of iron, bronze, pewter, gold and silver in France during the early
twentieth century. Includes jewelry.

863   Haedeke, Hanns-Ulrich. **Metalwork.** New York, Universe, 1970. 227p.
       illus. index. LC 75-90382.
Excellent, serious history of Western iron, pewter, bronze, brass and copper from
the early Middle Ages through art nouveau, with emphasis on the function of
metalwork within the general cultural perspective. Well illustrated with museum
pieces. Bibliography, pp. 213-18, is a good list of books in all languages.

864   Jenny, Wilhelm A. von. **Keltische Metallarbeiten aus heidnischer und
       christlicher Zeit.** Berlin, Verlag für Kunstwissenschaft, 1935. 62p. illus.
       index.
Good illustrated survey of Celtic metalwork from the La Tène period through the
eighth century A.D. Good but brief introductory essay, followed by good selection
of plates of major museum pieces. Bibliography of basic works, p. 62.

865   Lüer, Hermann, and Max Creutz. **Geschichte der Metalkunst.** Stuttgart,
       Ferdinand Enke, 1904-1908. 2v. illus. index.
Band I: Kunstgeschichte der unedlen Metalle: Schmiedeisen, Gusseisen, Bronze,
Zinn, Blei und Zink; Band II: Kunstgeschichte der edlen Metalle. Good, but old,
comprehensive history of metalwork, with emphasis on stylistic development
from ancient Egypt to the early twentieth century. Illustrated with museum
pieces. A classic, pioneering history.

866   Moore, Hannah. **Old Pewter, Brass, Copper, and Sheffield Plate**. Rutland,
       Vt., Tuttle, 1972. 224p. illus. index. LC 75-104206.
Popular history/handbook of American and British metalwork, with emphasis on
domestic pieces accessible to the collector. Brief bibliography of basic books.

BRASS AND COPPER

867   Burgess, Fred W. **Chats on Old Copper and Brass**. New York, Stokes, n.d.
       400p. illus. index.
Popular handbook/history of world copper, brass and bronze, including bronze
sculpture, bells and scientific instruments. Chapters on collecting.

868   Falke, Otto von, and Erich Meyer. **Romanische Leuchter und Gefässe.
       Giessgefässe der Gotik**. Berlin, Deutscher Verein für Kunstwissenschaft,
       1935. 121p. illus. index. (Bronzegeräte des Mittelalters, I Band)
Excellent, scholarly history/handbook of German Romanesque candelabras and
utensils and Gothic aquamanile. Brief introductory essay is followed by thorough
catalog with bibliographical references. A standard work on medieval bronze and
brass utensils.

869   Kauffmann, Henry J. **American Copper & Brass**. Camden, N.J., T. Nelson,
       1968. 288p. illus. index. LC 68-13938.
Serious handbook covering American domestic utensils in copper and brass to the
middle of the nineteenth century, with chapters on techniques and materials and
a list of documented coppersmiths and brass founders. Bibliography, pp. 282-83,
is an unclassified list of basic books and periodical articles.

870   Perry, John T. **Dinanderie; a History and Description of Medieval Art
       Work in Copper, Brass and Bronze** . . . New York, Macmillan; London,
       Allen, 1910. 238p. illus. index.
Popular history including bronze sculpture. Chapters treat types and countries.
Bibliography, pp. 221-22, is a dated list of books chiefly in English.

871   Pettorelli, Arturo. **Il bronze e il rame nell'arte decorativa italiana**. Milan,
       Hoepli, 1926. 314p. illus. index.
Good, serious history of Italian bronze and brass from Etruscan times to the early
twentieth century. Covers utensils as well as bronze and brass used in other decorative arts. Bibliographical footnotes.

872   Verster, A. J. C. **Bronze: altes Gerät aus Bronze, Messing und Kupfer**.
       Hanover, Fackelträger-Verlag, 1966. 71p. (text), 94 (plates). LC 67-97478.
Good, popular survey of Western bronze, brass and copper utensils and other
applied arts from the Middle Ages to the present. Bibliography of basic books in
all languages, pp. 71-72.

873   Wills, Geoffrey. **The Book of Copper and Brass.** London, Country Life, 1968. 96p. illus. index.

Popular handbook of English and American everyday copper and brass ware of the eighteenth and nineteenth centuries. Introduction, which discusses mining, smelting, manufacture and trade, is followed by a dictionary of copper and brass items. Illustrated with pieces accessible to the collector. Brief bibliography of books in English.

GOLD AND SILVER

Dictionaries of Marks

> Note: Only general dictionaries are included in this section. For dictionaries of gold and silver marks of specific countries, see the national categories below.

874   Beuque, E. **Dictionnaire des poinçons officiels français et étrangers, anciens et modernes.** Paris, C. Courtois, 1925-28. 2v. illus. index.

Comprehensive dictionary of gold and silver marks arranged in two parts: marks in the form of figurines and objects, and marks consisting of letters or numbers. Marks are given in facsimiles.

875   Ris-Paquot, Oscar E. **Dictionnaire des poinçons, symboles, signes figuratifs, marques et monogrammes des orfèvres français et étrangers, fermiers généraux, maîtres des monnaies, contrôleurs, vérificateurs, etc.** Paris, Laurens, 1890. 382p. illus.

Comprehensive dictionary of marks found on gold and silver, with emphasis on France. Covers jewelry makers as well. Special sections are devoted to the goldsmiths and jewelers of France, and specifically those of Paris. An older standard dictionary of French gold and silver marks still useful for specialized research on Parisian goldsmithery and jewelry making.

876   Rosenberg, Marc. **Der Goldschmiede Merkzeichen.** 3rd ed. Frankfurt am Main, Frankfurter Verlags-Anstalt, 1922-28. 4v. illus. index. Reprinted 1955.

Excellent, comprehensive dictionary of goldsmiths' marks, arranged by city and then by artist. Contents: Volumes 1-3, Deutschland; Volume 4, Ausland und Byzanz. Entries give smiths' basic bibliographical data, brief list of works, bibliography, and facsimiles of marks. Good collection of plates showing characteristic pieces. Each volume has an index by marks and names. The standard scholarly dictionary of goldsmiths' marks.

877   Tardy [firm]. **Les poinçons de garantie internationaux pour l'argent.** 4th ed. Paris, Tardy, n.d. 353p. illus. index.

Pocket-sized dictionary of major European silver marks, arranged by country and then by city. Identification of individual marks is facilitated by the subject index.

General Histories and Handbooks

878   Blakemore, Kenneth. **The Book of Gold.** New York, Stein and Day, 1971. 224p. illus. index. LC 73-16034.
Popular survey of gold and goldsmithery from ancient times to the present. Includes coins and jewelry.

879   Brunner, Herbert. **Old Table Silver: A Handbook for Collectors and Amateurs.** New York, Taplinger, 1967. 223p. illus. index. LC 67-16593.
Translation of *Altes Tafelsilber* (Munich, 1964). Good, serious history/handbook of European table silver to circa 1800. In addition to being a good historical survey, it also treats the use and production of table silver. Well illustrated with museum pieces, original designs, and works of art depicting table silver. Appendix with list of major silver marks. Bibliography, pp. 160-63, lists books and periodical articles in several languages.

880   Came, Richard. **Silver.** New York, Putnam, 1961. 128p. illus. index. LC 61-12197.
Popular illustrated survey of Western silver from the Middle Ages to the present. No bibliography.

881   Honour, Hugh. **Goldsmiths and Silversmiths.** New York, Putnam, 1971. 320p. illus. index. LC 77-14221.
Chronologically arranged series of serious biographies of Western gold and silversmiths from the early Middle Ages to the present. Well illustrated and supplied with a good bibliography, pp. 313-16, of books and periodical articles pertaining to the individual smiths.

882   Jones, Edward A. **Old Silver of Europe & America from Early Times to the Nineteenth Century . . .** Philadelphia, Lippincott, 1928. 376p. illus. index.
Older, popular survey of Western silver.

883   Link, Eva M. **The Book of Silver.** New York, Praeger, 1973. 301p. illus. index. LC 75-107153.
Good, serious history of gold and silver in the Western world from ancient Greece to the present. Useful features: outlines of types of table plate, list of principal cities with their marks, glossary of terms, and good chapter on technique and the history of silversmiths' guilds and hallmarks. Bibliography, pp. 291-96, is a thorough but unclassified list of books in many languages.

884   Meinz, Manfred. **Schönes Silber.** Munich, Keyser, 1964. 352p. illus. index.
Good, serious history of European silver from 1600 to the present, with emphasis on pieces in private collections and with dealers. Well illustrated; short lists of marks, and bibliography of basic books in all languages.

885   Rosenberg, Marc. **Geschichte der Goldschmiedekunst auf technischer Grundlage.** Frankfurt am Main, Baer, 1908-25. 7v. illus. index. Reprint: Osnabrück, Ohms, 1972.

Excellent, comprehensive history of Western goldsmithery with emphasis on technique. Volume one is an introduction treating material and general procedures and processes; Volume two covers niello; Volume three covers granulation; Volumes four and five are history of niello; Volumes six and seven treat the history of enamels through the ninth century A.D. Illustrated with museum pieces. Extensive bibliography in the footnotes. Although old, it is still a standard history of gold and enamel techniques.

886   Steingräber, Erich. **Der Goldschmied. Vom alten Handwerk der Gold- und Silberarbeiter.** Munich, Prestel, 1966. 96p. illus. (Bibliothek des Germanischen Nationalmuseums Nürnberg, Band 27)

Excellent, serious survey history of European goldsmithery, with emphasis on the general cultural context. Well-chosen illustrations of museum pieces, gold and silversmiths' tools, original designs, and works of art depicting gold and silver work. Excellent chapter on technique. Bibliography, pp. 94-95, of basic books in several languages.

887   Sutherland, Carol H. **Gold: Its Beauty, Power and Allure.** New York, McGraw-Hill, 1959. 196p. illus. index. LC 66-16097.

Popular history of the use of gold in both goldsmithery, jewelry and coinage. Chapters on early mining and processing. Bibliography, pp. 187-91, lists basic books.

888   Taylor, Gerald. **Art in Silver and Gold.** New York and London, Dutton, 1964. 160p. illus. LC 64-4439.

Popular history from ancient Egypt to the present. Covers only Western developments. Well-chosen illustrations of major pieces. No bibliography.

889   Taylor, Gerald. **Continental Gold and Silver.** London, Connoisseur, 1967. 120p. illus. LC 67-87709.

Popular, historical survey of Continental European gold and silver, directed to the collector. Bibliography, pp. 115-17, is a good list of basic histories and reference handbooks in all languages.

890   Wyler, Seymour B. **The Book of Old Silver, English, American, Foreign; with All Available Hallmarks Including Sheffield Plate Marks.** 9th ed. New York, Crown, 1947. 447p. illus. index.

Good, popular history/handbook with section on hallmarks arranged by country. Illustrated with museum pieces and pieces accessible to the collector. One-page bibliography of basic books in English.

Ancient and Medieval Gold and Silver

891   Belli Barsali, Isa. **Medieval Goldsmiths' Work**. London and New York,
       Hamlyn, 1969. 157p. illus. LC 77-481903.
Good popular history of medieval goldsmithery, including enamels and jewelry
from the fourth through the fifteenth century. Illustrated with museum pieces.
Plates have descriptive captions. No bibliography.

892   Busch, Harald, and Bernd Lohse, eds. **Wunderwelt der Schreine:**
       Meisterwerke mittelalterlicher Goldschmiedekunst. Frankfurt/Main,
       Umschau, 1959. 19p. (text), 80p. (plates).
Good pictorial survey of medieval gold and silver shrines from the twelfth through
the sixteenth centuries. Brief introductory essay is followed by good notes to the
plates. General bibliography on page xviii is amplified by bibliographies of
specialized literature in the notes to the plates.

893   Carducci, Carlo. **Gold and Silver Treasures of Ancient Italy**. Greenwich,
       Conn., New York Graphic Society, 1964. 85p. illus. LC 63-22472.
Illustrated survey of ancient Etruscan and Roman gold and silver based on pieces
exhibited at Turin in 1961. Good plates with descriptive notes. Bibliography,
pp. xxxi-xxxiii.

894   Coarelli, Filippo. **L'oreficeria nell'arte classica**. Milan, Fabbri, 1967. 158p.
       illus. index. LC 68-110814.
Popular history of gold and silver in the ancient world from the Greek Geometric
period through late Roman times. Bibliography, p. 155, lists basic books in all
languages.

895   Ebersolt, Jean. **Les arts somptuaires de Byzance; étude sur l'art impériale**
       de Constantinople. Paris, Leroux, 1923. 164p. illus. index.
Good, serious history of Byzantine gold and silver, including works in enamel.
Illustrated with museum pieces. Bibliographical footnotes.

896   Mujica Gallo, M. **The Gold of Peru**. Recklinghausen, Aurel Bongers, 1959.
       294p. illus.
Popular pictorial survey of Peruvian pre-Columbian and early colonial gold with
appendix of documents in Seville pertaining to sixteenth century seizure and
transfer of Peruvian gold to Spain. Chronological table and one-page bibliography
of basic books.

897   Strong, Donald E. **Greek and Roman Gold and Silver Plate**. Ithaca, N.Y.,
       Cornell University Press; London, Methuen, 1966. 235p. illus. index.
Excellent, scholarly handbook/history of ancient Greek and Roman gold and silver
work from the Bronze Age through the fifth century A.D. Excellent introduction
covers the use, position, supply and trade in gold and silver in ancient times. Subsequent chapters treat technique, the position of the ancient goldsmith trade and
the major periods in the history of ancient goldsmithery. Thorough bibliographical
footnotes, index of sites, museums and collections.

Modern Gold and Silver (19th and 20th Centuries)

898   Grandjean, Serge. **L'orfèvrerie du XIXe siècle en Europe.** Paris, Presses
       Universitaires de France, 1962. 161p. illus. index. LC 63-55026.
Good, popular history/handbook of European nineteenth century gold and silver.
Useful section on collectors and collections, good notes to the plates, and short
dictionary of marks. Bibliography, pp. 121-27, is a good classified and partially
annotated list of books and periodical articles in all languages.

899   Hughes, Graham. **Modern Silver Throughout the World 1880-1967.** New
       York, Crown, 1967. 256p. illus. index. LC 67-26050.
Well-illustrated, popular history of European and American silver and some jewelry.
Good section on techniques, and useful biographical dictionary of major makers.
Bibliography, p. 255, lists basic books and catalogs.

American Gold and Silver (U.S., Canada, and Latin America)

United States

900   Avery, Clara L. **Early American Silver.** New York and London, Century,
       1930. 378p. illus. index. Reprint: New York, Russell and Russell, 1968.
A good, popular history of American silver to the middle of the nineteenth century.
Arrangement is by states and cities and by types. Bibliography, pp. 361-64, lists
major works in English.

901   Bigelow, Francis H. **Historic Silver of the Colonies and Its Makers . . .**
       New York, Macmillan, 1917. 476p. illus. index.
Older, popular history/handbook of American Colonial silver; arranged by types,
with an index to silversmiths.

902   Currier, Ernest M. **Marks of Early American Silversmiths . . .** Portland,
       Me., Southworth-Anthoensen Press; London, Quaritch, 1938. Reprint:
       Harrison, N.Y., R. A. Green, 1970. 179p. illus. index. LC 74-111387.
Popular dictionary of American silver marks, arranged alphabetically and
illustrated with facsimiles. Covers American silversmiths to 1840.

903   Ensko, Stephen G. C. **American Silversmiths and Their Marks III.** New
       York, Ensko, 1948. 285p. illus.
Dictionary of American silversmiths and marks from 1650 to 1850. First part
is a list by name, giving basic biographical data, locations of businesses, records
of training, etc. Second section treats marks. Bibliography, pp. 281-85, gives a
brief list of basic books.

904   Fales, Martha G. **Early American Silver**. Rev. and enl. ed. New York,
       E. P. Dutton, 1973. 336p. illus. index.
First published as *Early American Silver for the Cautious Collector* (1970). An
excellent serious handbook of American silver from 1675 to 1825. Excellent
chapters on the American silversmith and special features of American silver.
Useful chapter on the care of old silver, glossary of terms, chart showing the
development of forms of silver. Excellent classified bibliography of books and
periodical articles, pp. 298-313.

905   French, Hollis. **A Silver Collectors' Glossary and a List of Early American
       Silversmiths and Their Marks.** New York, Walpole Society, 1917. 164p.
       illus. Reprint: New York, DaCapo, 1967. LC 67-27454.
Alphabetical dictionary of American silversmiths, with facsimiles of their marks.
Glossary covers decoration, objects and styles; illustrated with line drawings.

906   Graham, James. **Early American Silver Marks**. New York, n.p., 1936. 81p.
       illus.
Privately printed pocket-sized dictionary of American silver hallmarks of the
eighteenth and early nineteenth centuries.

907   Holland, Margaret. **Silver: An Illustrated Guide to American & British
       Silver.** London, Octopus, 1973. 144p. illus. index.
A good, popular handbook of American and British silver of the eighteenth and
early nineteenth centuries arranged by types or classes of silver ware. Chapter on
collecting has a brief list of major hallmarks. Well illustrated with major pieces.
No bibliography.

908   Hood, Graham. **American Silver: A History of Style, 1650-1900**. New
       York, Praeger, 1971. 255p. illus. index. LC 77-124854.
Good, popular history of American silver arranged by periods and illustrated
chiefly with museum pieces. Bibliography, pp. 247-50, is a good classified list
of books and catalogs.

909   Kovel, Ralph M., and Terry H. Kovel. **A Directory of American Silver,
       Pewter and Silver Plate.** New York, Crown, 1961. 352p. illus. index.
       LC 60-8620.
Popular dictionary of American makers and manufacturers of silver, pewter and
silver electroplate, arranged by makers' names. Entries give basic biographical
data and referral to reference books listed on pp. 345-47, a feature that makes
the work a useful bibliographical tool for specialized literature on individual
makers.

910   Phillips, John Marshall. **American Silver**. New York, Chanticleer Press,
       1949. 128p. illus.
Good, popular history of American silver from the sixteenth through the nine-
teenth centuries, with a chapter on the American silversmith and his craft.
Illustrated with museum pieces. Bibliography, pp. 127-28, lists basic books.

911   Thorn, C. Jordan. **Handbook of American Silver and Pewter Marks.** New York, Tudor, 1949. 289p. illus.
Popular dictionary of 3,500 marks, arranged by name of maker.

912   Turner, Noel D. **American Silver Flatware, 1837-1910.** South Brunswick, N.J., A. S. Barnes, 1972. 473p. illus. index. LC 68-27217.
Popular history covering sterling and electroplated American flatware. Contains a useful index of American and English manufacturers, trademarks and trade names. Bibliography, pp. 413-22, is an unclassified list of books and periodical articles.

913   Wenham, Edward. **The Practical Book of American Silver.** Philadelphia, Lippincott, 1949. 275p. illus. index.
A good but older popular history covering the period from the sixteenth century to circa 1925. Arranged by periods and types. Chapter on marks and collecting. Bibliography, pp. 265-67, lists basic books in English.

Canada

914   Langdon, John. **Canadian Silversmiths and Their Marks, 1667-1867.** Lunenburg, Vt., Stinehour Press, 1960. 190p. illus. index. LC 60-2484.
Good, serious handbook of Canadian silver to 1867, arranged by region. Each section has an historical sketch of the silver-working regions followed by a list of makers and their marks. Bibliography, pp. 175-79, is a classified list of basic books.

915   Langdon, John. **Canadian Silversmiths 1700-1900.** Toronto, Stinehour, 1966. 145p. illus. index. LC 66-28195.
Good, serious history/handbook consisting of an historical sketch and an alphabetical list of makers and their marks. Illustrated with pieces accessible to the average collector as well as museum pieces.

916   Langdon, John. **Guide to Marks on Early Canadian Silver, 18th and 19th Centuries.** Toronto, Ryerson, 1968. 104p. illus. LC 72-392416.
Useful pocket-sized dictionary of Canadian hallmarks, including manufacturers' marks found on late nineteenth century silver and electroplate.

917   Unitt, Doris J., and Peter Unitt. **Canadian Silver, Silver Plate and Related Glass.** Peterborough, Ont., Clock House, 1970. 256p. illus. index. LC 76-888154.
Popular history/handbook of Canadian sterling and electroplate, with a section on glass and silver vessels. List of major hallmarks. Bibliography of basic books and periodical articles, pp. 250-51.

Latin America

918   Anderson, L. L. **The Art of the Silversmith in Mexico, 1519-1936.** New
York, Oxford University Press, 1941. 2v. illus. index.
Good, scholarly history of colonial and modern silver in Mexico, with introductory
chapter on pre-Conquest silver. Well illustrated and with good list of marks in the
appendix. Bibliography, pp. 435-51, is a thorough but unclassified list of books and
periodical articles.

919   Duarte, Carlos F. **Historia de la orfebreria en Venezuela.** Caracas, Monte
Avila, 1970. 513p. illus. index.
Serious history of gold and silver plate in Venezuela from the sixteenth through the
middle of the nineteenth centuries, with dictionary of goldsmiths and silversmiths
and their marks.

920   Saville, Marshall H. **The Goldsmith's Art in Ancient Mexico.** New York,
Museum of the American Indian-Heye Foundation, 1920. 264p. illus.
index. (Indian Notes and Monographs, Miscellaneous, No. 7)
Good, but now somewhat out-of-date, history of pre-Columbian Mexican gold and
silver. Chapters on technique and symbolism. Bibliographical footnotes.

921   Taullard, Alfredo. **Plateria sudamericana** . . . Buenos Aires, Peuser, 1941.
285p. illus.
Comprehensive history of silver in South America from pre-Hispanic times through
the nineteenth century, arranged by place and type. Inadequate bibliography.

922   Valladares, José G. **Ourivesaria.** Rio de Janeiro, Ouro, 1968. 208p. illus.
index. LC 68-131074.
Popular illustrated history of Brazilian silver, both secular and ecclesiastical. List of
major marks is included; bibliography, pp. 185-208, lists basic books and periodical
articles.

923   Valle-Arizpe, Artemio de. **Notas de plateriá.** Mexico, Herrero Hermanos,
1961. 427p. illus. index. LC 62-2637.
Good, serious history/handbook of pre-Conquest silver in Mexico. Covers both
domestic and church plate. Good bibliography of books and periodical articles,
pp. 421-27.

European Gold and Silver

France

924   Babelon, Jean. **L'orfèvrerie française.** Paris, Larousse, 1946. 124p. illus.
index.
Good, popular survey of goldsmithery in France from ancient Gaul to the early
twentieth century. Illustrated with museum pieces. Bibliography, pp. 116-20, lists
basic books and periodical articles in French.

925 Beuque, E., and M. Frapsauce. **Dictionniare des poinçons des maîtres orfèvres français du XIVe siècle à 1838.** Paris, Beuque-Frapsauce, 1929. 343p. illus. index.
Good, comprehensive dictionary of French gold and silver marks, illustrated with facsimiles. Part one covers marks containing symbols and initials; Part two has marks with symbols but not with initials; Part three shows marks in lozenge form.

926 Bouilhet, Henri. **L'orfèverie française aux XVIIIe et XIXe siècle.** Paris, H. Laurens, 1902-1912. 3v. illus. index.
Comprehensive but popular history of French gold and silver of the eighteenth and nineteenth centuries. Illustrated with pieces in museums and with private and dealers' collections.

927 Brault, Solange, and Yves Bottineau. **L'orfèvrerie française du XVIIIe siècle.** Paris, Presses Universitaires de France, 1959. 189p. illus. index. LC 61-43045.
Popular illustrated survey of French eighteenth century silver, well illustrated with museum pieces. Bibliography, pp. 109-14, is a good list of books and periodical articles.

928 Carré, Louis. **A Guide to Old French Plate** . . . London, Chapman & Hall, 1931. 270p. illus. index.
Good, older handbook of French silver and goldsmiths' marks. Part one lists marks used before the Revolution; Part two, marks employed after the Revolution up to the early part of the present century.

929 Carré, Louis. **Les poinçons de l'orfèvrerie française du quatorzième siècle jusqu'au début du dix-neuvième siècle.** Paris, Carré, 1928. 355p. illus. index. Reprint: New York, B. Franklin, 1968. LC 69-19033.
Good, general dictionary of French goldsmiths' hallmarks to the beginning of the nineteenth century. Illustrated with facsimiles.

930 Cripps, Wilfred J. **Old French Plate; Its Makers and Marks** . . . 3rd ed. London, Murray, 1920. 115p. illus. index.
Older, handbook/history of French silver from the early Middle Ages to circa 1838, with facsimiles of principal hallmarks. Useful appendix of pieces with makers' names and marks.

931 Davis, Frank. **French Silver, 1450-1825.** New York, Praeger, 1970. 104p. illus. index. LC 72-516592.
Good, popular illustrated survey. Directed to the collector, yet illustrated chiefly with museum pieces. Bibliography of basic books in both French and English, pp. 99-100.

932   Dennis, Faith. **Three Centuries of French Domestic Silver.** New York,
        Metropolitan Museum of Art, 1960. 2v. illus. index. LC 60-9288.
Good, serious history of French silver, excluding church and court pieces, from the
sixteenth through the nineteenth century. Based on examples exhibited through a
loan exhibition at the Metropolitan Museum of Art in New York. Good bibliography of basic works, pp. 189-92.

933   Grandjean, Serge. **L'orfèvrerie du XIX siècle en Europe.** Paris, Presses
        Universitaires de France, 1962. 161p. illus. index. LC 63-55026.
Good, popular illustrated survey of nineteenth century European silver and gold.
Illustrated with museum pieces and pieces accessible to the collector.

934   Havard, Henry. **Histoire de l'orfèvrerie française.** Paris, May & Metteroz,
        1896. 472p. illus.
An early and classic history of French goldsmithery from the early Middle Ages
through the nineteenth century.

935   Helft, Jacques, ed. **French Master Goldsmiths and Silversmiths from the
        Seventeenth to the Nineteenth Century.** New York, French and European
        Publications, 1966. 333p. illus. LC 66-9055.
Good history consisting of essays by specialists. Well illustrated with museum pieces.
Section on the hallmarks of Paris from 1600 to 1838, with facsimiles. Bibliography,
p. 333, is a good but unclassified list of books, periodical articles and exhibition
catalogs.

936   Helft, Jacques. **Le poinçon des provinces françaises.** Paris, De Nobèle,
        1968. 612p. illus. LC 68-111690.
Excellent, comprehensive dictionary of French provincial gold and silver marks.
Arrangement is by region (*place de juridiction*), and marks are reproduced in both
facsimile and photographs of actual marks. Dictionary section is followed by an
excellent collection of plates illustrating major pieces of provincial French silver.
Bibliography, pp. 600-607, is a good but unclassified list of major books and
periodical articles.

937   Marquet de Vasselot, Jean Joseph. **Bibliographie de l'orfèvrerie et de
        l'émaillerie françaises . . .** Paris, Picard, 1925. 293p.
Excellent, classified bibliography of books and periodical articles on all aspects of
French goldsmithery and enamels. Approximately 2,700 entries of works published
up to 1923.

Germany, Austria and Switzerland

938   Braun, Joseph. **Meisterwerke der deutschen Goldschmiedekunst der
        vorgotischen Zeit.** Munich, Riehn and Reusch, 1922. 2v. illus. (Sammelbande
        zur Geschichte der Kunst und des Kunstgewerbes, Band VIII).
Good, scholarly history/handbook of German goldsmithery from the ninth through
the thirteenth centuries. Thorough illustrated catalog of works, with separate

bibliographies for each entry. A standard history of German early and high medieval goldsmiths' work.

939   Leitermann, Heinz. **Deutsche Goldschmiedekunst; das Goldschmiede-handwerk in der deutschen Kunst- und Kulturgeschichte.** Stuttgart, Kohlhammer, 1953. 156p. illus. index. (Urban Bücher, 8). LC A55-2431.
Good, popular illustrated survey of German gold and silver from the Middle Ages to the present, with emphasis on its cultural context. Bibliographical footnotes.

940   Lotz, W. **Gold und Silber: deutsche Goldschmiedearbeiten der Gegenwart.** Berlin, H. Reckendorf, 1926. 64p. illus.
Popular illustrated survey of German gold and silver including jewelry. No bibliography.

941   Redslob, Edwin. **Deutsche Goldschmiedeplastik.** Munich, Delphin, 1932. 45p. (text), 60p. (illus.).
Good, serious illustrated survey of German figurative gold and silver work from the early Middle Ages to the early eighteenth century. Good notes to the plates with separate bibliographies for each entry.

942   Schade, Günter. **Deutsche Goldschmiedekunst.** Leipzig, Koehler and Amelang, 1974. 241p. illus. index.
Good, serious history of German gold and silver from the Middle Ages to the beginning of the nineteenth century. Chapters on technique and manufacture. Illustrated with museum pieces and works of art depicting the use of silver and the work and life of German goldsmiths and silversmiths. Bibliography, pp. 235-38, lists books, catalogs and periodical articles.

943   Scheffler, Wolfgang. **Berliner Goldschmiede: Daten, Werke, Zeichen.** Berlin, Hessling, 1968. 647p. illus. index. LC 74-416236.
Excellent, scholarly and comprehensive dictionary of the goldsmith and silver-smith marks used in Berlin between 1600 and 1830. Provides full biographical data, list of items, bibliographical references and facsimiles of marks. Thoroughly indexed by name and marks. For other regional dictionaries of German gold and silver marks, see (944, 945).

944   Scheffler, Wolfgang. **Goldschmiede Niedersachsens: Daten, Werke, Zeichen.** Berlin, De Gruyter, 1965. 2v. illus. index. LC 66-50161.
Excellent, comprehensive dictionary/handbook of the goldsmiths and silversmiths of Lower Saxony, including Hamburg and Bremen. Arranged by place, it covers 1600 to 1830, giving full biographical data, list of marked works, bibliographical references and facsimiles of marks. Thoroughly indexed. One of the most thorough of silversmith and goldsmith dictionaries. For volumes covering other sections of Germany see (943, 945).

945   Scheffler, Wolfgang. **Goldschmiede Rheinland-Westfalens: Daten, Werke, Zeichen.** Berlin, De Gruyter, 1973. 2v. illus. index. LC 72-81568.
Excellent, scholarly and comprehensive dictionary of the goldsmiths and silver-smiths of the West German state of Rheinland-Westfalen. Arranged by place, it covers the period from 1600 to 1830, giving full biographical data, list of works, biographical references and facsimiles of marks. Thoroughly indexed. For other regional dictionaries of German gold and silversmiths' marks see (943, 944).

Great Britain

946   Ash, Douglas. **Dictionary of British Antique Silver.** New York, Hippocrene Books, 1972. 189p. illus. LC 72-80991.
Popular dictionary covering persons, places, types, techniques, periods and styles. Brief list of basic books, p. 189.

947   Banister, Judith. **English Silver.** New York, Hawthorn, 1966. 251p. illus. LC 66-16161.
Popular history/handbook covering English silver from 1500 to the present. Part one covers technique, hallmarks, and collecting and includes a glossary of terms and brief bibliography of basic works. Part two consists of short essays on the major periods in the history of English silver.

948   Bennett, Douglas. **Irish Georgian Silver.** London, Cassell, 1972. 369p. illus. index. LC 73-159885.
Good, serious history/handbook of Irish silver of the eighteenth and early nineteenth centuries. Illustrated with museum pieces, it includes a list of major hallmarks and a bibliography of basic books, p. 357.

949   Bennett, Douglas. **Irish Georgian Silver, 1714-1828.** London, Cassell, 1972. 448p. illus. index.
Good, serious handbook/history of Irish silver of the Georgian period. Well illustrated with pieces in museums and private collections. Major hallmarks are included. Brief bibliography of basic books, p. 357.

950   Bradbury, Frederick. **British and Irish Silver Assay Office Marks. 1544-1954** ... 9th ed. Sheffield, Northend, 1955. 90p. illus.
Good, pocket-sized handbook of silver marks, with appendices on gold and old Sheffield plate marks.

951   Bradbury, Frederick. **Guide to Marks of Origin on British and Irish Silver Plate from Mid-16th Century to the Year 1959.** 10th ed. Sheffield, Northend, 1959. 93p. illus.
Pocket-sized handbook of English, Scottish and Irish silver marks. References to further literature in the preface. Excellent portable guide to be used in conjunction with Jackson's comprehensive dictionary (961).

952   Chaffers, William. **Hall Marks on Gold & Silver Plate** . . . 10th ed. London,
          Reeves, 1922. 395p. illus. index.
Older, comprehensive handbook of hallmarks on English, Scottish and Irish silver
and gold, with table of statutes and ordinances affecting hallmarks, chronological
list of English plate, and table of London goldsmiths and silversmiths.

953   Clayton, Michael. **The Collector's Dictionary of Silver and Gold of Great
          Britain and North America.** New York, World, 1971. 351p. illus.
          LC 73-149055.
Good, serious dictionary of British and American silver, covering persons, materials,
techniques, objects, ornament, and styles. Well illustrated with museum pieces and
pieces accessible to collectors. Entries covering places include facsimiles of hallmarks, and most have literature references.

954   Cripps, Wilfred J. **Old English Plate; Ecclesiastical, Decorative and Domestic:
          Its Makers and Marks.** 11th ed. London, Murray, 1926. 540p. illus. index.
Older dictionary/handbook of English silver makers and marks with a useful appendix
of pieces used as authority for London date-letters and makers' marks, plus tables
of date-letters on English, Scottish and Irish silver.

955   Dennis, Jessie M. **English Silver.** New York, Walker, 1970. 83p. illus.
          LC 74-87071.
Popular history of English silver from circa 1500 to 1820, illustrated with museum
pieces.

956   Finlay, Ian. **Scottish Gold and Silver Work.** London, Chatto & Windus,
          1956. 178p. illus. index.
Good, serious history from early Celtic times to circa 1830, illustrated with museum
pieces. Bibliographical footnotes.

957   Grimwade, Arthur. **Rococo Silver, 1727-65.** London, Faber and Faber,
          1974. 96p. illus. index.
Good, serious history of English silver in the Rococo style made between 1727 and
1765. Contains chapters on style, development of the craft, and forms of plate;
a short bibliography, pp. 68-69, lists basic books and periodical articles. Illustrated
with museum pieces.

958   Heller, David. **A History of Cape Silver, 1700-1870.** Cape Town, D. Heller,
          1949. 276p. illus. index. LC A50-4836.
Popular, illustrated survey of Colonial silver made in South Africa with list of major
hallmarks. Bibliography of basic books and periodical articles, p. 270.

959   Holland, Margaret. **Old Country Silver: An Account of English Provincial
          Silver, with Sections on Ireland, Scotland and Wales.** New York, Arco,
          1971. 240p. illus. index. LC 79-160142.
Good, serious history/handbook on the provincial silver of Great Britain and Ireland,
arranged by region and place. Well illustrated with both museum pieces and pieces

accessible to the average collector, plus facsimiles of major hallmarks. Bibliography, pp. 227-30, is a good classified list of major books and periodical articles.

960   Hughes, George B., and Therle Hughes. **Three Centuries of English Domestic Silver, 1500-1820.** New York, Praeger, 1968. 248p. illus. index. LC 68-21582.
Popular history arranged by type of object, with a brief chapter on marks. Illustrated with pieces accessible to the average collector.

961   Jackson, Charles J. **English Goldsmiths and Their Marks; a History of the Goldsmiths and Plate Workers of England, Scotland, and Ireland . . .** 2nd ed. London, Macmillan, 1921. 747p. illus. index. Reprint: New York, Dover, 1964. LC 64-18852.
Excellent, comprehensive dictionary of British gold and silver marks. Introductory chapters treat legislation concerning goldsmiths and standards for gold and silver in Great Britain. Dictionary of marks is arranged by place and illustrated with facsimile. Standard work on the gold and silver marks of Great Britain and Ireland.

962   Jackson, Charles J. **An Illustrated History of English Plate, Ecclesiastical and Secular . . .** London, Country Life, 1911. 2v. illus. index.
Good illustrated history treating the Middle Ages to the end of the Georgian period. Useful companion to the author's handbook of hallmarks (961). Bibliographical references in the preface.

963   Okie, Howard P. **Old Silver and Old Sheffield Plate, a History of the Silversmith's Art in Great Britain and Ireland. . . .** 2nd ed. New York, Doubleday, 1952. 420p. illus. index.
Originally published in 1928. Handbook/history of British silver with a chapter on Sheffield plate. Provides lists of British, American and some Continental silver date-letters, place marks, and makers' marks.

964   Oman, Charles C. **English Church Plate, 597-1830.** London, Oxford University Press, 1957. 326p. illus. index.
Good, serious history of English ecclesiastical silver from the early Middle Ages to circa 1830, with special attention to the history of patronage and liturgical function. Illustrated with museum pieces. Good, classified bibliography, pp. 291-97, of books and periodical articles. Thorough indexing.

965   Oman, Charles C. **English Domestic Silver.** 7th ed. London, A. & C. Black, 1968. 240p. illus. index. LC 79-406854.
Good, popular history of English silver from the Middle Ages to the present. Chapters treat the goldsmith and his craft, development of style, major classes of plate, and hallmarks. Illustrated with museum pieces. Bibliography, pp. 233-34, is a brief classified list of major books.

966   Taylor, Gerald. **Silver.** 2nd ed. Baltimore, Penguin, 1963. 301p. illus. index.
       LC 63-25568.
Good, popular history of British and American silver from the Middle Ages through
the Regency period, with an epilogue on Victorian and modern silver. Illustrated
with museum pieces. Glossary of terms, table of major hallmarks and note on how
to clean silver. Good classified bibliography of books, pp. 286-96.

967   Ticher, Kurt. **Irish Silver in the Rococo Period.** Shannon, Irish University
       Press, 1972. 28p. (text), 105 plates. LC 73-152334.
Good, popular illustrated survey of Irish silver of the eighteenth century, with
emphasis on those pieces in the ornate rococo style. No bibliography.

968   Wenham, Edward. **Domestic Silver of Great Britain and Ireland.** New York,
       Oxford University Press, 1935. 186p. illus. index.
Good, older history from early Middle Ages through the nineteenth century, with
sections on evolution of types, techniques, and silversmiths and their marks. Brief
bibliography of basic books.

969   Wilkinson, Wynyard R. T. **Indian Colonial Silver: European Silversmiths
       in India, 1790-1860, and Their Marks.** London, Argent Press, 1973. 171p.
       illus. index.
Good, serious handbook of the hallmarks of Colonial silver made in India by
European silversmiths, mostly English. Bibliography of basic books, p. viii.

970   Wills, Geoffrey. **Silver for Pleasure and Investment.** New York, Arco, 1969.
       169p. illus. index. LC 71-108996.
Popular collector's handbook of old English silver, with index of makers and marks,
glossary of terms and dictionary of silver articles. Brief list of books in English,
p. 170.

Italy

971   Bulgari, Constantino G. **Argentieri, gemmari e orafi d'Italia** . . . Rome,
       Lorenzo del Turco, Ugo Bozzi and Fratelli Palombi, 1958-74. 5v. illus.
Excellent comprehensive dictionary of Italian gold, silver and jewelers' marks.
Parte prima: Roma (2v.); Parte secunda: Lazio, Umbria; Parte terza: Marche
Romagna; Parte quarta: Emilia. Well illustrated. Gives biographical data and
facsimiles of marks. Introductions to the various regions give control marks and
history of gold and silver work in the center or provinces. Standard work on
Italian gold and silver.

972   Churchill, Sidney J. A. **The Goldsmiths of Italy.** . . . London, Hopkinson,
       1926. 182p. illus. index.
Older popular history of Italian goldsmithery arranged by region. Includes jewelry.
Good bibliography of the older literature, pp. 161-73.

973   Denaro, Victor F. **The Goldsmiths of Malta and Their Marks.** Florence,
        L. S. Olschki, 1972. 241p. illus. index. (Arte e Archeologia, 3)
Good, serious handbook/history of Maltese silver, with list of marks. Bibliographical
footnotes.

974   Gregorietti, Guido. **Italian Gold, Silver and Jewelry: Their History and
        Centres.** Milan, Alfieri & Lacroix, 1971. 178p. illus. index. LC 72-190525.
Good, popular history with illustrations of museum pieces and list of major marks.
Brief bibliography of basic books in Italian.

975   Mariacher, Giovanni. **Argenti italiani.** Milan, Görlich, 1965. 31p. (text),
        242 illus.
Illustrated survey of Italian silver from the early Middle Ages to the present. Brief
introductory essay is followed by good selection of plates of museum pieces. One-
page bibliography of basic books in Italian.

976   Morassi, Antonio. **Antica oreficeria italiana.** Milan, Hoepli, 1936. 128p.
        illus. index.
Good, serious history of Italian goldsmithery, including jewelry from the Middle
Ages to the nineteenth century. Bibliographies at the end of each chapter.

Netherlands

977   Duyvené de Wit-Klinkhamer, Th. M., and M. H. Gans. **Dutch Silver.**
        London, Faber and Faber, 1961. 97p. illus. index. LC 70-356237.
Good, serious history/handbook of Dutch silver from the sixteenth century to
circa 1830, with chapters on marks, values, fakes, and use. Good bibliography,
pp. 89-93, of books and periodical articles.

978   Frederiks, J. W. **Dutch Silver.** The Hague, Nijhoff, 1952-1961. 4v. illus.
        index.
Volume one: Embossed Plaquettes, Tazze and Dishes from the Renaissance until
the End of the Eighteenth Century (1952); Volume two: Wrought Plate of North
and South-Holland from the Renaissance until the End of the Eighteenth Century
(1958); Volume three: Wrought Plate of the Central, Northern and Southern
Provinces from the Renaissance until the End of the Eighteenth Century (1960);
Volume four: Embossed Ecclesiastical and Secular Plate from the Renaissance
until the End of the Eighteenth Century (1961). Excellent, comprehensive handbook of Dutch silver arranged by region and then by artist, giving biographical
data and marks. Excellent corpus of illustrations. Standard reference work on
antique Dutch silver.

979   Schrijver, Elka. **Nederlands zilver.** Bussum, van Dishoeck, 1971. 104p.
        illus. LC 72-306046.
Good, popular history/handbook of Dutch silver from the Middle Ages through the
mid-nineteenth century. List of major hallmarks. Bibliography of basic reference
works, p. 102.

980   Voet, Elias, Jr. **Nederlands goud- en zilvermerken 1445-1951.** s'Gravenhagen, Nijhoff, 1951. 73p. illus.
Pocket-sized dictionary of Dutch gold and silver marks illustrated with facsimiles.

Scandinavia

981   Berg, Gosta, *et al.*, eds. **Svenskt Silversmide, 1520-1850.** Stockholm, Nordisk Rotogravyr, 1941-63. 4v. illus. LC 49-34806 rev.
Excellent serious history of Swedish silver, with emphasis on the major personalities. Contents: del 1., Renässans och Barock, 1520-1700; del. 2., Senbarock, Fredrik I:s Stil och Rokoko; del. 3., Gustaviansk Stil, Empire och Romantik, 1780-1850; del 4., Guld- och Silverstämplar. Volume four provides a good comprehensive dictionary of hallmarks and signatures. Bibliographies at end of each volume.

982   Bøje, Christian A. **Danske guld og sølv smedemaerker før 1870.** Copenhagen, Nyt Nordisk, 1946. 589p. illus. index.
Good, comprehensive dictionary of Danish gold and silver marks used before 1870. Illustrated with facsimiles. Supplement: *Tillaeg til Danske guld og sølv smedemaerker før 1870* (Copenhagen, 1949).

983   Bøje, Christian A. **Gammelt dansk sølvtøj.** 2nd ed. Copenhagen, Thaning & Appel, 1960. 102p. illus. index. LC 56-22999.
Good, serious history/handbook of Danish silver from the Middle Ages to the early twentieth century, with chapters on collecting and a list of major marks.

984   Boesen, Gudmund, and Christian A. Bøje. **Old Danish Silver.** Copenhagen, Hassing, 1949. 35p. (text), 496 plates. index.
Popular survey of Danish silver from circa 1570 to 1800. Good corpus of illustrations with descriptive notes. No bibliography.

985   Lassen, Erik. **Dansk sølv.** Copenhagen, Thaning & Appel, 1964. 294p. illus. index. LC 66-80842.
Good, serious history of Danish silver from the Middle Ages through the early nineteenth century. Illustrated with museum pieces. Bibliographical footnotes.

986   Polak, Ada. **Gullsmedkunsten in Norge før og nå.** Oslo, Dreyers Forlag, 1970. 178p. illus. index.
Good, serious history of Norwegian silver from the early Middle Ages to the present, illustrated with museum pieces. Chapters on technique and marks. English summary, pp. 164-71. Good classified bibliography, pp. 172-74, lists books and periodical articles.

987   Upmark, Gustaf. **Guld- och silversmeder i Sverige, 1520-1850.** Stockholm, Fröleen, 1943. 951p. illus. index.
Comprehensive dictionary of Swedish gold and silver marks, arranged geographically and illustrated with facsimiles. Standard work on Swedish gold and silversmiths and their marks.

Spain and Portugal

988   Johnson, Ada M. **Hispanic Silverwork** . . . New York, Hispanic Society,
       1944. 308p. illus. index.
Good, popular history of Spanish silver from the late Middle Ages through the
nineteenth century, with a catalog of examples in the Hispanic Society of America.
Bibliographical references in the footnotes. General bibliography, pp. 294-300.

989   Vidal, Manuel G. **Marcas de contrastas e ouvrives portugueses; desde o
       século XV a 1950.** Lisbon, Casa da Moeda, 1958. 560p. illus. LC 59-30601.
Good dictionary of Portuguese gold and silver hallmarks illustrated with facsimiles
of marks and plates of major signed pieces.

Oriental Gold and Silver

990   Roth, Henry L. **Oriental Silverwork, Malay and Chinese; a Handbook for
       Connoisseurs, Collectors, Students and Silversmiths.** Kuala Lumpur,
       University of Malaya Press, 1966, 300p. illus. index. LC 67-8882.
Popular history/handbook first published in 1910. Introduction is followed by
corpus of plates with descriptive captions. No bibliography.

IRON

991   Ayrton, Maxwell, and Arnold Silcock. **Wrought Iron and Its Decorative
       Use.** London, Country Life, 1929. 196p. illus. index.
Popular illustrated survey of European wrought iron from the Middle Ages to the
early twentieth century. No bibliography.

992   Baur-Heinhold, Margarete. **Geschmiedetes Eisen vom Mittelalter bis um
       1900.** Königstein, Langewies, 1963. 112p. illus.
Popular illustrated survey of wrought iron in German-speaking countries from the
Middle Ages to 1900. Introductory essay sketches the history and technique. No
bibliography.

993   Byne, Arthur, and Mildred Byne. **Spanish Ironwork** . . . New York,
       Hispanic Society, 1915. 143p. illus. index.
Good, illustrated survey of Spanish iron from the Middle Ages through the nineteenth century, with catalog of the pieces in the Hispanic Society of America's
collection.

994   Clouzot, Henri. **Le fer forgé.** Paris, A. Calavas, 1927. 29p. (text), 320
       (plates).
Popular illustrated survey of European wrought iron, with emphasis on French
examples from the Middle Ages to the end of the eighteenth century. No
bibliography.

995   D'Allemagne, Henri R. **Les anciens maîtres serruriers.** Paris, Gründ, 1943.
       2v. illus.
Good, serious history of French wrought iron, with emphasis on iron workers'
guilds, their techniques, equipment, regulations and training. Volume one is text;
Volume two has plates. Useful illustrations show works of art and also depict iron
mining, manufacture, and use. Covers the Middle Ages to the early twentieth
century.

996   Ferrari, Giulio. **Il ferro nell'arte italiana** . . . Milan, Hoepli, 1927. 197p.
       illus.
Good illustrated survey of Italian wrought iron from the Middle Ages through the
early nineteenth century. No bibliography.

997   Ffoulkes, Constance J. **Decorative Ironwork from the Eleventh to the
       Eighteenth Century.** London, Methuen, 1913. 148p. illus.
Popular history with emphasis on British wrought iron. Useful list of smiths and
ironworkers, pp. 141-44.

998   Frank, Edgar B. **Old French Ironwork; the Craftsman and His Art.**
       Cambridge, Mass., Harvard University Press, 1950. 221p. illus. index.
Good, serious history from the Middle Ages through the nineteenth century, with
emphasis on small pieces. Bibliography, pp. 217-18, lists basic books and catalogs
chiefly in French.

999   Gardner, John S. **English Ironwork of the XVIIth and XVIIIth Centuries;
       an Historical & Analytical Account of the Development of Exterior
       Smithcraft** . . . London, Batsford, 1911. 336p. illus. index.
Good, serious history with a chapter on medieval ironwork. Chapters treat classes
of objects (e.g., gates, railings, brackets, signs, etc.). Good list of smiths and designers,
pp. 321-23.

1000   Gardner, John S. **Ironwork.** Rev. ed. London, Board of Education,
       1922-30. 3v. illus. index. (Victoria and Albert Museum, Publication
       nos. 131, 195)
Good, serious history of European wrought iron from prehistoric times to the end
of the nineteenth century, based on examples in the Victoria and Albert Museum.
Contents: Part I, From the Earliest Times to the End of the Medieval Period;
Part II, Continental Ironwork of the Renaissance and Later Periods; Part III, A
Complete Survey of the Artistic Working of Iron in Great Britain from Earliest
Times. Bibliography of books in the Victoria and Albert Museum on Continental
wrought iron in Part II, pp. 112-14.

1001   Hoever, Otto. **An Encyclopedia of Ironwork; Examples of Hand Wrought
       Ironwork from the Middle Ages to the End of the 18th Century** . . .
       New York, Weyhe, 1927. 29p. (text), 320 plates.
Pictorial survey of European wrought iron work. Brief introductory essay traces
the development, followed by good collection of plates arranged chronologically.
No bibliography.

1002   Kauffmann, Henry J. **Early American Ironware Cast and Wrought**. Rutland,
        Vt., Tuttle, 1966. 166p. illus. index. LC 65-16743.
Popular history to the middle of the nineteenth century, with emphasis on main
types and techniques. Good illustrations of old forges and workshops. Pieces
illustrated are accessible to the collector. No bibliography.

1003   Lister, Raymond. **Decorative Wrought Ironwork in Great Britain**. Rutland,
        Vt., Tuttle, 1970. 267p. illus. index. LC 72-113903.
Reprint of 1957 edition (London). Popular history arranged according to main
types, with a chapter on the technique of the blacksmith. Covers from the Middle
Ages to the present. Glossary of terms. Good classified and annotated bibliography
of books and periodical articles, pp. 245-57.

1004   Sonn, Albert H. **Early American Wrought Iron**. New York, Scribner's,
        1928. 3v. illus. index.
Popular illustrated history covering decorative and utilitarian pieces. Bibliography
of basic books and periodical articles, v. 3, pp. 243-44.

1005   Stuttmann, Ferdinand. **Deutsche Schmiedeeisenkunst**. Munich, Delphin-
        Verlag, 1927-30. 5v. illus.
Good, comprehensive illustrated survey of German decorative wrought iron from
the early Middle Ages to the early twentieth century. Contents: Band 1, Mittelalter;
Band 2, Renaissance und Frühbarock; Band 3/4, Barock, Rokoko und Klassizismus;
Band 5, Gegenwart. Brief introductory essays are followed by good selection of
plates of major museum pieces.

1006   Zimelli, Umberto, and Giovanni Vergerio. **Decorative Ironwork**. London,
        Hamlyn, 1969. 159p. illus.
Popular illustrated survey of Western wrought iron from antiquity through the
baroque. Well illustrated. No bibliography.

PEWTER

General Histories and Handbooks

1007   Cotterell, Howard H. **Pewter Down the Ages; from Medieval Times to the
        Present Day** . . . London, Hutchinson, 1932. 237p. illus. index.
Good, serious history arranged by periods and illustrated with museum pieces and
pieces accessible to the collector. Plates of works of art depicting pewter. Glossary
of terms, list of British pewterers and their marks. No bibliography.

1008   Haedeke, Hanns-Ulrich. **Zinn. Ein Handbuch für Sammler und Liebhaber**.
        Braunschweig, Klinkhardt & Biermann, 1973. 498p. illus. index. (Handbuch
        für Kunst- und Antiquitätensammler, XVI)
Excellent serious history of Western pewter from prehistoric times to the present,
with chapters on collecting, manufacture and pewterers' guilds. Arranged by

period and country. Illustrated with museum pieces. Bibliography, pp. 483-88, is a good but unclassified list of major books and periodical articles in all languages.

American Pewter (U.S. and Canada)

1009   Coffin, Margaret. **The History & Folklore of American Country Tinware, 1700-1900.** Camden, N.J., T. Nelson, 1968. 226p. illus. index. LC 68-25512.
Popular history with chapters on the craft of the American tinsmith, identification and care of antique tinware, and glossary of terms. Bibliography, pp. 212-15, is an unclassified list of books and periodical articles.

1010   Ebert, Katherine. **Collecting American Pewter.** New York, Scribner's, 1973. 163p. illus. index. LC 72-12147.
A good handbook/history tracing pewter production in two periods: 1700-1825, and 1825-1860. Includes short biographical entries on prominent pewterers. Special attention to lamps, to cleaning, fakes and reproductions. Good lists of American pewterers, including many without reported examples, plus facsimiles of marks.

1011   Gould, Mary E. **Antique Tin & Tole Ware: Its History and Romance.** Rutland, Vt., Tuttle, 1958. 136p. illus. index. LC 57-8796.
Popular history of American tinware to the middle of the nineteenth century, with chapters on technique and the life of the tin peddler. No bibliography.

1012   Jacobs, Carl. **Guide to American Pewter.** New York, McBride, 1957. 216p. illus.
Good collectors' handbook, with a section on collecting and a checklist of American pewterers giving marks, biographical data and prices. Good selection of illustrations. Appendix with line drawings showing characteristic pewter forms. No bibliography.

1013   Jacobs, Celia. **Pocket Book of American Pewter; the Makers and the Marks.** 2nd ed. Boston, Herman, 1970. 93p. illus. index. LC 70-111761.
Good dictionary of major American pewterers, with facsimiles of their marks.

1014   Kauffman, Henry J. **The American Pewterer; His Techniques & His Products.** Camden, N.J., T. Nelson, 1970. 158p. illus. index. LC 77-113170.
Good, serious handbook of eighteenth and nineteenth century American pewter, arranged by types, with a good section on the craft of the pewterer. Also covers Britannia metal ware. Appendix is a useful reprint of the Metropolitan Museum of Art's *American Pewterers and Their Marks* (New York, 1942). Brief bibliography of basic books.

1015   Kerfoot, John Barett. **American Pewter** . . . New York, Houghton Mifflin, 1924. 239p. illus. index.
Good, serious history/handbook treating early Colonial times to circa 1850. Chapter on collecting. Illustrated with pieces in the author's collection. No bibliography. An older, standard work.

1016   Laughlin, Ledlie I. **Pewter in America, Its Makers and Their Marks.** Barre, Mass., Barre Pub., 1969-71. 3v. illus. index. LC 77-86912.
Volumes one and two are reprints of the first edition (Boston, 1940); Volume three is an update of the information in the first two volumes. Excellent, serious handbook/ history of American pewter to circa 1850, arranged by region and type, with a chapter on the craft of the pewterer and checklist of makers. Excellent corpus of illustrations with details of marks. Bibliography, Vol. 3, pp. 233-55, is an excellent classified list of books and periodical articles. The standard work on American pewter.

1017   Montgomery, Charles F. **A History of American Pewter.** New York and Washington, Praeger, 1973. 246p. illus. index. LC 77-141362.
Good, serious history of American pewter to 1880, illustrated with museum pieces. Chapter on the metallic composition of American pewter and Britannia metal, and list of marks of the objects illustrated. Useful bibliographical note, pp. 241-42.

European Pewter

General Histories and Handbooks

1018   Bedford, John. **Pewter.** New York, Walker, 1966. 63p. illus. LC 66-22380.
Popular handbook for the beginning collector with emphasis on English pewter from the sixteenth century through art nouveau. Arranged by types.

1019   Bell, Malcolm. **Old Pewter** . . . London, Newnes; New York, Scribner's, 1905. 186p. illus. index.
Older, popular history of European pewter to the early nineteenth century. Chapters on history, technique and collecting. No bibliography.

1020   Belloncle, Michel. **Les étains.** Paris, Gründ, 1968. 192p. illus. LC 70-358511.
Popular illustrated survey of European pewter, with emphasis on French examples. No bibliography.

1021   Dolz, Renate. **Antiquitäten-Zinn.** Munich, Heyne, 1970. 192p. illus. index. LC 70-58032.
Good, popular history/handbook of European pewter including utensils, figures and soldiers. Chapters on famous makers and workshops. Illustrated with major museum pieces and pieces accessible to the collector.

1022   Mory, Ludwig. **Schönes Zinn; Geschichte, Formen und Probleme.** 3rd ed. Munich, Bruckmann, 1972. 335p. illus. index. LC 72-312843.
Good, serious history of European pewter from the Middle Ages to the middle of the nineteenth century, with emphasis on German examples. Illustrated with museum pieces. Section on marks. Bibliography of basic books, pp. 317-18.

1023   Mory, Ludwig. **Zinn in Europa. Bildkarte der regionalen Krug und Kannentypen.** Munich, Bruckmann, 1972. 21p. illus. LC 73-303721.
Very useful pictorial outline of regional forms of pewter jugs and pitchers found in Europe from the Middle Ages through the early nineteenth century. Also lists some fifty major marks found on the pieces.

1024   Verster, A. J. G. **Old European Pewter.** London, Thames and Hudson, 1958. 80p. illus. index.
Good, popular history treating the subject from the fourteenth through the eighteenth centuries. Arranged by broad classes (e.g., home and tavern, church and cloister). Chapter on guilds, technique, and collecting. Bibliography, pp. 67-70, lists books and periodical articles in all languages.

National Histories and Handbooks

Czechoslovakia

1025   Tischer, Friedrich. **Böhmisches Zinn und seine Marken.** Leipzig, Hiersemann, 1928. 329p. illus. index. Reprint: Osnabrück, Ohms, 1973.
Good, scholarly handbook/history of Bohemian pewter with excellent lists of marks and dictionary of pewterers. Illustrated with museum pieces and pieces in major private collections. Bibliography, pp. xiv-xv, lists basic books in both German and Czech. Includes German pewterers working in Bohemia.

France

1026   Douroff, B. A. **Étains français des XVIIe et XVIIIe siècles.** Paris, Massin, n.d. 24p. (text), 36 plates.
Popular handbook of French pewter of the seventeenth and eighteenth centuries, with chapter on history, list of major marks, and good selection of plates illustrating pieces accessible to the collector. No bibliography.

1027   Tardy [firm]. **Les étains français.** Paris, Tardy, 1959. 843p. illus. index. LC 61-33100.
Originally issued as four separate volumes. Good, serious handbook of French pewter marks with chapters on manufacture, fakes, restoration and historical development. Dictionary section is arranged by place, each introduced with a history and some with documents.

1028   Tardy [firm]. **Les poinçons des étains français.** Paris, n.p., 1968. 284p. illus. LC 68-113754.
Pocket-sized handbook of French pewter marks. Introduction lists control marks followed by dictionary of masters' marks. Bibliography, pp. 239-43, is a list of basic books. Useful chapter on assaying pewterware.

Germany

1029   Hintze, Erwin. **Die deutschen Zinngiesser und ihre Marken** . . . Leipzig,
               Hiersemann, 1921-31. 7v. illus. index.
Excellent, comprehensive handbook of German pewter and its marks. Volume one
covers Saxony; Volume two, Nuremberg; Volume three, North Germany; Volume
four, Silesia; Volumes five through seven, South Germany. Within the volumes the
arrangement is geographical. Each volume has its own indexes by mark and pewterer.
The standard work on German pewter.

Great Britain

1030   Cotterell, Howard H. **Old Pewter, Its Makers and Marks in England,
               Scotland and Ireland** . . . London, Batsford, 1929. 432p. illus. index.
               Reprint: Rutland, Vt., Tuttle, 1963. LC 63-4599.
Excellent serious handbook/history with an historical introduction, dictionary of
pewterers and their marks, and bibliography, p. 423, listing basic books and
periodical articles. Marks are well indexed. Standard handbook.

1031   Jackson, Radway. **English Pewter Touchmarks, Including the Marks of
               Origin of Some of the Scottish and Irish Pewterers.** London and New
               York, Foulsham, 1970. 123p. illus. LC 77-866555.
Pocket-sized dictionary of major British pewter marks, with introduction covering
the history of touchmarks in England. Bibliography, pp. 121-23, lists major books
and periodical articles.

1032   Hatcher, John, and T. C. Barker. **A History of British Pewter.** London,
               Longman, 1974. 363p. illus. index. LC 73-93118.
Good, scholarly history with emphasis on the social and technological aspects.
Covers from the early Middle Ages to the present. Maps and tables of trade and
manufacturing statistics, appendix with retail prices. Numerous bibliographical
footnotes and good general bibliography, pp. 323-40, listing books, manuscripts
and periodical articles.

1033   Markham, C. A. **The "New" Pewter Marks and Old Pewter Ware; Domestic
               and Ecclesiastical** . . . London, Reeves & Turner, 1928. 355p. illus. index.
Dictionary of British pewter marks, with chapters on history, types, manufacture,
collecting and repair. No bibliography.

1034   Michaelis, Ronald F. **Antique Pewter of the British Isles.** London, Bell,
               1955. 118p. illus. index. Reprint: New York, Dover, 1971. LC 74-138387.
Good, serious handbook/history of the subject from the seventeenth through the
early nineteenth centuries. Chapters treat history, types, decoration, marks, and
collecting; each chapter has a separate bibliography. General bibliography, p. 114,
lists basic books in English.

1035   Peal, Christopher A. **British Pewter and Britannia Metal: For Pleasure and Investment.** London, Gifford, 1971. 200p. illus. index. LC 79-854003.
Popular history from the late Middle Ages through the nineteenth century, with emphasis on pieces accessible to the collector. Chapter on collecting and care. One section has list of major touchmarks.

Netherlands

1036   Dubbe, B. **Tin en Tinnegieters in Nederland.** Zeist, Netherlands, W. de Haan, 1965. 189p. illus. index. LC 72-222357.
Good, serious handbook of Dutch pewter, with good list of major pewterers and their marks. Bibliographies at the end of chapters.

Russia

1037   Gahlnbäck, Johannes. **Rüssisches Zinn.** Leipzig, Hiersemann, 1928-1932. 2v. illus. index.
Good scholarly history of Russian pewter manufactured in Moscow (Volume one) and Leningrad (Volume two) from the early Middle Ages through the eighteenth century, with good lists of marks. Thoroughly indexed and illustrated with museum pieces. Table of contents in Russian and German.

Scandinavia

1038   Bruzelli, Birger. **Tenngjutare i Sverige** . . . Stockholm, Forum, 1967. 606p. illus. index.
Good, serious handbook of Swedish pewterers and their marks from 1754 to 1912, with chapters on types of pewter and manufacture. Bibliography, pp. 602-606, is a good but unclassified list of books and periodical articles referred to in the text. Well illustrated.

1039   Möller, Johan. **Tennsamlarens uppslagsbok, Förteckning över tenngjutare i Sverige och Finland från 1600—talets början—till år 1900** . . . 3rd ed. Stockholm, Natur och Kultur, 1969. 151p. illus. index. LC 70-576665.
Popular handbook of Swedish and Finnish pewter, with lists of marks and chapters on types and techniques. Brief bibliography of basic books in Swedish.

Scotland

1040   Wood, Ingleby. **Scottish Pewterware and Pewterers.** Edinburgh, Morton, 1905. 223p. illus. index.
Older, serious history with large, useful section on the history of pewterers' guilds in various Scottish centers. Concentrates on the seventeenth and eighteenth centuries. Chapter on touchmarks. No bibliography.

Switzerland

1041   Bossard, Gustav. **Die Zinngiesser der Schweiz und ihr Werk.** Zug, Strübin, 1920-34. 2v. illus. index.
Excellent comprehensive dictionary of Swiss pewterers and their marks. Illustrates facsimiles of marks and major pieces. Brief bibliography of basic books, v. 1, p. 7.

CHAPTER SEVENTEEN

MUSICAL INSTRUMENTS

1042   Baines, Anthony. **European and American Musical Instruments.** New York,
         Viking, 1966. 174p. illus. index. LC 66-25611.
Good, serious illustrated history/handbook of Western European and American non-
keyboard instruments from the fifteenth through the mid-nineteenth century. Well-
chosen illustrations with descriptive notes. Excellent classified bibliography of books
and catalogs in all languages, pp. 161-66.

1043   Baines, Anthony, ed. **Musical Instruments through the Ages.** New York,
         Walker, 1966. 244p. illus. index. LC 66-22505.
Good, serious history/handbook of world musical instruments consisting of essays
on the major classes of instruments, written by various specialists. Useful glossary
of technical and acoustic terms. Good, classified bibliography, pp. 323-32, lists
books and periodicals in all languages.

1044   Clemenicie, R. **Old Musical Instruments.** London, Octopus, 1973. 96p. illus.
Popular illustrated history of world musical instruments. No bibliography.

1045   Galpin, Francis W. **Old English Instruments of Music.** 4th ed. London,
         Methuen, 1965. 254p. illus. index.
Good, scholarly history from prehistoric times through the eighteenth century with
emphasis on late medieval and Renaissance instruments. Well-chosen illustrations of
major museum pieces and works of art illustrating historic instruments. Contains
several useful appendices, including a list of illustrations of instruments in manuscripts and carvings, and classification of instruments. Unclassified but annotated
list of books of reference.

1046   Galpin, Francis W. **A Textbook of European Musical Instruments, Their
         Origin, History, and Character.** London, Williams and Norgate, 1937.
         256p. illus. index.
Good, popular handbook/history covering the period from prehistoric times to
1937. Arrangement is by class of instrument; emphasis is on technical features.
Poorly illustrated. General bibliography, pp. 19-22.

1047   Geiringer, Karl. **Musical Instruments: Their History in Western Culture
         from the Stone Age to the Present Day.** London, Allen & Unwin, 1943.
         340p. illus. index. 5th printing: 1965.
Good, serious history to circa 1940. Good selection of illustrations of museum
pieces and works of art illustrating historical instruments. Introduction discusses

the general acoustical qualities of all classes of instruments. Chapters following are arranged chronologically. Bibliography, pp. 318-23, lists book and periodical articles in all languages.

1048   Marcuse, Sibyl. **Musical Instruments: A Comprehensive Dictionary**. New York, Norton, 1975. 608p. illus.
Excellent scholarly dictionary covering all aspects of world musical instruments, with emphasis on the technical and musical historical aspects. Entries have bibliographical references to a list, pp. 603-608, of some 206 books and periodical articles.

1049   Ott, Alfons. **Tausend Jahre Musikleben, 800-1800**. Munich, Prestel, 1961. 95p. illus. (Bibliothek des Germanischen National-Museums zur deutschen Kunst- und Kulturgeschichte. Bilder aus deutschen Vergangenheit, Band 18/19)
Good, serious survey of German musical instruments, well illustrated with plates of major museum pieces and works of art illustrating musical instruments and their use. Brief bibliography of basic books in German.

1050   Sachs, Curt. **The History of Musical Instruments**. New York, Norton, 1940. 505p. illus. index.
Excellent, scholarly history of world musical instruments from prehistoric times through the early twentieth century. Well illustrated with plates and line drawings. Arrangement is by periods and regions. Excellent glossary of technical terms, pp. 454-67. Excellent, comprehensive bibliography, pp. 469-87, lists books and periodical articles in all languages, with special emphasis on German material. A standard history of musical instruments.

1051   Sachs, Curt. **Real-Lexikon der Musikinstrumente**. Enlarged and corrected edition. New York, Dover, 1964. 452p. illus. LC 63-19505.
First edition, Berlin, 1913. Excellent scholarly dictionary covering all aspects of world musical instruments. Illustrated with line drawings. List of major world collections of musical instruments. Good bibliography, pp. xv-xx, lists books and periodical articles. A standard reference tool for the history of musical instruments.

1052   Winternitz, Emanuel. **Musical Instruments of the Western World**. New York, McGraw-Hill, n.d. 259p. illus. index. LC 66-24889.
Excellent, serious history from the late Middle Ages to the mid-nineteenth century. Introductory essays treat form and function, historical aspects, history of collecting, organological literature, and classification. These essays are followed by excellent plates of one hundred major examples with excellent descriptive notes. Excellent classified bibliography of books, catalogs, and source treatises in all languages, pp. 254-256.

1053   Wright, Rowland. **Dictionnaire des instruments de musique: étude de lexicologie**. London, Battley, 1941. 196p. illus.
Good, serious dictionary of musical terms applied to musical instruments. No illustrations. Bibliography, pp. xi-xiv, is a good classified list of books and periodical articles chiefly in French.

CHAPTER EIGHTEEN

TEXTILES

BIBLIOGRAPHIES

1054   "Bibliographie," in: *Bulletin de Liaison du Centre International d'Étude des Textiles Anciens.* v. 21-Lyon, 1965– .
Annual bibliography of books and periodical articles on the history, restoration and preservation of all kinds of textiles, including costume. A standard reference tool for serious study of the history of textiles.

1055   Wilckens, Leonie von. "Textilien in Westeuropa. Literatur von 1945-1961," in: *Zeitschrift für Kunstgeschichte*, v. 24, 1961, pp. 261-75.
Excellent, scholarly essay critically evaluating the scholarly literature, books and periodical articles, that appeared on all aspects of Western textiles between 1945 and 1961. The works are cited in footnotes.

DICTIONARIES AND ENCYCLOPEDIAS

1056   **AF Encyclopedia of Textiles.** By the Editors of American Fabrics Magazine. 2nd ed. Englewood Cliffs, N.J., Prentice Hall, 1972. 636p. illus. index. LC 70-167915.
Comprehensive encyclopedia with emphasis on materials and techniques. Part two, covering the history and origin of textiles, has a section on inventors and inventions in textile manufacture. Part eight treats textile terminology.

1057   Harmuth, Louis. **Dictionary of Textiles.** 2nd ed. New York, Fairchild, 1920. 222p. illus.
Good, serious, comprehensive dictionary of textiles. Although the emphasis is on technique, materials and manufacture, there is much related to historical and modern textiles. No bibliography.

1058   Heiden, Max. **Handwörterbuch der Textilkunde aller Zeiten und Völker für Studierende, Fabrikanten, Kaufleute, Sammler und Zeichner der Gewerbe, Stickereien, Spitzen, Teppiche . . .** Stuttgart, Enke, 1904. 664p. illus.
Older comprehensive dictionary of textiles covering mechanized textile manufacture as well as terms applicable to the history of traditional textiles. Still a useful reference tool.

1059   Linton, George E. **The Modern Textile Dictionary**. New York, Duell,
        Sloan and Pearce, 1954. 772p. illus.
Good, general dictionary of textile terminology, with emphasis on modern materials.
Appendix provides a brief list of books on textile technology.

GENERAL HISTORIES AND HANDBOOKS

1060   Birrell, Verla L. **The Textile Arts**. New York, Harper, 1959. 524p. illus.
        index.
Popular handbook of world textiles, with emphasis on techniques of historical and
recent times. Illustrated with representative examples and detailed sketches of
weaves and of looms and other machinery. Glossary of terms. Bibliography,
pp. 493-500, lists books in all languages.

1061   Dreger, Moriz. **Künstlerische Entwicklung der Weberei und Stickerei**.
        Vienna, K. K. Hof- und Staatsdruckerei, 1904. 3v. illus. index.
Comprehensive scholarly history of Western textiles from late Roman times to the
early nineteenth century. Illustrated with museum pieces. Thorough bibliographical
footnotes throughout. A classic, pioneering work. Although out of date in many
details, it is still one of the best histories of textiles emphasizing the artistic
development.

1062   Falke, Otto von. **Decorative Silks** . . . New ed. New York, Helburn, 1922.
        47p. (text) 126 plates.
Good serious illustrated history of Western patterned silks from the fourth century
to about 1800, with a short section on Oriental silk tapestries. Good plates with
descriptive captions. No bibliography.

1063   Glazier, Richard. **Historic Textile Fabrics, a Short History of the Tradition
        and Development of Pattern in Woven & Printed Stuffs** . . . London,
        Batsford; New York, Scribner's, 1923. 119p. illus. index.
Serious history of world woven textiles from ancient Greece through the eighteenth
century. Chapters on materials, weaving, printing methods, and dyeing. Bibliography,
pp. 115-16, lists basic books in English, German, and French.

1064   Hunter, George L. **Decorative Textiles; an Illustrated Book on Coverings
        for Furniture, Walls and Floors** . . . Philadelphia and London, Lippincott;
        Grand Rapids, Mich., The Dean-Hicks Co., 1918. 457p. illus. index.
Good, serious history/handbook of textiles used in interior decoration. Covers all
types: woven and embroidered textiles, lace, wallpapers and leather. Excellent
collection of plates. Glossary of terms. Good classified and annotated bibliography,
pp. 438-47, of books in Western languages (all in the Library of the Metropolitan
Museum of Art, New York). An old standard work.

1065   Jaques, Renate, and Ernst Flemming. **Encyclopedia of Textiles, Decorative Fabrics from Antiquity to the Beginning of the 19th Century Including the Far East and Peru.** New York, Praeger, 1958. 32p. (text), 500 illus. LC 58-8171.

Good, pictorial handbook of world textiles. An introductory essay, covering history from ancient Egypt to the early nineteenth century, is followed by a good corpus of chronologically arranged plates of museum pieces. No bibliography.

1066   Migeon, Gaston. **Les arts du tissu** . . . Nouv. éd., revue et augmentée. Paris, Renouard, 1929. 468p. illus.

Older comprehensive history of world textiles from Sassanian Persia to Europe and the Far East in the nineteenth century. Arranged by types, then by country and period. Bibliographies at the end of each chapter. Chronological table.

1067   Schmidt, Heinrich J. **Alte Seidenstoffe; ein Handbuch für Sammler und Liebhaber.** Braunschweig, Klinkhardt & Biermann, 1958. 483p. illus. index. (Bibliothek für Kunst- und Antiquitätenfreunde, Bd. 10)

Excellent, scholarly history/handbook of world patterned silks from earliest times through the eighteenth century. Chapters on collecting and care.

1068   Weibel, Adèle Coulin. **Two Thousand Years of Textiles; the Figured Textiles of Europe and the Near East.** New York, Pantheon, 1952. 169p. illus. Reprint: New York, Hacker, 1972. LC 77-143367.

Good, scholarly history from prehistoric times to the end of the eighteenth century, with introduction treating materials and techniques. Illustrated with pieces in U.S. museums, with descriptive catalog. Bibliography, pp. 165-67, is a good list of books and periodical articles in all languages.

PRE-COLUMBIAN TEXTILES

1069   Bird, Junius, and Louisa Bellinger. **Parcas Fabrics and Nazca Needlework.** Washington, National Publishing Co., 1954. 126p. illus. index.

Excellent, scholarly history/handbook of pre-Hispanic Peruvian textiles, with emphasis on the technique. Good plates with very thorough catalog, numerous charts and diagrams, and list of terms. Bibliography, pp. 117-22 is an excellent, critically annotated list of books and periodical articles in all languages.

1070   Harcourt, Raoul d'. **Textiles of Ancient Peru and Their Techniques.** Seattle, University of Washington Press, 1962. 186p. illus. index. LC 62-17150.

Revised edition and translation of the author's *Les textiles anciens du Pérou et leurs techniques* (Paris, 1935). Good, scholarly history with emphasis on technique. Good selection of plates (poorly reproduced from 1935 edition) with descriptive notes. Bibliography, pp. 141-46, is a chronological list of basic books and periodical articles.

1071   Means, Philip A. **Peruvian Textiles.** New York, Metropolitan Museum of
        Art, 1930. 27p. (text), 24 plates.
Good, serious handbook of Peruvian textiles of the pre-Hispanic period. Plates
illustrate pieces from the collections of the Metropolitan Museum of Art; they
are accompanied by an excellent descriptive catalog. Bibliography of basic books.

1072   O'Neale, Lila M. **Textile Periods of Ancient Peru.** Berkeley, Calif., University
        of California Press, 1930. 188p. illus. index.
Good, scholarly history/handbook of pre-Hispanic Peruvian textiles. Part one deals
with the Nazca region, Part two, the Parcas. Plates with detailed catalog. Glossary,
bibliographical footnotes.

1073   Vanstan, I. **The Fabrics of Peru.** Leigh-on-Sea, England, F. Lewis, 1966. 16p.
        (text), 60p. (illus.).
Pictorial survey of pre-Columbian textiles in Peru. Brief introductory text and
descriptive notes to the plates are followed by good selection of plates. No
bibliography.

AMERICAN TEXTILES (U.S.)

1074   Little, Frances. **Early American Textiles** . . . New York and London,
        Century, 1931. 267p. illus. index.
Popular history of American textiles from the seventeenth through mid-nineteenth
centuries. Bibliography, pp. 249-53, is an unclassified list of major books and
periodical articles.

1075   Pettit, Florence H. **America's Printed and Painted Fabrics; 1600-1900.**
        New York, Hastings House, 1970. 256p. illus. index.
Popular history with good chapter on methods of printing and painting textiles.
Excellent plates with descriptive captions. List of major textile exhibitions,
p. 242, and bibliography listing books and periodical articles, pp. 245-47.

EUROPEAN TEXTILES

1076   Algoud, Henri. **La soie, art et histoire.** Paris, Payot, 1928. 255p. illus.
Good serious history of Western patterned silks from antiquity to the early twentieth
century. No bibliography.

1077   Branting, Agnes, and Andreas Lindblom. **Medieval Embroideries and
        Textiles in Sweden.** Stockholm, Almquist & Wiksells Boktryck, 1932.
        2v. illus. index.
Excellent, scholarly history of woven and embroidered textiles, both foreign and
Swedish, from the tenth to the mid-fifteen century. Excellent collection of plates
with descriptive captions. No bibliography. A standard work.

1078   Clouzot, Henri. **Painted and Printed Fabrics; the History of the Manufactory at Jouy and Other Ateliers in France 1760-1815** . . . New Haven, Yale University Press, 1927. 108p. illus. index.
Scholarly history/handbook of French printed and painted textiles, with a note on printed cottons in England and America (pp. 75-89). Useful appendix lists centers of cotton printing in France from 1760 to 1815. Bibliography, pp. 91-96, is an unclassified list of books in all languages.

1079   Cole, Alan Summerly. **Ornament in European Silks.** London, Debenham & Freebody, 1899. 220p. illus. index.
Older, serious history of European patterned silks from the sixth through the eighteenth centuries, with chapters on Islamic and Byzantine silks. Includes embroidered pieces. Plates with descriptive captions. No bibliography.

1080   Hunton, W. Gordon. **English Decorative Textiles; Tapestry and Chintz, Their Design and Development from the Earliest Times to the Nineteenth Century.** London, Tiranti, 1930. 9p. (text), 18 plates.
Illustrated survey with brief introductory essay and descriptive captions. Bibliography, p. 10, lists books and museum catalogs.

1081   Jaques, Renate. **Deutsche Textilkunst: ihrer Entwicklung bis zur Gegenwart** . . . Berlin, Rembrandt Verlag, 1942. 319p. illus. index.
Good, serious history of German textiles from the Romanesque to the early twentieth century. Illustrated with museum pieces. No bibliography.

1082   Kendrick, Albert F. **English Decorative Fabrics of the Sixteenth to Eighteenth Centuries** . . . Benfleet, England, Lewis, 1934. 88p. illus. index.
Good, popular history covering embroidery, carpets, and tapestry. Good plates with descriptive notes. Emphasis on style rather than technique.

1083   Majkowski, Karol. **Polish Textiles.** Leigh-on-Sea, England, Lewis, 1968. 62p. illus.
Pictorial survey of Polish textiles from the early Middle Ages through the nineteenth century. No bibliography.

1084   Montgomery, Florence M. **Printed Textiles; English and American Cotton and Linens, 1700-1850.** New York, Viking, 1970. 379p. illus. index.
Good, serious history with section on use. Part one is a history and discussion of trade and use; Part two, a catalog of classes of printed cottons and linens. Excellent illustrations with good descriptive captions. Contemporary prices occasionally given. Good classified and annotated bibliography of books, periodical articles and catalogs, pp. 361-71.

1085   Percival, Maciver. **The Chintz Book** . . . London, Heinemann, 1923. 103p. illus.
Serious handbook/history of printed cotton chintz from circa 1630 to 1800 covering English, French and occasionally Indian products. Section on manufacture, list of

important dates in the history of printed cottons, and glossary of terms. Good collection of plates. Brief bibliography of basic books in English, French and German.

1086   Podreider, Fanny. **Storia dei tessuti d'arte in Italia, sècolo XII-XVIII.**
        Bergamo, Istituto Italiano d'Arti Grafiche, 1928. 312p. illus. index.
Good, serious history of Italian textiles of the twelfth through the eighteenth centuries with chapters on technique and guide to collection of textiles in Italian museums. Bibliographical footnotes.

1087   Potrescu, Paul. **Romanian Textiles.** Leigh-on-Sea, England, Lewis, 1966.
        71p. illus.
Pictorial survey from the early Middle Ages through the nineteenth century. No bibliography.

1088   Réal, Daniel. **Tissus espagnoles et portugais.** Paris, Calavas, 1925. 9p.
        (text), 49 plates.
Pictorial survey of Spanish and Portuguese textiles from the ninth to the twentieth centuries. Brief introductory essay is followed by plates with descriptive captions. No bibliography.

1089   Santangelo, Antonino. **Tessuti d'arte italiani dal XII° al XVIII° sècolo.**
        Milan, Electra, 1959. 241p. illus. index. LC A60-2242.
Good, serious history of Italian textiles from the early twelfth through the eighteenth centuries. Well illustrated with color plates with descriptive captions. Bibliography, pp. 55-57, is an unclassified list of books and periodical articles.

1090   Santangelo, Antonino. **A Treasury of Great Italian Textiles.** New York,
        Abrams, 1964. 239p. illus. index. LC 64-14691.
Good, serious history of Italian textiles from the early twelfth through the eighteenth centuries. Well illustrated with color plates, which have descriptive captions. Bibliography, pp. 55-57, is an unclassified list of books and periodical articles chiefly in Italian.

1091   Thornton, Peter. **Baroque and Rococo Silks.** New York, Taplinger, 1965.
        209p. illus. index. LC 65-14391 rev.
Good, scholarly history of Western European silk textiles from 1640 to 1770 covering technique, manufacture, style and ornament. Good selection of plates with informative notes; separate bibliographies for each piece illustrated. Additional bibliographic references in the footnotes to the text.

1092   Volbach, Wolfgang F. **Early Decorative Textiles.** London and New York,
        Hamlyn, 1969. 157p. illus. LC 79-437236.
Good, popular illustrated survey of Western textiles from Coptic Egypt through the eleventh century in Byzantium. Well-chosen illustrations. No bibliography.

1093   Walton, Perry. **The Story of Textiles; a Bird's-eye View of the History of the Beginning and the Growth of the Industry by Which Mankind Is Clothed.** New York, Tudor, 1937. 274p. illus. index.
Popular history of Western textiles from prehistoric times to the early twentieth century, with emphasis on the development of textile technology. No bibliography.

1094   Weigert, Roger-Armand. **Textiles en Europe sous Louis XV.** Fribourg, Office du Livre, 1964. 168p. illus.
Good, scholarly history of woven and embroidered textiles from 1720 to 1735 in the Richelieu Collection. Historical introduction appears in English at end. Excellent plates with descriptive notes. No bibliography.

1095   Ysselsteyn, G. T. van. **White Figurated Linen Damask from the 15th to the Beginning of the 19th Century.** The Hague, Van Goor Zonen, 1962. 255p. illus. index.
Good, serious history. Excellent selection of plates with detailed descriptive catalog; each entry has a bibliography. The bibliography on pp. 192-196 lists basic books in all languages.

ORIENTAL TEXTILES

1096   Bunt, Cyril, G. E. **Persian Fabrics.** Leigh-on-Sea, England, F. Lewis, 1963. 9p. (text), 55p. (illus.).
Pictorial survey from the sixth century to the end of the nineteenth century. No bibliography.

1097   Gunsaulus, Helen C. **Japanese Textiles.** New York, Japan Society of New York, 1941. 94p. illus.
Popular handbook/history covering Japanese textiles from 463 A.D. to the mid-nineteenth century. Good plates with good descriptive notes. Bibliography, pp. 93-94, lists books and periodical articles in English and Japanese.

1098   Kybalová, Ludmilla. **Coptic Textiles.** London, Hamlyn, 1967. 157p. illus. LC 68-98613.
Good, popular history/handbook of Coptic textiles with chapters on the history of the Copts, the relationship of textiles to Coptic major arts, technique, and symbolism. Illustrated with examples in East European museums. One-page bibliography of basic books in all languages.

1099   Langewis, Laurens, and Fritz A. Wagner. **Decorative Art in Indonesian Textiles.** Amsterdam, Van der Peet, 1964. 211p. illus.
Good, well-illustrated survey of nineteenth and twentieth century Indonesian textiles. Brief bibliography, pp. 44-45, lists basic books in all languages.

1100   Öz, Tahsin. **Turkish Textiles and Velvets.** Ankara, Turkish Press Broadcasting and Tourist Department, 1950. 119p. illus.
Popular history from the fourteenth through the sixteenth centuries. Illustrated with color plates of museum pieces with explanatory notes and works of art depicting the use of textiles in Turkey during the period under study. Some bibliographical footnotes.

1101   Réal, Daniel. **Tissus des Indes Néerlandaises.** Paris, Calavas, n.d. 6p. (text), 49 plates.
Pictorial survey of Indonesian textiles of the pre-Colonial period, with brief introductory essay. No bibliography.

1102   Reath, Nancy A., and Eleanor B. Sachs. **Persian Textiles and Their Technique from the Sixth to the Eighteenth Centuries** . . . New Haven, Yale University Press; London, Milford, Oxford University Press, 1937. 133p. illus. index.
Scholarly history/handbook with emphasis on the evolution of technique. Table of textile classification. Definitions of terms. Good selection of plates with descriptive notes. No bibliography.

1103   Riefstahl, R. M. **Persian and Indian Textiles from the Late Sixteenth to the Early Nineteenth Century.** New York, Weyhe, 1923. 14p. (text), 36 plates.
Good, serious pictorial survey with introductory essay on the historical development and descriptive captions of the well-chosen plates. No bibliography.

1104   Volbach, Wolfgang F., and Ernst Kühnel. **Late Antique Coptic and Islamic Textiles of Egypt.** New York, Weyhe, 1926. 15p. (text), 100 plates.
Good, illustrated survey with brief but excellent scholarly introduction. Excellent plates with short descriptive captions. No bibliography.

1105   Wiet, Gaston. **Soieries persanes.** Cairo, Institut Français d'Archéologie Oriental, 1947. 251p. illus.
Good, scholarly history of Persian silks of the ancient and medieval periods. Modestly illustrated with black and white plates and maps. List of collections. Good bibliography of books, periodical articles and catalogs, pp. xi-xix.

AFRICAN TEXTILES

1106   Boser-Sarivaxévanis, Renée. **Les tissus de l'Afrique Occidentale. Tome 1: Sénégal, Gambie, Mali, Haute-Volta, Niger, Guinée portugaise, Guinée, Sierre Leone, Libéria, Côte d'Ivoire, Ghana.** Basel, 1972. 227p. illus. index. (Basler Beiträge zur Ethnologie, 13). LC 73-310716.
Good, scholarly handbook of West African textiles providing a detailed classification by technique, use, material and decoration. Bibliographical footnotes.

1107   Clouzot, Henri. **Tissue Nègres**. Paris, Calavas, n.d. 7p. (text), 48 illus.
Pictorial survey of sub-Saharan textiles with brief introductory essay. No
bibliography.

1108   Sieber, Roy. **African Textiles and Decorative Arts**. New York, Museum
        of Modern Art, 1972. 239p. illus. LC 72-76268.
Good serious, illustrated survey covering costume, painted and dyed textiles,
scarification, jewelry and woven textiles. Illustrated with examples from the
eighteenth, nineteenth and twentieth centuries in a special exhibition at The
Museum of Modern Art in New York. Good classified bibliography of books
and periodical articles, pp. 230-38, compiled by Roslyn Walker Randall.

CARPETS AND RUGS

General Histories and Handbooks

1109   Franses, Jack. **European and Oriental Rugs for Pleasure and Investment**.
        New York, Arco, 1970. 176p. illus. index. LC 75-123397.
Popular handbook of carpets for the beginning collector, with emphasis on nine-
teenth and twentieth century examples. Covers Islamic world, Europe, India and
China.

1110   Holt, Rosa B. **Oriental & Occidental Rugs, Antique & Modern** . . . New
        and rev. ed. Garden City, N.Y., Garden City Publishing Co., 1937. 208p.
        illus. index.
Older popular handbook with chapters on history of rug weaving in the Orient,
Europe and the United States. Dated bibliography, pp. 175-78.

1111   Hubel, Reinhard G. **The Book of Carpets**. New York, Praeger, 1970.
        347p. illus. index. LC 71-107152.
A good, serious handbook/history of Western and Oriental carpets. Introductory
chapters cover the early history of the carpet, production, structure, material,
colors, dyeing, design and pattern; these are followed by well-illustrated chapters
on the major regions of carpet production. Plates, which illustrate primarily pieces
within reach of the experienced collector, have very detailed notes with much
information concerning technique. Useful chapters on collecting and care of
carpets. Good bibliography, pp. 345-46, lists books in all languages.

1112   Kendrick, Albert F., and Creassey E. C. Tattersall. **Hand-woven Carpets,
        Oriental and European** . . . New York, Scribner's, 1922. 2v. illus.
Popular history/handbook with good selection of plates of both museum pieces
and pieces accessible to the collector. Brief, dated bibliography, pp. 193-94.

1113   Schlosser, Ignace. **The Book of Rugs–Oriental and European.** New York, Crown, 1963. 318p. illus. index. LC 62-11812.
Good, popular history/handbook of Western and Oriental carpets. Text consists of an historical and regional outline followed by a catalog of nineteenth and twentieth century rugs illustrating examples of interest to the average collector. Also includes chapters on techniques (with good weaving drawings), glossary of terms; bibliography, pp. 307-09, lists books in all languages.

European Carpets and Rugs

1114   Campana, P. Michele. **European Carpets.** Feltham, England, and New York, Hamlyn, 1969. 158p. illus. LC 70-550059.
Popular history of carpets in Spain, Portugal, England and France well illustrated with color plates of museum pieces. Emphasis on eighteenth and nineteenth century carpets. No bibliography.

1115   Faraday, Cornelia B. **European and American Carpets and Rugs** . . . Grand Rapids, Mich., Dean-Hicks, 1929. 383p. illus. index.
Good, serious history of non-Oriental carpets up to the twentieth century. Contains a chapter on technique. Includes machine-made carpets and American Indian rugs. No bibliography. An old standard work.

1116   Tattersall, Creassey E. C. **A History of British Carpets, from the Introduction of the Craft until the Present Day** . . . New rev. and enl. ed. Leigh-on-Sea, England, F. Lewis, 1966. 139p. illus.
Good, serious history from the sixteenth through the twentieth century, including machine-made carpets. List of carpet manufacturers includes short histories of the firms. Section on historical carpets has good descriptive notes to the plates, plus bibliographical references.

1117   Weeks, Jeanne G., and Donald Treganowan. **Rugs and Carpets of Europe and the Western World.** Philadelphia, Chilton, 1969. 251p. illus. index. LC 70-99605.
Popular history of rug weaving in Spain, France, Great Britain, Scandinavia, Greece and America. Section on America also includes American Indian rugs. Illustrated with pieces in museums and private collections. Bibliography, pp. 243-44, is a brief list by title.

Oriental Carpets and Rugs

General Histories and Handbooks

1118   Bronimann, André. **Splendeur du tapis d'Orient.** Paris, La Bibliothèque des Arts, 1974. 242p. illus.
Good, serious history/handbook of Islamic carpets, with emphasis on technique and production. Maps, glossary of terms, and appendix with documents and statistics relating to trade in Oriental carpets. Well illustrated. No bibliography.

1119   Calatchi, Robert de. **Oriental Carpets.** Rutland, Vt., Tuttle, 1967. 223p.
        illus. index. LC 67-28904.
Popular collector's handbook covering all major regions that produce Oriental
carpets, including China. Useful but too brief chapter on motifs and symbolism.
Catalog, pp. 206-15, provides useful comparisons of decorative motifs in various
regions through juxtaposed photographic details. Bibliography, p. 217, lists books
in English.

1120   Campana, R. Michele. **Oriental Carpets.** London and New York, Hamlyn,
        1969. 157p. illus. LC 70-437385.
Popular handbook of all major classes of Oriental carpets, with a chapter on the
historical and technical background. Good selection of color plates illustrating
chiefly pieces from the nineteenth and twentieth centuries. No bibliography.

1121   Dilley, Arthur U. **Oriental Rugs and Carpets; A Comprehensive Study.**
        New York and London, Scribner's, 1931. 303p. illus. index. Reprint:
        Philadelphia, Lippincott, 1959. LC 59-13247.
A serious history/handbook of Oriental carpets written by one of the best
connoisseurs of the past. A treasury of much useful information despite its age.

1122   Edwards, A Cecil. **The Persian Carpet.** 4th ed. London, Duckworth, 1974.
        384p. illus. index.
Good, serious handbook with introduction on craft and carpets of the great period.
Appendix with chronological table. Some bibliographical footnotes. Well illustrated
with emphasis on nineteenth and twentieth century pieces.

1123   Erdmann, Kurt. **Oriental Carpets: An Essay on Their History.** New York,
        Universe, 1960. 78p. illus. index. LC 60-14504.
Excellent, scholarly history of Oriental carpets through the sixteenth century.
Chapter on the role of Oriental rugs in Europe. Excellent bibliography, pp. 59-69,
is a classified list of books, catalogs and periodical articles in all languages.

1124   Erdmann, Kurt. **Seven Hundred Years of Oriental Carpets.** Berkeley,
        University of California Press, 1970. 238p. illus. index. LC 69-12473.
Scholarly history/handbook of Oriental carpets with an important chapter on
Spanish and other early European carpets. Chapters treat special problems as well
as histories of major regional styles. Excellent chapter on the great rug collection
formerly in the Kaiser-Friedrich-Museum, Berlin. Thorough notes to the plates
and footnotes to text give reference to specialized literature. A standard work on
Oriental carpets by one of the leading scholars in the field.

1125   Formenton, Fabio. **Oriental Rugs and Carpets.** New York, McGraw-Hill,
        1972. 251p. illus. index. LC 71-179881.
A good, popular handbook of Oriental carpets covering Turkey, Caucasia, Iran,
Turkestan and China. Well illustrated with more recent carpets within the reach
of the average collector.

1126   Gans-Ruedin, Erwin. **The Connoisseur's Guide to Oriental Carpets.**
        Rutland, Vt., Tuttle, 1971. 430p. illus. index. LC 70-157255.
Good, serious handbook covering Islamic, Central Asian, Chinese, Indian and Balkan
carpets. Has chapters on the history, technique and collecting of Oriental carpets.
Well illustrated with pieces from the late nineteenth and twentieth centuries. One-
page bibliography of basic books.

1127   Grote-Hasenbalg, Werner. **Der Orientteppich. Seine Geschichte und seine
        Kultur.** Berlin, Scarabaeus, 1922. 3v. illus. index.
Good, older handbook of Oriental carpets including China and India and with
chapters on technique, aesthetic, use, care and collecting. Good selection of plates
with emphasis on nineteenth and early twentieth century pieces. No bibliography.

1128   Hackmack, Adolf. **Chinese Carpets and Rugs.** Tientsin, China, Librairie
        Française, 1924. 78p. illus. index. Reprint: New York, Dover, 1973.
        LC 72-93765.
Popular handbook with emphasis on early twentieth century pieces. Chapters on
development, color, design and weave. No bibliography.

1129   Hawley, Walter A. **Oriental Rugs, Antique and Modern.** New York, Tudor,
        1937. 320p. illus. index. Reprint: New York, Dover, 1970. LC 79-105665.
Serious handbook of Oriental rugs and carpets for the beginning and experienced
collector. Covers rugs of Persia, Asia Minor, Central Asia and China. Emphasis on
technique of weaving. Although written over sixty years ago, it is still useful for its
detailed analysis of weaves and its charts of comparative ornamental motifs.

1130   Hopf, Albrecht. **Oriental Carpets and Rugs.** New York, Viking, 1962. 140p.
        illus. index. LC 62-11771.
Popular handbook excluding India and China. Consists of brief essays on the various
regions followed by plates of pieces dating from the eighteenth through the twentieth
centuries, with descriptive notes. No bibliography.

1131   Jacobsen, Charles W. **Oriental Rugs, a Complete Guide.** Rutland, Vt., Tuttle,
        1962. 479p. illus. LC 62-14117.
Popular handbook of Oriental rugs and carpets for the beginning collector, written
by a major dealer. Covers Chinese, Indian and Balkan rugs as well as Islamic rugs.
Chapters on collecting, uses, and care with much helpful information. Illustrated
with collectible pieces in the antique, semi-antique and new classes.

1132   Kühnel, Ernst, and Wilhelm von Bode. **Antique Rugs from the Near East.**
        4th ed. Braunschweig, Klinkhardt und Biermann, 1958. 180p. illus.
Scholarly history of early Near Eastern carpets, covering those made before the
eighteenth century in Turkey, Caucasia, Egypt, Persia and India. Illustrated with
pieces in major European museums. Excellent annotated bibliography, pp. 176-79.
A standard history of early Islamic carpets.

1133   Larson, Knut. **Rugs and Carpets of the Orient.** London, F. Warne, 1967.
        219p. illus. index. LC 67-91266 rev.
Popular handbook including China, India and Pakistan with chapters on material,
technique, collecting and care. Glossary of Oriental terms. Illustrated with nineteenth and twentieth century pieces, with emphasis on pieces produced since 1941.
No bibliography.

1134   Lewis, George G. **The Practical Book of Oriental Carpets . . .** New rev. ed.
        Philadelphia and New York, Lippincott, 1945. 317p. illus. index.
Older, popular handbook with chapters on technique, decoration and symbolism,
and on the major regions and centers of Oriental rug production. Bibliography,
pp. 307-309, is a good guide to the older literature.

1135   Liebetrau, Preben. **Oriental Rugs in Color.** New York, Macmillan, 1963.
        131p. illus. index. LC 63-18408.
Popular handbook of Oriental carpets and rugs covering Islamic and Chinese
examples. Brief but factual text, with chapters on technique, material, decoration,
and collecting as well as chapters covering the major regional types. Descriptive
notes to the plates, and brief bibliography.

1136   Mumford, John K. **Oriental Rugs . . .** New York, Scribner's, 1929. 278p.
        illus. index.
Serious handbook of Oriental rugs and carpets, excluding Chinese. Chapters on
technique, materials and history, and useful tables of technical features of the
various regional types. No bibliography.

1137   Neugebauer, Rudolf, and Siegfried Troll. **Handbuch der orientalischen
        Teppichkunde.** Leipzig, Hiersemann, 1930. 111p. illus. index.
Good, older serious handbook of Oriental rugs and carpets, including central Asian
but excluding Chinese. Good chapter on the development before 1800. Chapters
on technique, design, care and collecting. Bibliographical footnotes.

1138   Orendi, Julius. **Das Gesamtwissen über antike und neue Teppiche des
        Orients.** Vienna, Julius Orendi, 1930. 2v. illus.
Useful handbook in the form of 312 alphabetically arranged essays on various
aspects of the history, collecting, care, identification and use of Oriental rugs
and carpets. No bibliography.

1139   Reed, Stanley. **Oriental Rugs and Carpets.** New York, Putnam, 1967.
        120p. illus. LC 67-21989.
Popular history/handbook concentrating on Islamic rugs. Introductory chapter
on history is followed by brief chapters on the major regions. No bibliography.

1140   Ropers, Hinrich. **Morgenländische Teppiche; ein Handbuch für Sammler
        und Liebhaber.** 9th ed. Braunschweig, Klinkhardt & Biermann, 1961. 331p.
        illus. index. (Bibliothek für Kunst- und Antiquitätenfreunde, Bd. 19).
        LC 66-75973.

Good, serious handbook of Oriental carpets including China and India. Arranged by region, it contains chapters on manufacture, ornament, care and collecting. Emphasis is on nineteenth and twentieth century pieces. One-page bibliography of basic books in all languages.

1141   Sarre, Friedrich, and Hermann Trenkwald. **Old Oriental Carpets.** Vienna, Schroll, 1926-29. 2v. illus. index.
Scholarly history/handbook concentrating on penetrating analyses of sixty outstanding examples of early Islamic carpets, most in the Österreichisches Museum für Kunst und Industrie in Vienna. Although old, the illustrations are of extraordinary quality. Very thorough bibliography, Vol. 2, pp. 37-42, compiled by Kurt Erdmann. A classic and standard work on Oriental carpets.

1142   Schürmann, Ulrich. **Oriental Carpets.** London, Hamlyn, 1966. 80p. illus.
Popular handbook covering the rugs and carpets of Asia Minor, North Africa, Persia, Caucasia, Central Asia, India, Pakistan and China. Each region is introduced with a brief description and history, followed by good plates of both early and later examples with brief descriptive notes.

1143   Turkhan, Kudret H. **Islamic Rugs.** New York, Praeger, 1969. 112p. illus. index. LC 73-75418.
Popular collector's handbook covering carpets made in Persia, Turkey, Caucasia and Armenia. Chapters on history and construction as well as chapters describing the major regional types. Good maps and diagrams of weaves.

Caucasian and Central Asian Carpets and Rugs

1144   Bidder, Hans. **Carpets from Eastern Turkestan, Known as Khotan, Samarkand and Kansu Carpets.** New York, Universe, 1964. 96p. illus. LC 64-22109.
Excellent, scholarly history/handbook, with emphasis on the carpets of Khotan. The art historical background, manufacture and trade are all thoroughly treated, together with the identification of types. Good selection of plates and diagrams. Extensive bibliographical footnotes.

1145   Schürmann, Ulrich. **Central-Asian Rugs.** London, Allen and Unwin, 1970. 176p. illus. LC 70-569162.
Good, serious handbook of Turkoman carpets including Afghanistani, Belouchi and East-Turkestan work. Concentrates on eighteenth and nineteenth century examples. Excellent plates with good descriptive captions. Map, bibliographical footnotes and classified bibliography, pp. 75-76, of books and periodical articles chiefly in German.

1146   Tschebull, Raoul. **Kazak; Carpets of the Caucasus.** New York, Near Eastern Art Research Center, 1971. 104p. illus. LC 78-165292.
Good popular collector's handbook of nineteenth and early twentieth century Caucasian rugs. Brief introduction is followed by good plates with descriptive notes. Bibliography, pp. 100-101, lists books in English.

Chinese Carpets and Rugs

1147   Lorentz, H. A. **A View of Chinese Rugs from the 17th to the 18th Century.**
London and Boston, Routledge Kegan Paul, 1972. 194p. illus. index.
Good, serious handbook/history of Chinese and Central Asian rugs and carpets.
Well illustrated. Good bibliography, pp. 185-88, lists books and periodical articles
in all languages. Additional bibliography in the footnotes.

1148   Ripley, Mary C. **The Chinese Rug Book** . . . New York, Stokes, 1927.
66p. illus.
Popular handbook with chapters on history, technique, colors, designs and classification. No bibliography.

EMBROIDERY

Dictionaries and Encyclopedias

1149   Caulfield, Sophia F. A., and Blanche C. Saward. **The Dictionary of
Needlework, and Encyclopaedia of Artistic, Plain and Fancy Needlework** . . .
2nd ed. London, Gill, 1885. 528p. illus.
Old but still useful dictionary treating terms, materials, techniques and designs of
historical and modern needlework. Numerous useful line drawings. No bibliography.

1150   Dillmont, Thérèse de. **Encyclopedia of Needlework.** New ed. rev. and enl.
Mulhouse. France, T. de Dillmont, n.d. 809p. illus.
Older, popular handbook of Western needlework, with emphasis on techniques and
identification. Includes hand and machine work in embroidery, plain sewing,
knitting, tapestry, crochet work, tatting, macramé, netting, laces and needlework
trimmings. No bibliography.

General Histories and Handbooks

1151   Antrobus, Mary S., and Louisa Preece. **Needle Work Through the Ages;
a Short Survey of Its Development in Decorative Art** . . . London, Hodder
and Stoughton, 1928. 413p. illus. index.
Good, older, serious history of embroidery from ancient times to the end of the
nineteenth century. Good collection of plates arranged chronologically. Bibliography, pp. 391-98, lists books and periodical articles chiefly in English.

1152   Christie, Grace. **Embroidery and Tapestry Weaving; a Practical Text-book
of Design and Workmanship** . . . London, Hogg, 1906. 414p. illus. index.
4th ed. London, Putnam, 1933. 403p. illus. index.
Good, serious handbook of embroidery and tapestry weaving, particularly useful
for the numerous illustrations of stitches and weaves. No bibliography.

1153   Christie, Grace. **Samplers and Stitches; a Handbook of the Embroiderer's Art** . . . London, Batsford; New York, Dutton, 1929. 144p. illus. 4th ed. New York, Hearthside Press, 1959. 152p. illus. LC 59-15824.
Good, serious handbook to the various stitches, methods, and techniques of embroidery. Many useful diagrams of weaves and stitches. No bibliography.

1154   Farcy, Louis de. **La broderie du XIe siècle jusqu'à nos jours d'après des spécimens authentiques et les anciens inventaires.** Angers, Belhomme, 3 portfolios. 1890-1900.
Good, older history of Western embroidery from the early Middle Ages to the middle of the nineteenth century, arranged by countries and periods. Bibliographical footnotes. Classic pioneering history of embroidery.

1155   Johnstone, Pauline. **The Byzantine Tradition in Church Embroidery.** London, Tiranti, 1967. 144p. illus. index.
Good, serious history with chapters on iconography, ornament, inscriptions and technique. Appendix with list of Byzantine church vestments. Good bibliography, pp. 132-35, of books and periodical articles. Further literature in the footnotes.

1156   Jones, Mary E. **A History of Western Embroidery.** London, Studio Vista; New York, Watson-Guptill, 1969. 159p. illus. index. LC 77-83369.
Good, popular history of European and American embroidery from ancient Egypt to twentieth century America. Covers all classes including ecclesiastical and folk embroidery. Chapter on the evolution of technique. Glossary of terms, list of museums in Britain and America with noted collections of embroidery. One-page bibliography of basic books in English.

1157   Millet, Gabriel. **Broderies religieuses du style Byzantin.** Paris, Presses Universitaires de France, 1947. 117p. illus.
Good, scholarly history of Byzantine religious embroideries. Part one treats vestments, Part two altar paraments. Bibliographical footnotes and bibliography of works cited, pp. 110-14. A standard history.

1158   Schuette, Marie, and Sigrid Müller-Christensen. **The Art of Embroidery.** London, Thames and Hudson, 1964. 336p. illus. index.
Excellent, serious history/handbook of Western embroidery from the fourth and fifth centuries A.D. to the present. Examples of Oriental embroidery are included to demonstrate links and influences. Brief historical introduction is followed by excellent selection of plates of major museum pieces, accompanied by a thorough catalog that gives descriptions and bibliographies for each piece. Good section on materials and techniques.

1159   Seligman, G. Saville, and Talbot Hughes. **Domestic Needlework, Its Origins and Customs Throughout the Centuries.** London, Country Life, 1926. 95p. illus.
Popular history of Western embroidery arranged by types of object (e.g., samplers, bookbindings, etc.). No bibliography.

National Histories and Handbooks

Germany

1160   Schuette, Marie. **Gestickte Bildteppiche und Decken des Mittelalters.**
        Leipzig, Hiersemann, 1927-30. 2v. illus.
Good scholarly history of German medieval embroideries. Volume one covers the
works in Kloster Wienhausen and Kloster Lüne; Volume two, those in Braunschweig,
Kloster Ebstorf, Kloster Isenhagen, Wernigerode, Kloster Drubeck, and Halberstadt.
Thorough catalog. Bibliographical footnotes.

Great Britain

1161   Christie, A. G. I. **English Medieval Embroidery, a Brief Survey of English
        Embroidery Dating from the Beginning of the Tenth Century until the
        End of the Fourteenth** . . . Oxford, Clarendon, 1938. 206p. illus. index.
Excellent scholarly history consisting of an introductory essay followed by a
catalog of existing pieces. Fully illustrated, with thorough bibliographical references
in the entries. Appendices give documents referring to English embroidery and
embroidery workers. A standard work on English medieval embroideries.

1162   Digby, George Wingfield. **Elizabethan Embroidery.** New York, Yoseloff,
        1964. 151p. illus. index. LC 64-54751.
Good, serious history of all classes of embroidery during the reign of Elizabeth I.
Part one deals with style and design sources and has an interesting chapter on two
important women embroiderers. Part two treats the major classes of embroidery
for furnishing. Good selection of illustrations. Good classified bibliography of
books and catalogs, pp. 142-46.

1163   Kendrick, Albert F. **English Embroidery.** London, Newnes; New York,
        Scribner's, 1905. 125p. illus. index. 2nd ed. revised by Patricia Wardle.
        London, Black, 1967. 212p. illus. index. LC 67-87510.
Good, general survey from the early Middle Ages to the beginning of the nineteenth
century. Modest but well-chosen selection of plates.

1164   Morris, Barbara J. **Victorian Embroidery.** New York, Universe, 1970.
        238p. illus. index.
Good, serious history/handbook of English and American embroidery of the
second half of the nineteenth century. Illustrated with good selection of pieces
in museums, churches and private collections. Bibliography of basic books.

Italy

1165   Ricci, Elisa. **Ricàmi italiani antichi e moderni.** Florence, Felice le Monnier,
        1925. 310p. illus.
Good, serious history of Italian embroidery from ancient Roman times to the
twentieth century. Bibliographical footnotes.

United States

1166   Kassell, Hilda. **Stitches in Time: The Art and History of Embroidery.** New
        York, Duell, Sloan and Pearce, 1967. 108p. illus. LC 67-2273.
Popular history of American embroidery from early Colonial times to the present,
with a chapter on how to execute various stitches. Bibliography, pp. 107-108, lists
basic books in English.

1167   Wheeler, Candace. **The Development of Embroidery in America.** New York
        and London, Harper, 1921. 151p. illus.
Popular history from early Colonial times to the late nineteenth century. Includes
tapestry. No bibliography.

LACE

Dictionaries and Encyclopedias

1168   Brooke, Margaret L. **Lace in the Making with Bobbins and Needle . . .**
        London, Routledge, 1923. 164p. illus. index.
Useful technical guide to the principal kinds of Western lace, a brief dictionary of
centers of lace making, and glossary of terms. Bibliography, pp. 156-58, includes
some books on the history of lace making together with works on lace technology.
Illustrated with examples in the Victoria and Albert Museum.

1169   Clifford, Chandler R. **The Lace Dictionary.** New York, Clifford & Lawton,
        1913. 156p. illus. index.
Popular dictionary covering historic and modern lace.

1170   Whiting, Gertrude. **A Lace Guide for Makers and Collectors; with Bibliog-
        raphy and Five-Language Nomenclature . . .** New York, Dutton, 1920.
        415p. illus.
Useful reference tool giving lace terminology in English, French, Italian, Spanish,
and German and clear illustrations of various types. Bibliography, pp. 243-401, is
an excellent list of nearly two thousand books, catalogs and periodical articles in
all languages.

General Histories and Handbooks

1171   Bath, Virginia C. **Lace.** Chicago, Regnery, 1974. 320p. illus. index.
        LC 73-20671.
Popular handbook of basic types, with emphasis on modern art lace. No bibliography.

1172   Caplin, Jessie F. **The Lace Book.** New York, Macmillan, 1932. 166p. illus.
        index.
Popular handbook for the identification of the chief kinds of lace, with chapter on
care, and glossary of terms. Bibliography, pp. 163-64, is a list of basic books.

1173   Frauberger, Tina. **Handbuch der Spitzkunde. Technisches und Geschichtliches
        über die Näh-, Klöppel- und Maschinenspitzen.** Leipzig, Seemann, 1894.
        272p. illus. index.
Good, older scholarly history/handbook of lace, with section on the technique of
lace making. Bibliography of basic books, p. 263. A classic and pioneering work on
lace.

1174   Head, Mrs. R. E. **The Lace & Embroidery Collector; a Guide to Collectors
        of Old Lace and Embroidery.** London, Jenkins, 1922. Reprint: Detroit,
        Gale, 1974. 252p. illus. index. LC 74-2031.
Good, popular handbook/history of European lace and embroidery from the early
Middle Ages to 1820. Glossary of terms. Appendix A gives list of ecclesiastical
embroidery in the English provinces; Appendix B is a list of basic older books.

1175   Henneberg, Alfred von. **Stil und Technik der alten Spitze.** Berlin, Wasmuth,
        1931. 181p. illus.
Excellent scholarly history/handbook of Western European lace. Part one gives a
general history of lace, Part two a detailed analysis of technique, and Part three a
developmental history of lace with emphasis on technique. Bibliographical footnotes
and general bibliography of basic books, p. 52.

1176   Jackson, Emily N. **A History of Hand-Made Lace.** London, Upcott Gill;
        New York, Scribner's, 1900. 245p. illus. index. Reprint: Detroit, Tower
        Books, 1971. LC 70-136558.
Good, older, comprehensive history of Western lace from ancient Egypt through
the nineteenth century, with chapters on ecclesiastical lace, folk lace, care and
collecting. Second part is a useful dictionary of lace, with long and short entries
treating the various types and techniques. A chapter titled "The Literature of
Lace" provides a good introduction to the older literature.

1177   Jones, Mary E. **The Romance of Lace.** London, Spring, n.d. 172p. illus.
Popular history/handbook arranged by countries. No bibliography.

1178   Jourdain, M. **Old Lace; a Handbook for Collectors . . .** London, Batsford,
        1907. 121p. illus. index.
Older popular history of Western European lace by type and country. Illustrated
with works of art illustrating lace and examples of lace in museum collections. No
bibliography.

1179   Meulen-Nulle, L. W. van der. **Lace.** New York, Universe, 1964. 79p. illus.
        index. LC 64-10343.
Good, popular handbook of lace with chapters on types of lace, use and origin of
lace. Good selection of illustrations of actual pieces and works of art depicting
persons wearing lace. Bibliography, pp. 70-71, is a good list of basic books in all
languages.

1180   Moore, H. Hudson. **The Lace Book.** New York, Tudor, 1937. 206p. illus. index.

Popular history of Italian, Flemish, French, Spanish and Irish lace with introductory chapter covering the general development. Illustrated with museum pieces and portraits of persons wearing lace. No bibliography.

1181   Morris, Frances, and Marian Hague. **Antique Laces of American Collectors.** New York, William Helburn for the Needle and Bobbin Club, 1920-26. 5v. illus. index.

Good, serious history of the laces of Italy, France and the Netherlands from the sixteenth through the eighteenth centuries. Illustrated with works in American private collections. Bibliography, vol. 5, pp. 131-35, lists basic works of reference in all languages.

1182   Overloop, E. van. **Catalogue des ouvrages se rapportant à l'industrie de la dentelle.** Brussels, H. Lamertin, 1906. 433p. illus. index.

Excellent older history of Belgian lace from the Middle Ages to 1900 featuring pieces in the Musées Royaux des Arts Décoratifs et Industriels in Brussels. Bibliographical footnotes.

1183   Palliser, Fanny M. **History of Lace, Entirely Revised, Rewritten and Enlarged Under the Editorship of M. Jourdain and Alice Dryden . . .** London, Sampson Low, Marston, 1919. 536p. illus index. Reprint: (3rd ed.). Detroit, Tower Books, 1971. LC 75-78219.

Good, older history of Western lace. Arranged by countries, with an introduction on types and techniques. Chapter on machine-made lace. Appendix with list of pattern books. Bibliographical footnotes.

1184   Pethebridge, Jeanette E. **A Manual of Lace.** London, Cassell, 1947. 71p. illus.

Popular handbook of types of lace, with brief introduction on the history, care and restoration of lace. No bibliography.

1185   Pollen, F. N. **Seven Centuries of Lace.** New York, Macmillan, 1908. 53p. illus. index.

Popular handbook/history arranged by types. Glossary of terms. Good collection of plates with descriptive captions.

1186   Powys, Marian. **Lace and Lace-making.** Boston, Branford, 1953. 219p. illus. index. LC 52-14187.

Good, popular handbook; well illustrated and with a useful key to lace types. No bibliography.

1187   Schuette, Marie. **Alte Spitzen: Nadel- und Klöppelspitzen. Ein Handbuch für Sammler und Liebhaber.** 4th ed. Braunschweig, Klinkhardt & Biermann, 1963. 247p. illus. index. (Bibliothek für Kunst- und Antiquitätenfreunde, Bd. 6)

Excellent scholarly handbook of Western lace. Part one treats technique, Part two history of lace by country. Well illustrated. Good, annotated and classified bibliography of basic books, pp. 246-47. Specialized literature in the foot-notes to the text. A standard handbook of lace.

1188   Seguin, Joseph. **La dentelle. Histoire description—fabrication—bibliographie.** Paris, J. Rothschild, 1875. 214p. illus. index.
Good, serious history/handbook of European lace illustrated with excellent engravings. In spite of its age, it is filled with much useful information.

1189   Wardle, Patricia. **Victorian Lace.** New York, Praeger, 1969. 286p. illus. index. LC 69-11863.
Good, serious history of nineteenth century lace in Belgium, England, France and Ireland including machine-made lace. Illustrations show details and entire garments. Appendix describes basic techniques. Lists of prices are given in the text. Good, classified bibliography, pp. 267-70, of books and periodical articles.

National Histories and Handbooks

Belgium

1190   Paulis. L. **Pour connaître la dentelle.** Antwerp, De Nederlandsche Boekhandel, 1947. 135p. illus. index.
Excellent, scholarly history/handbook of European lace with emphasis on Belgian work. Bibliographical footnotes.

Italy

1191   Ricci, Elisa. **Old Italian Lace.** Philadelphia, Lippincott, 1913. 2v. illus.
Good, older handbook/history arranged by type and by place of manufacture. Well illustrated. Occasional bibliographical footnote.

Spain

1192   May, Florence L. **Hispanic Lace and Lace Making.** New York, Hispanic Society of America, 1939. 417p. illus. index.
Good, serious history from the Middle Ages to the twentieth century, with section on Hispanic lace in the Azores, Philippine Islands, Mexico, and South and Central America. Bibliographical footnotes and general bibliography, pp. 400-405, lists books and periodical articles in all languages.

United States

1193   Vanderpoel, Emily N. **American Lace and Lace-makers** . . . New Haven, Yale University Press, 1924. 14p. (text), 110 plates.
Popular pictorial survey with introductory essay and descriptive notes to the well-chosen selection of plates. No bibliography.

TAPESTRY

Bibliographies

1194   Guiffrey, Jules M. J. **La tapisserie; bibliographie critique de la tapisserie dans les différents pays de l'Europe, depuis ses origines jusqu'à nos jours.** Paris, Picard, 1904. 128p. index.
Good, classified bibliography of some 1,083 entries covering books, catalogs and periodical articles on all aspects of European tapestry published up to 1904.

General Histories and Handbooks

1195   Ackerman, Phyllis. **Tapestry, the Mirror of Civilization** . . . New York, Oxford University Press, 1933. 451p. illus. index.
Popular history of world tapestries from ancient Egypt through the nineteenth century, with sections on the Far East and America and a chapter on technique. List of collectors and collections, pp. 318-42. Bibliography, pp. 431-33, lists books in all languages.

1196   Demotte, G. J. **La tapisserie gothique.** Paris and New York, Demotte, 1924. 10p. (text), 100 plates.
Pictorial survey of Western tapestries of the fourteenth through sixteenth centuries with descriptive notes and bibliography accompanying the plates.

1197   Göbel, Heinrich. **Wandteppiche.** Leipzig, Klinkhardt und Biermann, 1923-24. 3v. in 6. illus. index.
Excellent, scholarly history/handbook of Western tapestries from the Middle Ages through the eighteenth century. Arranged by major geographical regions. Chapters treat all aspects of the history. Facsimiles of signatures and marks. Well illustrated and thoroughly indexed. Extensive bibliographical footnotes. A standard work on tapestry.

1198   Guiffrey, Jules M. J., *et al.* **Histoire générale de la tapisserie.** Paris, Société Anonyme de Publications Périodiques, 1878-85. 3v. illus. index.
Good, older history of Western European tapestry consisting of essays on the major countries by early experts. Occasional bibliographic footnotes. A classic, pioneering work.

1199   Heinz, Dora. **Europäische Wandteppiche; ein Handbuch für Sammler und Liebhaber. Band I: Von den Anfängen der Bildwirkerei bis zum Ende des 16. Jahrhunderts.** Braunschweig, Klinkhardt & Biermann, 1963. 338p. illus. index. (Bibliothek für Kunst- und Antiquitätenfreunde, Band 37). LC 64-6573.
Excellent, scholarly history/handbook of Western European figurative tapestries covering the period from the fourteenth century to the end of the sixteenth century. Chapter on technique and care. Excellent bibliography of books and periodical articles in all languages, pp. 319-331. A standard work on European late medieval tapestries.

1200 Heinz, Dora. **Medieval Tapestries.** New York, Crown, 1967. 14p. (text), 20 plates. LC 67-15642.
Good, brief popular survey. Well-chosen selection of color plates, accompanied by excellent descriptive and interpretive notes. One-page bibliography of basic books.

1201 Hunter, George L. **The Practical Book of Tapestries . . .** Philadelphia and London, Lippincott, 1925. 302p. illus. index.
Popular history from ancient Egypt to early twentieth century, with emphasis on design and technique. Bibliography, pp. 281-92, is a good annotated list of basic books up to that time.

1202 Hunter, George L. **Tapestries, Their Origin, History and Renaissance.** New York, Lane, 1913. 438p. illus. index.
Older handbook; poorly illustrated but with useful chapter on restoration. Bibliographical references in Chapter XV.

1203 Janneau, Guillaume. **Évolution de la tapisserie.** Paris, Compagnie des Arts Photomécaniques, 1937. 91p. (text), 63 illus.
Good, scholarly history of Western European tapestry from the fourteen through the early nineteenth century. Good notes to the plates, with bibliographies. Further bibliography in the footnotes to the text.

1204 Jarry, Madeleine. **World Tapestry, from Their Origins to the Present.** New York, Putnam, 1969. 358p. illus. LC 68-22257.
Popular history from Coptic examples to the present. Chapter on technique with illustrations of work processes. Good classified bibliography of books and catalogs, pp. 349-54.

1205 Müntz, Eugène. **A Short History of Tapestry: From the Earliest Times to the End of the 18th Century . . .** London and New York, Cassell, 1885. 399p. illus.
English translation of the second edition of *La tapisserie.* An early, pioneering history of Western tapestries still useful for its list of marks and monograms and its list of painters who designed cartoons for tapestry. Illustrated with line drawings.

1206 Plourin, Marie-Louise. **Historia del tapiz en Occidente.** Barcelona, Editorial Seix Barral, 1955. 427p. illus.
Serious history of Western tapestries to the twentieth century. Good notes to the plates. Bibliography, pp. 189-92, is a chronological list of books in all languages.

1207 Schmitz, Hermann. **Bildteppiche; Geschichte der Gobelinwirkerei.** Berlin, Verlag für Kunstwissenschaft, 1919. 352p. illus. index.
Good, serious history of Western tapestry from the fifteen through the eighteenth centuries, with emphasis on Germany, the Low Countries, and France. Good list of tapestry marks. Bibliography, pp. 349-52, is good source for older literature.

1208   Sevensma, W. S. **Tapestries**. New York, Universe, 1966. 110p. illus.
        LC 65-24049.
Good, popular history of Western tapestry from the fourteenth century to the
present with a discussion of Byzantine and Islamic work. Well illustrated, including
maps and line drawings. Facsimiles of major marks. Bibliography, pp. 106-108, is
a chronological list of basic books, catalogs, and periodical articles in German,
French and English.

1209   Spina Barelli, Emma. **L'arazzo in Europa**. Novara, Agostini, 1963. 380p.
        illus. index. LC 67-41102.
Good, serious history of European tapestries from the late Middle Ages to the
present. Illustrated with museum pieces. Bibliography of basic books in all languages.

1210   Thomson, William G. **A History of Tapestry from the Earliest Times until
        the Present Day**. Rev. ed. New York, Putnam, 1931. 550p. illus. index.
        Reprint: Wakefield, E. P. Publishing, 1973.
Good, older, serious history of Western tapestries from ancient Egypt to the
twentieth century. Chapter on tapestry marks. Frequent reference to documents
on tapestries. Well indexed. Some bibliographical footnotes.

1211   Verlet, Pierre, *et al.* **Great Tapestries: The Web of History from the 12th
        to the 20th Century**. Lausanne, Edita S.A., 1965. 278p. illus. index.
Good, popular history of Western tapestries comprised of essays on Gothic, classical
(16th through 18th centuries) and contemporary tapestries with a chapter on technique. Brief section of marks and signatures and list of prices of select tapestries
sold between 1960 and 1964. Bibliography, pp. 269-70, is a brief unclassified list
of books and exhibition and museum catalogs.

1212   Viale, Mercedes. **Tapestries**. London, Hamlyn, 1969. 159p. illus.
Popular illustrated history of Western tapestries from the Middle Ages through the
eighteenth century. No bibliography.

1213   Viale, Mercedes, and Vittorio Viale. **Arazzi e tappeti antichi**. Turin, ILTE,
        1952. 242p. illus.
Good encyclopedia on the rugs and tapestries of the world; divided into two parts,
according to the respective technique. Articles on countries and places, and a fine
selection of plates. Good bibliographies at the end of each article.

1214   Ysselteyn, G. T. van. **Tapestry: the Most Expensive Industry of the XVth
        and XVIth Centuries . . .** The Hague, Van Goor Zonen, 1969. 232p. illus.
        index.
Good, serious history of Western European tapestry by country and center of
manufacture. Good selection of plates. Bibliography, pp. 204-15, is an unclassified
list of books and periodical articles.

National Histories and Handbooks

France

1215   Kurth, Betty. **Gotische Bildteppiche aus Frankreich und Flandern.** Munich, Riehn & Reusch, 1923. 12p. (text). illus. (Sammelbände zur Geschichte der Kunst- und des Kunstgewerbes, Band 7)
Good, illustrated survey of French and Flemish tapestries of the fourteenth through the sixteenth centuries. Brief but informative introductory essay is followed by good selection of plates with descriptive captions.

1216   Lejard, André, ed. **French Tapestry.** London, Elek, 1946. 107p. illus.
Good, serious history of French tapestry from the fourteenth century to mid-20th century consisting of articles by various specialists, including one on technique and one on the modern revival of tapestry in France. Well illustrated. One-page bibliography of basic books.

1217   Marquet de Vasselot, Jean J., and Roger-Armand Weigert. **Bibliographie de la tapisserie, des tapis et de la broderie en France.** Paris, Colin, 1935. 354p. index. (Archives de l'art français. Nouv. pér., t. XVIII)
Excellent classified bibliography of approximately 2,700 entries. Covers books and periodical articles on all aspects of French tapestry, embroidery, and rugs published up to 1932. Standard reference tool.

1218   Salet, Francis. **La tapisserie française.** Paris, Vincent, Fréal, 1946. 23p. (text), 103 illus.
Pictorial survey from the Middle Ages to the twentieth century. No bibliography.

1219   Weigert, Roger-Armand. **French Tapestry.** London, Faber and Faber, 1962. 214p. illus. index.
Translation of *La tapisserie française* (1956). A good, serious history from the fourteenth to the twentieth century with glossary of terms, dictionary of designers and manufacturers, and good bibliography, pp. 206-212, of books and periodical articles up to 1956.

Germany

1220   Kurth, Betty. **Die deutschen Bildteppiche des Mittelalters.** Vienna, Schroll, 1926. 3v. illus. index.
Excellent scholarly history/handbook of German medieval pictorial tapestries, with chapters on techniques, sources, and an excellent catalog of the pieces illustrated. Thorough bibliographical footnotes. Also has an index of subjects depicted.

Low Countries

1221   D'Hulst, Roger A. **Tapisseries flamandes.** Brussels, Éditions L'Arcade, 1960.
318p. illus. index.
Good, illustrated survey covering the period from the fourteenth to the early
eighteenth century. Consists of an introduction followed by essays on major pieces.
Good bibliographies are given for each piece in the notes on pp. 296-303.

1222   Göbel, Heinrich. **Tapestries of the Lowlands.** New York, Brentano, 1924.
98p. illus. Reprint: New York, Hacker, 1974.
Good, serious history from the fourteenth through the eighteenth century, with a
chapter on technique and a section of marks. An older standard work.

1223   Ysselsteyn, G. T. van. **Geschiedenis der Tapijtweverijen in de noordelijke
Nederlanden** . . . Leiden, Leidsche Uitgeversmaatschappij, 1936. 2v. illus.
index.
Good, scholarly history of tapestry in the northern Netherlands through the
eighteenth century. English summaries by chapters in Volume two. List of marks.
Bibliography, vol. 2, pp. 47-76, is an alphabetical list of major books.

CHAPTER NINETEEN

TOYS AND DOLLS

1224   Allemagne, Henry R. d'. **Histoire des jouets** . . . Paris, Hachette, 1902.
          316p. illus. index.
Older, serious history of toys from prehistory to the end of the nineteenth century.
Occasional bibliographical footnotes.

1225   Bachmann, Manfred, and Claus Hansmann. **Dolls the Wide World Over.**
          New York, Crown, 1973. 204p. illus. LC 72-94617.
Good, popular history from prehistoric and ancient times to the present. Well
illustrated. Good bibliography, pp. 200-204, lists basic books and catalogs in all
languages.

1226   Boehn, Max von. **Dolls and Puppets.** New York, Cooper Square, 1966.
          521p. illus. index. LC 65-25496.
Translation of *Puppen und Puppenspiele*. First part (volume one of the German
edition) was reprinted (New York, Dover, 1972. 269p. illus. LC 73-189341).
Excellent scholarly history of Western dolls and puppets from the early Middle Ages
to the end of the nineteenth century. Excellent bibliography of books and periodical
articles in all languages, pp. 481-506. A standard history of dolls.

1227   Coleman, Dorothy E., and Evelyn J. Coleman. **The Collector's Encyclopedia**
          of Dolls. New York, Crown, 1968. 697p. illus. LC 68-9101.
Good, serious dictionary with entries covering types, styles, materials, construction
details, and makers with their marks. Good basic bibliography, pp. 672-75.

1228   Culf, R. **The World of Toys.** London, Hamlyn, 1969. 146p. illus.
Well-illustrated, popular history from prehistoric and ancient times to the present,
with emphasis on nineteenth century dolls and toys. Includes Oriental toys. No
bibliography.

1229   Fawcett, Clara H. **Dolls.** Boston, Charles T. Branford, 1964. 282p. illus.
          index. LC 64-16263.
Good, popular history with emphasis on nineteenth century and modern dolls.
Chapter on early history, restoration and repair, list of doll museums in the U.S.,
and list of collectors' dolls patented in America. Bibliography, pp. 268-73, provides
a classified list of basic books.

1230   Fraser, Antonia. **Dolls.** New York, Putnam, 1963. 128p. illus. index. LC 63-15526.
Good, popular history of world dolls from antiquity to the present, with emphasis on English and American dolls of the nineteenth century. Brief bibliography of basic books.

1231   Fraser, Antonia. **A History of Toys.** New York, Delacorte, 1966. 256p. illus. index. LC 66-20120. Another edition: New York and London, Spring, 1972. LC 72-170632.
Good, popular history of toys from ancient Egypt to the present. Good selection of plates and line drawings. Bibliography, pp. 249-50, lists basic books in all languages.

1232   Fritzsch, Karl E., and Manfred Bachmann. **An Illustrated History of Toys.** London, Abbey, 1965. 194p. illus.
Good, serious history of German toys from the Middle Ages to 1960, illustrated with pieces in German museums. Bibliography, pp. 193-94, lists basic books and catalogs, chiefly in German.

1233   Gordon, Lesley. **Peepshow into Paradise, a History of Children's Toys.** London, Harrap, 1953. 264p. illus. index. LC 54-9928.
American edition published by De Graff (New York, 1954). Good, popular history of world dolls from prehistory to the present. Illustrations chosen from museum pieces and pieces accessible to the collector.

1234   Gröber, Karl. **Kinderspielzeuge aus alter und neuer Zeit.** 2nd ed., edited by Juliane Metzger. Hamburg, M. von Schröder, 1965. 221p. illus. index. LC 66-57981.
Excellent, serious history of Western toys from prehistory to the end of the nine-teenth century, illustrated with major museum pieces. Brief bibliography of basic books. First edition (1927) was translated under the title: *Children's Toys of Bygone Days* (London, Batsford, 1932). A standard history of toys.

1235   Hillier, Mary. **Dolls and Doll-makers.** New York, Putnam, 1968. 256p. illus. index. LC 68-20629.
Good, popular history from prehistoric and ancient times to the present, including primitive and Oriental dolls. Chapter on folk dolls and useful list of doll-makers and their marks. Brief bibliography of basic books in all languages.

1236   McClintock, Inez, and Marshall McClintock. **Toys in America.** Washington, D.C. Public Affairs Press, 1961. 480p. illus. index. LC 59-13657.
Good, popular history of dolls and toys in the United States from early Colonial times through the nineteenth century. Illustrations feature chiefly pieces of interest to the collector.

1237   Noble, John. **Dolls.** New York, Walker, 1967. 84p. illus. LC 67-23093.
Popular history of European dolls from the beginning of the eighteenth century to
1914, with a chapter on collecting. No bibliography.

1238   Rabecq-Maillard, Marie-M. **Histoire du jouet.** Paris, Hachette, 1962. 95p.
        illus. LC 63-56243.
Popular illustrated survey of toys from prehistoric times to the present, with emphasis
on nineteenth century Continental toys and dolls of the nineteenth century.

1239   White, Gwen. **Antique Toys and Their Background.** New York, Arco, 1971.
        260p. illus. index. LC 74-153651.
Good, popular handbook/history covering games and novelties as well as toys, with
emphasis on the nineteenth century. Good chapter on earlier history, a section on
marks, with index, and a bibliography of general books, pp. 254-55.

1240   White, Gwen. **European and American Dolls and Their Marks and Patents.**
        London, Batsford; New York, Putnam, 1966. 274p. illus. index. LC 66-
        24567.
Good, serious handbook with chapters on materials, construction, special or novelty
dolls and very good dictionary of makers' marks and biographical dictionary of
major makers. Glossary of terms. Brief bibliography of basic books in all languages.
Well illustrated with plates and line drawings.

AUTHOR INDEX

References are to entry number, not to page number. In addition to authors, main entry titles are also listed here.

Abrahams, E., 472
Ackerman, P., 1195
Adam, P., 815
AF Encyclopedia of Textiles, 1056
Aldred, C., 778
Alexandre, A., 35
Alfassa, P., 324, 361
Algoud, H., 1076
Allemagne, H. d', 445, 995, 1224
Anderson, L., 918
Andren, E., 654
Antrobus, M., 1151
Aprà, N., 637
Armand, A., 840
Armstrong, N., 793
Arnold, J., 434, 446
Aroldi, A., 150
Aronson, J., 527
Art populaire; travaux artistiques et scientifiques du 1er congrès international des arts populaires, 97
Ash, D., 606, 946
Ashdown, C., 141
Aslin, E., 607
Auscher, E., 325
Avery, C., 900
Ayer, J., 499
Ayrton, M., 991

Babelon, J., 841, 924
Bacci, M., 314
Bachmann, M., 1225, 1232, 1233
Baillie, G., 390, 392, 402
Baines, A., 1042, 1043
Baker, H., 544
Ballardini, G., 223, 374, 375
Barber, E., 191, 236, 237
Barker, T., 1032
Barrelet, J., 719
Barth, H., 773
Basanta Campos, J., 400
Bassermann-Jordan, E. von, 403, 404
Bath, V., 1171
Baud-Bovy, D., 130
Baur-Heinhold, M., 992

Beard, G., 50
Becatti, G., 779
Beckwith, J., 751
Bedford, J., 1018
Behse, A., 199
Beigbeder, O., 585, 752
Beihoff, N., 747
Bell, M., 1019
Belli Barsali, I., 512, 891
Bellinger, L., 1069
Belloncle, M., 1020
Bemrose, G., 334
Béné-Petitclerc, F., 573
Bennett, D., 948, 949
Berchem, E. von, 842
Berg, G., 981
Berges, R., 205
Berlin, Kunstbibliothek. *Katalog der Lipperheideschen Kostümbibliothek*, 435
Berliner, R., 77
Bernt, W., 675
Beuque, E., 874, 925
Beurderley, C., 293
Beurderley, M., 293
Beyer, K., 681
Bidder, H., 1144
Biehn, H., 774
Bigelow, F., 901
Birch, W., 843
Bird, A., 419
Bird, J., 1069
Birrell, V., 1060
Bjerkoe, E., 548
Bjerkoe, J., 548
Blackmore, H., 142, 179, 180
Blair, C., 151, 152
Blair, D., 745
Blakemore, K., 878
Bloch, J., 361
Boccia, L., 153
Bochnak, A., 60
Bode, W. von, 1132
Boeheim, W., 154, 155
Boehn, M. von, 447, 448, 1226
Boesen, C., 984

Boesen, G., 984
Bogeng, G., 816
Boger, L., 1, 192, 530
Bøje, C., 982, 983
Bonnet, H., 144
Bosc, E., 2
Boschkov, A., 107
Boser-Sarivaxévanis, R., 1106
Bossard, G., 1041
Bossert, H., 17, 78, 79, 102
Bott, G., 775
Bottineau, Y., 927
Boucher, F., 449
Bouilhet, H., 926
Boulanger, G., 574
Bourgeois, E., 23
Bowes, J., 65
Brackett, O., 608
Bradbury, F., 950, 951
Bradford, E., 3, 785, 794
Branigan, K., 860
Branting, A., 1077
Brassington, W., 817
Brault, S., 927
Braun, J., 938
Braun-Ronsdorf, M., 450
Britten, F., 405
Brockhaus, A., 766
Brøndsted, J., 80
Bronimann, A., 1118
Brooke, I., 473, 484, 485, 486, 487, 488
Brooke, M., 1168
Brosio, V., 376, 638, 639
Brückner, W., 112
Brugmans, H., 844
Bruhn, W., 451
Bruhn de Hoffmeyer, A., 156
Brunner, H., 879
Bruton, E., 393, 406, 407
Bruzelli, B., 1038
Bucher, B., 18
Buck, A., 489
Buckley, W., 676
Bueno, L., 662
Bulgari, C., 971
Bulletin de Liaison du Centre International d'Étude des Textiles Anciens.
   "Bibliographie," 1054
Bunt, C., 1096
Burger, W., 513
Burgess, F., 867
Burr, G., 660
Burton, W., 200, 310
Busch, H., 892
Buschor, E., 224
Bushell, R., 767, 768, 769
Bushnell, G., 218
Butler, A., 285

Butler, J., 549
Byne, A., 661, 993
Byne, M., 661, 993

Caiger-Smith, A., 353
Calatchi, R., 1119
Calthrop, D., 490
Came, R., 880
Cameron, I., 4
Campana, R., 1114, 1120
Caplin, J., 1172
Carducci, C., 893
Carrà, M., 753
Carré, L., 928, 929
Carrillo y Gariel, A., 550
Caulfield, S., 1149
Cescinsky, H., 420, 609, 610
Chaffers, W., 201, 202, 206, 952
Chambon, R., 720
Chamot, M., 514
Champfleury, J., 189
Chapuis, A., 431, 432
Charles, R., 315
Charleston, R., 207, 225, 335
Chavagnac, X., 326
Chenakal, V., 399
Chiesa, G., 54, 55, 56
Chompret, J., 361, 377
Christensen, E., 81, 98
Christie, A., 1161
Christie, G., 1152, 1153
Churchill, S., 972
Cinotti, M., 193
Cipolla, C., 408
Cito-Filomarino, A., 57, 640
Clavert, A., 157
Clayton, M., 953
Clemenicie, R., 1044
Clemmenson, T., 655
Clifford, C., 1169
Clouzot, H., 507, 861, 862, 994, 1078, 1107
Clutton, C., 409
Coelho, E., 153
Coffin, M., 1009
Cohn-Wiener, E., 66
Colas, R., 436
Cole, A., 1079
Coleman, D., 1227
Collard, E., 238
Comoli Sordelli, A., 531
Complete Encyclopedia of Antiques, 5
Comstock, H., 30, 551
Connoisseur's Complete Period Guides, 6
Conti, G., 378
Cook, D., 441
Cooper, E., 208
Coraelli, F., 780, 894
Cosgrove, M., 525

Cotterell, H., 1007, 1030
Couissin, P., 145
Cox, W., 209
Coysh, A., 7
Creswell, K., 171
Creutz, M., 865
Creux, R., 131
Cripps, W., 930, 954
Crompton, S., 725
Csányi, K., 282, 343
Culf, R., 1228
Cundall, J., 818
Cunnington, C., 491, 492, 493, 494, 495
Cunnington, P., 493, 494, 495
Cunynghame, H., 515
Currier, E., 902
Curtil, H., 362
Cushion, J., 203, 249, 254, 259
Cuss, T., 410
Cust, A., 754
Czarnecka, I., 124

D'Allemagne, H., 445, 995, 1224
Danckert, L., 316
Daniel, D., 690
Daniels, G., 409, 421
D'Assailly, G., 452
Davenport, C., 802
Davenport, M., 453
Davis, D., 727
Davis, F., 532, 711, 726, 931
Dawson, E., 510
Day, L., 511
Dean, M., 611
Debes, D., 82
Demmin, A., 158
Demotte, G., 1196
Denaro, V., 973
Deneke, B., 597
Dennis, F., 932
Dennis, J., 955
Devauchelle, R., 819
Dexel, W., 244
D'Hulst, R., 1221
Diehl, E., 820
Digby, A., 218
Digby, G., 1162
Dilley, A., 1121
Dillmont, T., 1150
Dillon, E., 311, 677
Doane, E., 8
Dolz, R., 1021
Doménech, R., 662
Douroff, B., 1026
Dreger, M., 1061
Dreppard, C., 191, 427
Droz, E., 432
Duarte, C., 552, 919

Dubbe, B., 1036
Du Boulay, A., 294
Ducharte, P., 111
Ducret, S., 255, 317
Dugas, C., 226
Dunbar, J., 496
Duncan, G., 673
Dupont, M., 67, 668
Duyvené de Wit-Klinkhamer, T., 977

Earle, A., 479
Eberlein, H., 210, 641
Ebersolt, J., 895
Ebert, K., 1010
Ecke, G., 669
Edley, W., 417
Edwards, A., 1122
Edwards, R., 612, 613, 627
Egerton, W., 172
Eicher, J., 504
Eisen, G., 686
Ellsworth, R., 670
Elville, E., 674
Ensko, S., 903
Erdmann, K., 1123, 1124, 1142
Eriksen, S., 41
Erixon, S., 656
Ernould-Gandouet, M., 250
Eudel, P., 800
Evans, J., 83, 474, 786, 795
Evans, M., 454
Evers, J., 533
Ewald, W., 845

Fabriczy, C., 846
Fairservis, W., 500
Fales, M., 904
Falke, O., 379, 516, 598, 868, 1062
Faraday, C., 1115
Farcy, L., 1154
Fastnedge, R., 614
Fawcett, C., 1229
Feddersen, M., 68, 69, 348, 349, 808
Feduchi, L., 663
Félice, R., 575, 576, 577, 578
Felletti Maj, B., 545
Ferrari, G., 996
Feulner, A., 567
Ffoulkes, C., 159, 181, 997
Finlay, I., 61, 956
Fischer, E., 657
Fisher, S., 260, 261
Fleet, S., 411
Flower, C., 505
Flower, M., 796
Folk Art in Rumania, 126
Folsom, R., 227
Fontaine, G., 251

Formenton, F., 1125
Forrer, L., 847
Fořtova-Sámalová, P., 84
Fourest, H., 363
Frank, E., 998
Franses, F., 1109
Frantz, H., 252
Frapsauce, M., 925
Fraser, A., 1230, 1231
Frauberger, H., 516
Frauberger, T., 1173
Frederiks, J., 978
Frégnac, C., 787
French, H., 905
*French Cabinetmakers of the Eighteenth
  Century*, 579
Friedländer, J., 848
Fritzsch, K., 1232
Frohne, J., 387
Frothingham, A., 743
Früh, M., 256
Fryer, D., 160
Fuchs, L., 678
Furtwängler, A., 803
Furumark, A., 228

Gahlnbäck, J., 1037
Gall, G., 821
Galpin, F., 1045, 1046
Galter, J., 129
Gamber, O., 170
Gandilhon, R., 849
Gans, M., 798
Gans-Ruedin, E., 1126
Gardner, J., 161, 999, 1000
Gardner, R., 134
Garner, H., 526
Garnier, E., 194, 517
Gauthier, M., 518
Gebhart, H., 804
Geiringer, K., 1047
Gelfer-Jørgensen, M., 39
Gélis, E., 412, 431
Gelli, J., 135
Gere, C., 788
Gernsheim, A., 478
Ghelardini, A., 642
Ghurye, G., 501
Giacommotti, J., 364
Giltay-Nijssen, L., 789
Gink, K., 118
Glazier, R., 85, 1063
Gloag, J., 51, 528, 534, 615, 616
Gluckman, A., 186
Goaman, M., 422
Godden, G., 262, 263, 264, 265, 266, 336,
  371
Göbel, H., 1197, 1222

Goidsenhoven, J., 295
Goldschmidt, A., 755, 756, 757
Gompertz, G., 304
González Marti, M., 279
Gonzalez-Palacios, A., 42
Gordon, L., 1233
Gorham, H., 302
Gorsline, D., 455
Gould, M., 1011
Grässe, J., 211
Graham, J., 906
Grandjean, P., 850
Grandjean, S., 568, 898, 933
Grange, R., 497
Gray, B., 296
*Great Styles of Furniture: English, Italian,
  French, Dutch, Spanish*, 569
Gregorietti, G., 776, 974
Gribble, E., 610
Grierson, P., 851
Grimwade, A., 957
Gröber, K., 1234
Grollier, C., 326, 327
Gros-Galliner, G., 679
Grote-Hasenbalg, W., 1127
Grotemeyer, P., 852
Grotz, G., 553
Grover, L., 691
Grover, R., 691
Gruel, L., 822
Guérin, J., 324, 361
Guiffrey, J., 1194, 1198
Guilmard, D., 86
Guimaraes, A., 664
Gulland, W., 297
Gunsaulus, H., 1097
Guye, S., 413
Gyngell, D., 136

Haberlandt, M., 104
Habich, G., 853, 854
Hackenbroch, Y., 519
Hackmack, A., 1128
Haedecke, H., 863, 1008
Haggar, R., 195, 270
Hague, M., 1182
Hamlin, A., 87
Hannover, E., 212
Hansen, H., 103
Hansmann, C., 1225
Harcourt, R. d', 219, 1070
Harmuth, L., 1057
Harper, G., 20
Hatcher, J., 1032
Hauglid, R., 122
Havard, H., 9, 382, 934
Hawley, W., 1129
Haynes, E., 680

Hayward, C., 617
Hayward, H., 535
Hayward, J., 182
Head, R., 1174
Heiden, M., 1058
Heinz, D., 1199, 1200
Helft, J., 935, 936
Heller, D., 958
Helwig, H., 823, 824, 825
Henneberg, A., 1175
Henschen Ingvar, I., 658
Henzke, L., 356
Herberts, K., 809
Herbst, H., 831
Hernmarck, C., 277
Hetherington, A., 298
Hettes, K., 722
Hewitt, J., 162
Higgins, R., 781
Hildburgh, W., 520
Hiler, H., 437
Hiler, M., 437
Hill, G., 855, 856
Hillier, B., 245
Hillier, M., 1235
Himmelheber, G., 599, 600
Hinckley, F., 536, 580
Hintze, E., 1029
Hobson, R., 200, 299
Hoever, O., 1001
Hofmann, F., 321
Holland, M., 907, 959
Holme, C., 105, 120, 127
Holstein, P., 173
Holt, R., 1110
Holzhausen, W., 810
Honey, W., 203, 246, 267, 290, 303, 328
Honour, H., 881
Hood, G., 908
Hood, K., 389
Hopf, A., 1130
Hopstock, C., 59
Hornung, C., 31
Houston, M., 475, 476
Huard, F., 581
Hubel, R., 1111
Huenefeld, I., 438
Hüseler, K., 368
Hughes, G., 213, 268, 269, 372, 728, 729, 899, 960
Hughes, T., 10, 268, 618, 960, 1159
Hungarian Decorative Folk Art, 119
Hunter, G., 1064, 1201, 1202
Hunton, W., 1080
Huth, H., 811

Internationale Volkskundliche Bibliographie, 96

Jackowski, A., 125
Jackson, C., 961, 962
Jackson, E., 1176
Jackson, H., 183
Jackson, R., 1031
Jacobs, C., 1012, 1013
Jacobsen, C., 1131
Jacquemart, A., 214
Jahss, B., 812
Jahss, M., 812
Janneau, G., 692, 1203
Jaques, R., 1065, 1081
Jaquet, E., 426
Jarry, M., 1204
Jedding, H., 318
Jenny, W., 864
Jenyns, S., 350, 351
Jervis, S., 619
Jervis, W., 196
Jessup, R., 782
Jexlev, T., 738
Johnson, A., 988
Johnstone, P., 1155
Jones, E., 882
Jones, M., 1156, 1177
Jones, O., 88
Jonge, C., 383, 650
Jourdain, M., 613, 620, 621, 622, 1178
Journal of Glass Studies. Check List of Recently Published Articles and Books on Glass, 672
Joy, E., 623
Juaristi Sagarzazu, V., 521

Kämpfer, F., 681
Karlinger, H., 113
Kassell, H., 1166
Kates, G., 671
Kauffman, H., 869, 1002, 1014
Kelly, F., 456, 457
Kendrick, A., 1082, 1112, 1163
Kerfoot, J., 1015
Ketchum, W., 239
Kiegeland, B., 394
Kim, C., 304
Kingsley-Rowe, E., 4
Kirk, J., 554
Kisa, A., 687
Kittel, E., 857
Klingenberg, K., 47
Knittle, R., 700
Koechlin, R., 758
Köhler, K., 458, 459
Köllmann, E., 320
König, R., 460
Kohlhaussen, H., 36, 48
Kondakov, N., 522

Kovel, R., 357, 909
Kovel, T., 357, 909
Koyama, F., 291, 305
Kreisel, H., 600
Kris, E., 805
Kühnel, E., 70, 770, 1132
Kümmel, O., 71
Kunz, G., 748
Kurth, B., 1215, 1220
Kybalová, L., 439, 1098
Kyriss, E., 826
Kyster, A., 827

Labarte, J., 37
Lacy, A., 229
Laking, G., 163
Lambert, M., 117
Lamm, C., 746
Lane, A., 230, 286, 287, 338, 365
Langdon, J., 914, 915, 916
Langewis, L., 1099
Larsen, A., 739
Larsen, S., 827
Larson, K., 1133
Lassen, E., 985
Laufer, B., 771
Laughlin, L., 1016
Laver, J., 461, 462, 463, 477
Lavine, S., 52
Lazar, V., 506
Lee, R., 693, 694
Lee, S., 72
Leeds, E., 89
Lehmann, H., 220
Lehmann, O., 114
Lehnert, G., 21
Leitermann, H., 939
Lejard, A., 1216
Leloir, M., 440, 464
Lenormant, F., 858
Lenygon, F., 624
Lessard, M., 32
Lester, K., 465
Lesur, A., 366
Lewis, G., 373
Lewis, G. G., 1134
Lichten, F., 24
Liebetrau, P., 1135
Lindblom, A., 1077
Lindsay, M., 184
Lindsey, B., 701
Link, E., 883
Linton, G., 1059
Lipman, J., 99, 100
Lippold, G., 806
Lister, R., 1003
Litchfield, F., 247
Little, F., 1074

Liverani, G., 380
Lloyd, H., 395, 414
Llubiá Munné, L., 280
Lockwood, L., 529
Lohse, B., 892
Longhurst, M., 759
Longnon, H., 581
Lorentz, H., 1147
Lotz, W., 940
Loubier, H., 228
Lozoya, J., 665
Lüer, H., 865
Luff, R., 636
Lukomsij, G., 345
Lüthi, M., 64
Luzzato-Bilitz, O., 813

McClelland, E., 508
McClelland, Elisabeth, 480, 481
McClintock, I., 1236
McClintock, M., 1236
McClinton, K., 25
Macdonald-Taylor, M., 11, 625
McKearin, G., 702, 703
McKearin, H., 702, 703
McLean, R., 829
Macquoid, P., 626, 627
Maindron, M., 143
Majkowski, K., 1083
Mankowitz, W., 270
Mannelli, V., 643
Marangoni, G., 22
Marcuse, S., 1048
Mariacher, G., 682, 712, 736, 737, 975
Marius Michel (firm), 830
Markham, C., 1033
Marquet de Vasselot, J., 937, 1217
Marquis, H., 32
Marryat, J., 215
Mårtenson, G., 278
Martin, P., 164
Marx, E., 117
Maskell, A., 760
Mason, A., 777
Maurice, K., 433
Maxwell-Hyslop, K., 801
May, F., 1192
Mazzariol, G., 644
Means, P., 1071
Meinz, M., 884
Mejer, W., 831
Mercer, E., 537
Meulendyke, E., 99
Meulen-Nulle, L., 1179
Meyer, E., 868
Meyer, F., 90
Meyer, H., 283
Meyer-Heisig, E., 115, 369

Michaelis, R., 1034
Michel, H., 413
Michon, L., 832
Middlemas, K., 713
Migeon, G., 73, 1066
Miller, E., 555
Millet, G., 1157
Mikami, T., 306
Mingazzini, P., 231
Minghetti, A., 197
Minnich, H., 502
Mitsuoka, T., 307
Molinier, E., 38, 509, 523, 761
Möller, J., 1039
Möller, L., 601
Monro, I., 441
Montgomery, C., 1017
Montgomery, F., 1084
Moore, H., 714, 866
Morassi, A., 976
Morazzoni, G., 339, 645
Morpurgo, E., 397, 398
Morris, B., 1164
Morris, F., 1181
Mory, L., 1022, 1023
Mrlian, R., 108
Mujica Gallo, M., 896
Muller, P., 799
Müller, S., 538, 1158
Mumford, J., 1136
Munsterberg, H., 132, 308
Müntz, E., 1205
Muraoka, K., 133
Musciarelli, L., 137
Musgrave, C., 628

Nagel, C., 556
Natanson, J., 762, 763
Neuburg, F., 688
Neugebauer, R., 1137
Neurdenburg, E., 384
Newman, H., 198
Nickel, H., 165, 166
Nickerson, D., 629, 630
Nicolay, J., 582
Nielsen, K., 40
Noble, J., 1237
Nomura, S., 502
Norbury, J., 26
Norman, V., 167
Norris, H., 466
Nutting, W., 557

Overloop, E. van, 1182

Palardy, J., 562
Palliser, F., 1183
Palmer, B., 428, 429

Passarge, W., 49
Paulis, L., 1190
Payne, B., 467
Pazaurek, G., 257, 695, 696, 697
Peal, C., 1035
Pearse, G., 651
Pedaret, A., 434
Pedrini, A., 647
Pelka, O., 764
Penderei-Brodhurst, J., 631
Penkala, M., 292, 360
Percival, M., 1085
Perez Bueno, L., 744
Perry, J., 870
Peterson, H., 138, 168
Pethebridge, J., 1184
Petrie, F., 91
Pettit, F., 1075
Pettorelli, A., 871
Peyre, R., 253
Philip, P., 539
Philippe, J., 689
Philippovich, E. von, 765
Phillips, J., 910
Phillips, P., 13
Picken, M., 442
Pignatti, T., 648
Pileggi, A., 240
Pinto Cardoso, A., 666
Planché, J., 443
Plath, I., 63
Plourin, M., 1206
Poche, E., 344
Podreider, F., 1086
Polak, A., 698, 740, 986
Pollard, H., 185
Pollen, F., 1185
Polley, R., 101
Potrescu, P., 1087
Powys, M., 1186
Preece, L., 1151
Prideaux, S., 833
Pronin, A., 128

Rabecq-Maillard, M., 1238
Racinet, A., 92, 468
Rackham, B., 272, 273, 381, 385
Rademacher, F., 723
Ramsay, J., 241
Ramsdell, R., 210, 641
Randell, R. W., 1108
Random House Collector's Encyclopedia: Victoriana to Art Deco, 27
Read, H., 272
Réal, D., 1088, 1101
Reath, N., 1102
Redslob, E., 941
Reed, S., 1139

Reitzenstein, A., 169
Renan, A., 483
Rettelsbusch, E., 93
Revi, A., 699, 704, 705
Ricci, E., 1165, 1191
Ricci, S. de, 583
Richter, G., 546
Riefstahl, R., 1103
Riismøller, P., 739
Ripley, M., 1148
Ris-Paquot, O., 875
Ritz, G., 570, 571, 602
Ritz, J., 602, 603
Rivero, M., 242
Rivière, H., 288
Robinson, H., 174
Roche, O., 977
Roman, J., 859
Ropers, H., 1140
Roquet, A., 836
Rosa, G., 58, 322
Rosenberg, M., 876, 885
Rosenthal, L., 721
Rosenthal, R., 783
Rossi, F., 797
Roth, H., 990
Rozembergh, A., 347
Rudofsky, B., 469
Rust, W., 342
Ryerson, E., 772
Ryszard, S., 346

Sachs, C., 1050, 1051
Sachs, E., 1102
Sack, A., 563
Salazar Bondy, S., 221
Salet, F., 1218
Salonen, E., 146
Salverte, F. de, 584
Salvy, C., 585
Sanchez-Mesa, M., 62
Sandão, A., 667
Sandon, H., 274
Santangelo, A., 1089, 1090
Santos, J., 564
Santos, R. dos, 386
Sarre, F., 1141
Satterlee, L., 186
Saulnier, R., 111
Savage, G., 14, 44, 198, 216, 217, 275, 329,
    331, 337, 354, 683
Saville, M., 920
Saward, B., 1149
Schade, G., 604, 724, 942
Schedelmann, H., 170, 187
Scheffler, W., 943, 944, 945
Schlosser, I., 684, 1113
Schlüter, M., 739

Schmidt, H., 1067
Schmidt, L., 106, 605
Schmidt, R., 300, 312, 572, 715
Schmitz, H., 540, 598, 1207
Schnorr von Carolsfeld, L., 320
Schönberger, A., 332
Schottmüller, F., 649
Schreiber, H., 834
Schrijver, H., 340, 716, 979
Schuette, M., 1158, 1160, 1187
Schuppisser, P., 460
Schürmann, U., 1142, 1145
Schwabe, R., 456, 457
Schwartz, M., 243, 313, 706
Seguin, J., 1188
Seitz, H., 177, 741
Seligman, G., 1159
Seling, A., 15
Seling, H., 16
Sellink, J., 425
Sevensma, W., 1208
Sidenbladh, E., 401
Sieber, R., 1108
Silcock, A., 991
Simmingskold, B., 717
Simoni, A., 424
Singleton, E., 652
Smith, H., 790
Snodgrass, A., 147, 148
Solon, L., 190
Sonn, A., 1004
Souchal, G., 586
Sourek, K., 109
Speltz, A., 94
Spiess, K. von, 116
Spina Barelli, E., 1209
Staehelin, W., 258
Stafford, M., 95, 632
Stany-Gauthier, J., 587, 588
Steenberg, E., 717, 742
Steenbock, F., 835
Steensberg, A., 659
Steingräber, E., 791, 886
Stevens, G., 707
Stewart, J., 123
Stibbert, F., 470
Stiles, H., 233
Stillinger, E., 33
Stitt, I., 309
Støckel, J., 139
Stoehr, A., 370
Stone, G., 140
Strange, T., 45, 53
Strauss, K., 284
Strong, D., 897
Stuttmann, F., 1005
Sutherland, C., 887
Symonds, R., 423, 633, 634
Sypesteyn, C., 341

Tardieu, S., 589
Tardy (firm), 248, 391, 396, 418, 749, 877, 1027, 1028
Tattersall, C., 1116
Taullard, A., 565, 921
Taylor, G., 888, 889, 966
Theunissen, A., 590
Thoinan, E., 836
Thomas, B., 170
Thomson, R., 430
Thomson, W., 1210
Thorn, C., 204, 911
Thornton, P., 1091
Thorpe, W., 730, 731
Ticher, K., 967
Tilke, M., 457, 503
Tilmans, E., 330, 367
Tischer, F., 1025
Toschi, P., 121
Treganowan, D., 1117
Trenkwald, H., 1141
Trowell, K., 76
Truman, N., 471
Tschebull, R., 1146
Turk, F., 74
Turkhan, K., 1143
Turner, N., 912
Tyler, E., 415

Uldall, K., 110, 388
Unitt, D., 709, 917
Unitt, P., 709, 917
Upmark, G., 987

Valente, V., 281
Valladares, J., 922
Valle-Arizpe, A. de, 923
Vanderpoel, E., 1193
Vanstan, I., 1073
Van Tassel, V., 708
Vergerio, G., 1006
Verlet, P., 541, 591, 592, 593, 1211
Verster, A., 872, 1024
Vever, H., 792
Viale, M., 1212, 1213
Vianello, G., 175
Vidal, M., 989
Viaux, J., 594, 595
Villard, F., 234
Viollet-le-Duc, E., 46
Voet, E., 980
Vogelsang, W., 653
Volbach, W., 1092, 1104

Wagner, F., 1099
Wallis, H., 235
Walton, P., 1093
Wanscher, O., 542

Wardle, P., 1163, 1189
Ware, D., 95
Ware, G., 333
Warren, P., 732
Waterer, J., 837, 838
Watkins, L., 710
Watson, F., 596
Webber, N., 733
Webster, D., 34, 358, 359
Webster, M., 420
Weeks, J., 1117
Weibel, A., 1068
Weigert, R., 1094, 1217, 1219
Weiss, G., 355, 685
Weisweiler, M., 839
Wenham, E., 913, 968
Wessel, K., 524
Wheeler, C., 1167
Whineray, B., 634
White, G., 1239, 1240
Whiting, G., 1170
Wiet, G., 1105
Wilckens, L. von, 1055
Wilcox, R., 444, 482
Wilkinson, A., 784
Wilkinson, F., 178, 188
Wilkinson, O., 718
Wilkinson, W., 969
Williams, C., 547
Williams, H., 566
Wills, G., 276, 635, 734, 735, 750, 873, 970
Willsberge, J., 416
Winchester, A., 100
Windisch-Graetz, F., 543
Winternitz, E., 1052
Wolf, W., 149
Wolfe, R., 313
Wolsey, S., 636
Wood, I., 1040
Wood, V., 28
Woodhouse, C., 29
Wright, R., 1053
Wuthenau, A. von, 222
Wyler, S., 890
Wynter, H., 323

Yamada, C., 75
Yarwood, D., 498
Yoshida, M., 289
Ysselsteyn, G. van, 1095, 1214, 1223
Yu-kuan, L., 814

Zimelli, U., 1006
Zimmermann, E., 301, 352

SUBJECT INDEX

The chief purpose of this subject index is to complement the table of contents, which is the main subject access tool of the book. By supplying synonyms to terms used in the table of contents and by indexing the individual arts under variant terminologies, the subject index expands the vocabulary of the applied and decorative arts. It functions, thus, as a cross-reference tool and, indirectly, as a lexicon.

Accessories. *See* Chapter Seven–Costume, and Chapter Twelve–Jewelry.
African applied and decorative arts, 76
African costume, 504, 506
African jewelry, 1108
African textiles, 1106-1108
American applied and decorative arts, 30-34
American arms and armor, 168
American cabinetmakers, 548
American ceramic marks, 236
American ceramics, 236-243
American clocks, 427-430
American copper and brass, 869
American costume, 479-482
American coverlets. *See* American textiles.
American design, 81
American embroidery, 1166-1167
American folk art, 98-101
American furniture, 548-566
American glass, 700-710
American Indian crafts, 79
American Indian rugs, 1116, 1117
American lace, 1193
American musical instruments, 561
American pewter, 1009-1017
American pewter marks, 1010, 1012, 1014, 1016
American porcelain, 313
American potters' marks, 236, 239, 241
American pottery, 356-359
American silver, 900-913
American textiles, 1074, 1075
American wrought iron, 1002, 1004
Ancient arms and armor, 144-149
Ancient ceramics, 223-234
Ancient costume, 472-477
Ancient furniture, 544-547
Ancient glass, 686-689
Ancient gold and silver, 891-897
Ancient jewelry, 778-784
Ancient ornament, 91
Anglo-Saxon ornament, 80
Antwerp lace. *See* Belgian lace.
Apostles spoons. *See* English silver.
Applied and decorative arts
  general. *See* Chapter One–Applied and Decorative Arts–General.
  dictionaries and encyclopedias, 1-16
Appliqué. *See* Embroidery.
Armorers' marks, 136, 139
Arms and armor, 440, 443, 451, 453, 455, 457, 468, 470, 476. *See also* Chapter Four–Arms and Armor.
  dictionaries and encyclopedias, 134-140

Arras tapestries. *See* Flemish tapestry.
Art deco, 25, 27. *See also* Modern applied and decorative arts.
Art nouveau. *See* Modern applied and decorative arts.
Arts and crafts movement. *See* Modern applied and decorative arts.
Asian . . . *See* Oriental . . .
Assay marks. *See* Goldsmiths' marks; Silversmiths' marks.
Aubusson carpets. *See* European carpets and rugs.
Australian costume, 505
Australian pottery, 389
Australian applied and decorative arts. *See* German applied and decorative arts.
Austrian ceramics. *See* German ceramics.
Austrian folk art, 104-106
Austrian pewter. *See* German pewter.
Austrian porcelain. *See* German porcelain.
Austrian silver. *See* German silver.
Automata. *See* Chapter Six–Clocks, Watches and Automata.

Baccarat glass. *See* French glass.
Batavian ware. *See* Chinese porcelain.
Battersea enamels. *See* English enamels.
Batik. *See* Indonesian textiles.
Belgian glass, 720
Belgian lace, 1190
Berlin work. *See* German embroidery.
Bibelots. *See* Chapter Twelve–Jewelry.
Biedermeier furniture. *See* German furniture.
Blackwork embroidery. *See* English embroidery.
Blanc de chine. *See* Chinese porcelain.
Blown glass. *See* glass.
Blue and white Canton ware. *See* Chinese porcelain.
Blue and white Delft ware. *See* Dutch porcelain.
Bohemian ceramics, 283
Bohemian pewter, 1025
Bohemian porcelain, 344
Bookbinding. *See* Chapter Fourteen–Leather and Bookbinding.
  bibliographies, 831
Boulle marquetry. *See* French furniture.
Brass, 867-873
Brazilian ceramics, 240
Brazilian furniture, 564
Breech-loader. *See* Firearms.
Britannia ware, 1014, 1017, 1035

British applied and decorative arts, 50-53
British carpets and rugs, 1116
British ceramic marks, 259, 263, 264
British ceramics, 259-276
British clocks, 419-423
British costume, 484-498
British embroidery, 1161-1164
British folk art, 117
British furniture, 605-636
British glass, 725-735
British jewelry, 793-796
British pewter, 1030-1035
British pewter marks, 1030, 1031
British porcelain, 334-337
British pottery, 371-373
British silver, 946-980
British silversmiths' marks, 950-952, 954, 961
British wrought iron, 997, 999, 1003
Brussels lace. See Belgian lace.
Bulgarian folk art, 107
Byzantine ceramics, 235
Byzantine enamels, 522, 524
Byzantine gold and silver, 895
Byzantine ivories, 755
Byzantine textiles, 1092

Cameo glass. See Ancient glass.
Cameos, 802, 804, 806
Canadian applied and decorative arts, 32, 34
Canadian ceramics, 238
Canadian furniture, 562
Canadian pottery, 356, 357
Canadian silver, 914-917
Canton ware. See Chinese porcelain.
Cape silver, 651, 958
Carolingian ivories, 757
Carpets, 1109-1148
Cassone. See Italian furniture.
Caucasian carpets and rugs, 1114-1146
Celadon ware. See Chinese porcelain, Japanese porcelain, Korean porcelain.
Celtic ornament, 89
Central Asian carpets and rugs, 1114, 1145
Ceramic marks, 199-204
Ceramics. See Chapter Five-Ceramics.
  bibliographies, 189, 190
  dictionaries and encyclopedias, 191-198
  dictionaries of marks and signatures, 199-204
Champlevé. See Enamels.
China. See Chapter Five–Ceramics, especially porcelain.
Chinese carpets and rugs, 1147, 1148
Chinese ceramics, 290-301
Chinese furniture, 668-671
Chinese lacquer, 808, 809, 814
Chinese porcelain, 349-351
Chintz, 1085. See also Printed textiles.

Clocks. See Chapter Six–Clocks, Watches, and Automata.
Cloisonné. See Enamels.
Clothing. See Costume.
Colored ornament, 78, 92
Copper, 867-873
Coptic textiles, 1098, 1092, 1104
Costume. See Chapter Seven–Costume.
  bibliographies, 434-437
  dictionaries and encyclopedias, 438-444
Crackle glass. See Italian glass.
Creamware. See English pottery.
Crêpe-de-chine. See silk.
Crewel work. See American embroidery; English embroidery.
Cristallo. See Italian glass.
Crockery. See Ceramics.
Crystal. See Glass.
Cuir cielé. See German bookbinding.
Cut glass. See Glass.
Cycladic ceramics, 226. See also Ancient ceramics.
Czechoslovakian folk art, 108, 109
Czechoslovakian pewter, 1025

Daggers. See Edged weapons.
Damascene work. See Edged weapons, iron.
Danish applied and decorative arts, 39, 40
Danish bookbinding, 827
Danish faience, 387, 388
Danish folk art, 110
Danish furniture, 655, 659
Danish glass, 738, 739
Danish seals, 850
Danish silver, 982-985
Date letters. See Silversmiths' marks.
Decoration. See Chapter Two–Ornament.
Delftware. See Dutch porcelain.
Derby porcelain. See English porcelain.
Designs. See Chapter Two–Ornament.
Dinanderie, 870
Directoire. See French applied and decorative arts; French furniture.
Dolls. See Chapter Nineteen–Toys and Dolls.
Dresden china. See German porcelain.
Dress. See Costume.
Dutch clock and watchmakers, 398
Dutch clocks, 425
Dutch faience, 382-385
Dutch furniture, 650-652
Dutch jewelry, 798
Dutch pewter, 1036
Dutch porcelain, 340-342
Dutch porcelain marks, 340, 341
Dutch pottery, 382-385
Dutch seals, 844
Dutch silver, 977-980
Dutch silversmiths' marks, 978, 980
Dutch tapestry, 1223

Early Christian ivories, 762
Earthenware. *See* Pottery.
Ebéniste. *See* French furniture.
Ecclesiastical dress, 451, 453, 471, 474, 476
Edged weapons, 176-178
Egyptian ornament, 84
Elizabethan embroidery, 1162
Embroidery, 1149-1167
Empire style, 23. *See also* Modern applied and decorative arts.
Empire style furniture. *See* American furniture; French furniture.
Enamels. *See* Chapter Eight – Enamels.
  bibliographies, 508
  dictionaries and encyclopedias, 507, 509
English applied and decorative arts, 50-53
English arms and armor, 161
English ceramic marks, 259, 263, 264
English ceramics, 259-276
English clocks, 419-420
English costume, 484-498
English embroidery, 1161-1164
English enamels, 514
English furniture, 606-636
English pewter, 1030-1035
English pewter marks, 1030, 1031
English porcelain, 334-337
English pottery, 371-373
English silver, 946-970
English silversmiths' marks, 950-952, 954, 961
English textiles, 1080, 1082, 1084
English wrought iron, 997, 999, 1003
Estonian ceramics, 284
European arms and armor, 151, 154, 155, 158-160, 163-167, 169, 170
European carpets and rugs, 1114-1117
European ceramics, 244-248
European folk art, 102, 103
European furniture, 567-572
European glass, 711-718
European jewelry, 785-791
European lacquer, 810, 811
European pewter, 1018-1024
European porcelain, 314-323
European porcelain marks, 316
European textiles, 1076-1093

Fabrics. *See* Chapter Seven – Costume; Chapter Eighteen – Textiles.
Faience. *See* Chapter Five – Ceramics.
Famille rose, verte. *See* Chinese porcelain.
Far Eastern . . . *See* Oriental . . .
Fashion. *See* Costume.
Fashion accessories. *See* Chapter Seven – Costume; Chapter Twelve – Jewelry.
Federal style. *See* American applied and decorative arts.
Finnish ceramics, 278

Finnish pewter, 1039
Firearms, 179-188
Flemish furniture, 588. *See also* Dutch furniture.
Flemish tapestry, 1221, 1222
Flint-lock. *See* Firearms.
Folk art. *See* Chapter Three – Folk Art.
  bibliographies, 96
Folk costume. *See* Folk art; *See also* Costume.
Folk furniture, 570, 597, 602, 605
Frankenthal china. *See* German porcelain.
French applied and decorative arts, 41-46
French bookbinding, 819, 830, 832, 836
French ceramic marks, 249, 253. *See also* French faience marks; French porcelain marks.
French ceramics, 249-253
French clock and watchmakers, 396
French clocks, 417, 418
French costume, 483
French faience, 361-367
French faience marks, 362, 366
French folk art, 111
French furniture, 573-596
French glass, 719, 721
French jewelry, 792
French pewter, 1026-1029
French porcelain, 324-330
French porcelain marks, 326, 327
French pottery, 361-367
French provincial furniture, 574, 581, 585, 587, 588, 589
French seals, 849, 859
French silver, 924-937
French silversmiths, 935
French silversmiths' marks, 925, 928, 935, 936
French tapestry, 1215-1219
French wrought iron, 994, 995
Furniture. *See* Chapter Nine – Furniture.
  dictionaries and encyclopedias, 527-529

Gem engravers, 847
Gems, 774, 777, 791. *See also* Jewelry.
Georgian silver. *See* English silver.
Georgian style. *See* English applied and decorative arts.
German applied and decorative arts, 47-49
German bookbinding, 823, 826
German ceramic marks, 254, 257. *See also* German faience marks; German porcelain marks.
German ceramic painters, 257
German ceramics, 254-257
German embroidery, 1160
German enamels, 516
German faience, 368-370

German folk art, 112-116
German folk furniture, 597, 602, 603, 605
German furniture, 597-605
German glass, 722-724
German gold. *See* German silver.
German medals, 842, 852, 853
German pewter, 1029
German pewterers, 1025
German porcelain, 331-333
German porcelain marks, 331, 333. *See also*
  German ceramic marks.
German pottery, 368-370
German silver, 938-945
German silversmiths' marks, 942-945
German tapestry, 1220
German textiles, 1081
German wrought iron, 992, 1005
Glass. *See* Chapter Ten–Glass.
  bibliographies, 672, 673
  dictionaries and encyclopedias, 674
Gobelins. *See* French tapestry.
Gold. *See* Chapter Sixteen–Metalwork.
Goldsmiths' marks, 874-877
Greek ceramics, 224, 227, 229-231, 234.
  See also Ancient ceramics.
Grolier. *See* French bookbinding.
Gros point. *See* Embroidery.
Guns. *See* Firearms.
Gunsmiths' marks, 134, 136, 139, 184, 186,
  187

Hallmarks. *See* Silversmiths' marks.
Hausmaler. *See* German ceramic painters.
Hepplewhite style. *See* English furniture.
Hungarian ceramics, 282
Hungarian folk art, 118, 119
Hungarian porcelain, 343

Imari porcelain. *See* Japanese porcelain.
Indian (American) crafts, 19
Indian (American) rugs, 1116, 1117
Indian (East) arms and armor, 172, 173, 174
Indian (East) costume, 499, 500, 501, 503
Indian Colonial silver, 969
Indonesian textiles, 1099, 1101
Inro. *See* Japanese lacquer; Netsuke.
Intaglios, 803-807
Intarsia. *See* European furniture.
Irish . . . *See* British . . .
Iron, 991-1006. *See also* Metalwork.
Islamic arms and armor, 171, 174
Islamic bookbinding, 839
Islamic ceramics, 285-289
Islamic ivories, 770
Italian applied and decorative arts, 54-58
Italian arms and armor, 150, 153
Italian brass and bronze, 871
Italian ceramics. *See* Italian pottery.

Italian clock and watchmakers, 397
Italian clocks, 424
Italian embroidery, 1165
Italian enamels, 519
Italian folk art, 120, 121
Italian furniture, 637-649
Italian glass, 736-737
Italian gold, 971-974, 976
Italian gold and silversmiths' marks, 971
Italian jewelry, 797, 971, 972
Italian lace, 1191
Italian majolica, 374-381
Italian medals, 840, 846, 854, 855, 856
Italian porcelain, 338-339
Italian pottery, 374-381
Italian silver, 971-976
Italian textiles, 1086, 1089, 1090
Italian wrought iron, 996
Ivory. *See* Chapter Ten–Ivory.

Jacobean . . . *See* English . . .
Japanese ceramics, 302, 305-309
Japanese glass, 745
Japanese lacquer, 812, 814
Japanese porcelain, 348, 352
Japanese textiles, 1097
Japanning. *See* Lacquer.
Jewelers' marks, 875, 878, 899
Jewelry, 443, 449, 464, 467. *See also*
  Chapter Twelve–Jewelry.

Kazak carpets and rugs. *See* Caucasian
  carpets and rugs.
Kilim. *See* Oriental carpets and rugs.
Korean ceramics, 303, 304
Korean lacquer, 814
Korean porcelain. *See* Korean ceramics.

Lace, 1168-1193
Lacquer. *See* Chapter Thirteen–Lacquer.
Latvian ceramics, 284
Leather. *See* Chapter Fourteen–Leather
  and Bookbinding.
Lenox china. *See* American porcelain.
Linen damask, 1095
Lithuanian ceramics, 284

Majolica, 374-381
Makers' marks. *See* Armorers' marks,
  Pewterers' marks; Silversmiths' marks.
Maltese silver, 973
Marquetry. *See* European furniture; French
  furniture; German furniture; Italian
  furniture.
Mechlin lace. *See* Belgian lace.
Medallions. *See* Medals.
Medallists, 847
Medals. *See* Chapter Fifteen–Medals and
  Seals.

Medieval bookbinding, 826, 835
Medieval brass and bronze, 868
Medieval gold and silver, 891, 892
Medieval ivories, 751, 756, 757, 758, 763
Meissen china. *See* German porcelain.
Mennecy porcelain. *See* French porcelain.
Metalwork. *See* Chapter Sixteen–Metalwork.
Mexican furniture, 550, 565
Mexican silver, 918, 920, 923
Military dress, 451, 453, 455, 470, 471, 474
Millefiori glass. *See* Ancient glass; French glass; Italian glass.
Millinery. *See* Chapter Seven–Costume.
Modern applied and decorative arts, 23-29
Modern costume, 478
Modern glass, 690-699
Modern gold and silver, 898, 899
Musical instruments. *See* Chapter Seventeen–Musical Instruments.
Mycenean ceramics, 228. *See also* Ancient ceramics.

Nazca textiles, 1069, 1072
Near Eastern . . . *See* Islamic . . .
Needlework. *See* Embroidery. *See also* Costume.
Neo-classicism. *See* Modern applied and decorative arts.
Netsuke, 766, 767, 768, 769, 772
Niello. *See* Metalwork.
Norwegian applied and decorative arts, 59
Norwegian folk art, 122, 123
Norwegian glass, 740
Norwegian silver, 986

Opal glass. *See* English glass; German glass.
Opus anglicanum. *See* English embroidery.
Oriental applied and decorative arts, 65-75
Oriental arms and armor, 171-175
Oriental carpets and rugs, 1118-1148
Oriental costume, 499-503
Oriental folk art, 132; 133
Oriental furniture, 668-671
Oriental glass, 745, 746
Oriental ivories, 766-772
Oriental jewelry, 800, 801
Oriental lacquer, 809, 813, 814
Oriental porcelain, 348-352
Oriental silver, 990
Oriental textiles, 1096-1105
Ornament. *See* Chapter Two–Ornament.
  bibliographies, 82
  dictionaries, 88, 90, 95
Ornament designers, 77, 86
Ornament designs, 77, 86
Ornament history, 83, 87, 94
Ottonian ivories, 757

Painted textiles, 1075, 1078
Palissy ware. *See* French ceramics.
Paperweights. *See* Glass.
Paroas textiles, 1069, 1072
Patterns. *See* Ornament.
Peasant art. *See* Folk art.
Pennsylvania Dutch decorative arts. *See* American folk art.
Persian carpets and rugs. *See* Oriental carpets and rugs.
Persian pottery, 289. *See also* Islamic ceramics.
Persian textiles, 1096, 1102, 1103, 1105
Peruvian ceramics, 219, 221. *See also* Pre-Columbian ceramics.
Petit point. *See* Embroidery.
Pewter, 1007-1041
Polish applied and decorative arts, 60
Polish folk art, 124, 125
Polish porcelain, 346
Polish textiles, 1083
Porcelain, 310-352
Porcelain marks, 199-204
Portrait medallions. *See* Chapter Fifteen–Medals and Seals.
Portuguese ceramics, 281
Portuguese faience, 386
Portuguese furniture, 664, 666, 667
Portuguese pottery, 386
Portuguese silver, 989
Portuguese textiles, 1088
Pottery, 353-389
Prayer-rugs. *See* Oriental carpets and rugs.
Pre-Columbian ceramics, 218-222
Pre-Columbian textiles, 1069-1073
Pressed Glass. *See* Glass.
Printed textiles, 1078, 1084, 1085

Quilting. *See* Textiles; American textiles; European textiles.

Raku. *See* Japanese ceramics.
Régence style. *See* French applied and decorative arts.
Regency furniture, 628. *See also* English furniture.
Reja. *See* Spanish wrought iron.
Roman ceramics, 223, 225, 232. *See also* Ancient ceramics.
Roman costume. *See* Ancient costume.
Roman furniture. *See* Ancient furniture.
Roman glass. *See* Ancient glass.
Roman gold and silver, 893, 897
Roman jewelry. *See* Ancient jewelry.
Rugs. *See* Carpets.
Rumanian folk art, 126
Rumanian textiles, 1087

Russian clock and watchmakers, 399
Russian folk art, 127, 128
Russian pewter, 1037
Russian porcelain, 345, 347
Russian porcelain marks, 347

Samplers. See American embroidery;
  English embroidery.
Savonnerie carpets. See European
  carpets and rugs.
Scandinavian . . . See Danish . . .;
  Finnish . . .; Norwegian . . .;
  Swedish . . .
Scandinavian ceramics, 277-278
Scientific instruments, 455
Scottish applied and decorative arts, 61.
  See also British applied and decorative
  arts.
Scottish dress, 496, 497
Scottish pewter, 1040. See also British
  pewter.
Scottish silver, 956
Scottish tartans, 496, 497
Seal engravers, 847
Seals. See Chapter Fifteen—Medals and
  Seals.
Sèvres porcelain. See French porcelain.
Sezession. See German applied and
  decorative arts.
Sheffield plate. See English silver.
Sheraton style. See English furniture.
Silks, 1076, 1079, 1091
Silver, 874-990
Silversmiths' marks, 874-877
South African ceramics, 651
South African furniture, 651
South African glass, 651
South African silver, 651, 958
South American silver, 921
Spanish applied and decorative arts, 62
Spanish arms and armor, 157
Spanish ceramics, 279, 280
Spanish clock and watchmakers, 400
Spanish enamels, 520
Spanish folk art, 129
Spanish furniture, 641, 660-663, 665
Spanish glass, 743, 744
Spanish jewelry, 799
Spanish lace, 1192
Spanish silver, 988
Spanish textiles, 1088
Spanish wrought iron, 993
Stoneware, 353-389
Swedish applied and decorative arts, 63
Swedish ceramics, 277
Swedish clock and watchmakers, 401
Swedish furniture, 654, 656, 657, 658
Swedish glass, 741, 742
Swedish pewter, 1038, 1039

Swedish silver, 981, 987
Swedish textiles, 1077
Swiss applied and decorative arts, 64
Swiss ceramics, 256, 258
Swiss folk art, 130, 131
Swiss pewter, 1041
Swiss silver. See German silver.
Swiss textiles. See German textiles.
Swiss watches, 426
Swords, 176-178

Tapestry, 1194-1223
Tartans, 496, 497
Terra sigillata, 232
Textiles. See Chapter Eighteen—Textiles.
Tiffany glass. See American glass; Modern
  glass.
Timepieces. See Chapter Six—Clocks,
  Watches and Automata.
Toiles de Jouy. See French textiles;
  Printed textiles.
Tole and tinware, 1011
Touchmarks. See Pewter; Silversmiths'
  marks.
Toys. See Chapter Nineteen—Toys and Dolls.
Turcoman rugs. See Central Asian carpets
  and rugs.
Turkey work. See European carpets and
  rugs.
Turkish carpets. See Oriental carpets and
  rugs.
Turkish textiles, 1100

Uniforms. See Military dress.

Venezuelan ceramics, 242
Venezuelan furniture, 552
Venezuelan silver, 919
Victorian applied and decorative arts, 24,
  27-29
Victorian bookbinding, 829
Victorian embroidery, 1164
Victorian furniture, 559, 561
Victorian porcelain, 266, 269. See also
  American ceramics.
Victoriana, 24, 27-29

Watches. See Chapter Six—Clocks, Watches
  and Automata.
Weapons. See Chapter Four—Arms and Armor.
Wedgwood china. See English porcelain.
Willow ware. See American ceramics; English
  ceramics; English porcelain.
Wrought iron, 991-1006

Zwischengoldglas. See Bohemian glass;
  German glass.

Temp cd

LSL
Ref
Z
5956
A68
E47

50000